Organisation Structures and Processes

by:

Christine Swales

 BTEC

 BLACKWELL *Business*

THE OPEN LEARNING FOUNDATION

Copyright © Open Learning Foundation Enterprises Ltd 1995

First published 1995

Blackwell Publishers Ltd
108 Cowley Road
Oxford OX4 1JF, UK

238 Main Street
Cambridge, Massachusetts 02142, USA

Every effort has been made to trace all copyright owners of material used in this book but if any have been inadvertently overlooked the publishers will be pleased to make necessary arrangements at the first opportunity.

British Library Cataloguing-in-Publication Data
A CIP catalogue record for this book is available from the British Library

Library of Congress Cataloging-in-Publication Data
A catalogue record for this book is available from the Library of Congress

ISBN 0-631-19667-6

Printed in Great Britain by Alden Press

This book is printed on acid-free paper

Contents

Contents

Foreword

BTEC is committed to helping people of any age to acquire and maintain the up-to-date and relevant knowledge, understanding and skills they need for success in current or future employment.

These aims are greatly enhanced by this series of open learning books for the new BTEC HND and HNC in Business Studies.

These books will provide more students with the opportunity to achieve a widely recognised national qualification in business by allowing flexible study patterns combined with an innovative approach to learning.

Our active involvement in a partnership with the Open Learning Foundation and Blackwell Publishers ensures that each book comprehensively covers the specific learning outcomes needed for a module in this Higher National programme.

Acknowledgments

Author
Christine Swales
Additional Material supplied by: Des Hickie (Liverpool John Moores University)

Open Learning Editor: Peter Gaukroger

For the Open Learning Foundation:
Director of Programmes: Leslie Mapp
Design and Production: Stephen Moulds
Text Editor: Paul Stirner
Academic Co-ordinator: Glyn Roberts (Bradford & Ilkley Community College)
Academic Reviewers: Martin Gibson (University of Central Lancashire)

Bob McClelland (Liverpool John Moores University)

The Open Learning Foundation wishes to acknowledge the support of Bradford & Ilkley Community College during the preparation of this workbook.

For BTEC
Diane Billam: Director of Products and Quality Division
John Edgar: Consultant
Françoise Seacroft: Manager of Futures Department
Mike Taylor: Deputy Head of Department of Service Sector Management, University of Brighton

For Blackwell Publishers
Editorial Director: Philip Carpenter
Senior Commissioning Editor: Tim Goodfellow
Production Manager: Pam Park
Development Editors: Richard Jackman and Catriona King
Pre-production Manager: Paul Stringer
Sub-editorial team: First Class Publishing
Reviewers: Sue Gauntlett-Gilbert (Highbury College)
Marilyn Farmer (West Herts College)
Mary Mroczek (London Guildhall University)

Copyright acknowledgments

The publishers are grateful for permission to reproduce material from the following sources:

In section 2, session 2, figures 2.1 to 2.7 and table 2.1 are from Mintzberg, H. and Quinn J.B., The Strategy Process: Concepts, Contexts, Cases, 2nd edn, © 1991, pp. 330–350. Reprinted by permission of Prentice Hall, Upper Saddle River, New Jersey.

In section 2, session 3, table 3.1 is adapted and reprinted by permission of Harvard Business Review. An exhibit from 'Choosing Strategies for Change' by John P. Ketter and Leonard A. Schlesinger, March-April 1979. Copyright © 1979 by the President and Fellows of Harvard College; and all rights reserved. In James A. Stoner and R. Edward Freeman, 1989, Management, Prentice Hall, Englewood Cliffs, New Jersey, p. 370.

In section 3, session 1, table 1.1 is from Robbins, S.P., Organizational Behavior: Concepts, Controversies and Applications, 5th edn, © 1991, p. 321, and figure 1.7 is from Baron, R.A. and Greenberg, J., Behavior in Organizations, 3rd edn, © 1990. Both are reprinted with permission of Prentice Hall, Upper Saddle River, New Jersey.

In section 3, session 2, tables 2.1 and 2.2 are from Clampitt, P.G., Communicating for Managerial Effectiveness, p. 83 and p. 199, © 1991 by Sage Publications, Inc. Both are reprinted by permission of Sage Publications, Inc.

In section 4, session 2, table 2.1 is from Hofstede's Culture and Organization, © 1991 and is reproduced with the permission of McGraw-Hill Book Company Europe.

Resources 2 and 3 are from Jones, G.R., Organizational Theory: Text and Cases, © 1995 Addison-Wesley Publishing Company, Inc. Reprinted by permission of Addison-Wesley Publishing Company, Inc.

Reource 4 © The Economist, 29 July 1989.

Introduction

Welcome to this workbook for the BTEC module Organisation Structures and Processes.

This is a book specifically designed for use by students studying on BTEC Higher National programmes in Business, Business and Finance, Business and Marketing and Business and Personnel. However, it can be also used by people who wish to learn about this aspect of business.

How to use the workbook

Please feel free to:

- write notes in the margins

- underline and highlight important words or phrases.

As you work through this module, you will find activities have been built in. These are designed to make you stop to think and answer questions.

There are four types of activities.

Memory and recall These are straightforward tests of how much text you are able to remember.

Self-assessed tasks (SATs) These are used to test your understanding of the text you are studying or to apply the principles and practices learnt to a related problem.

Exercises These are open-ended questions that can be used as a basis for classroom or group debate. If you do not belong to a study group, use the exercises to think through issues raised by the text.

Assignments These are tasks set for students studying at a BTEC centre which would normally require a written answer to be looked at by your tutor. If you are not following a course at college, the assignments are still a useful way of developing and testing your understanding of the module.

There are answer boxes provided below each activity in this module. Use these boxes to summarise your answers and findings. If you need more space, use the margins of the book or separate sheets of paper to make notes and write a full answer.

SAT:
allow 10 mins

Managing tasks and solving problems ✔

EXAMPLE ACTIVITY

As an 'icebreaker' try this exercise.

What are the fundamental characteristics of an organisation? Give three or four examples of organisations you regularly come into contact with.

Commentary...

An organisation is a group (or groups) of people working together to achieve a particular goal (or goals). Examples you might have chosen could include schools, football clubs, supermarket chains, the church or any company supplying goods or services.

The emphasis of the workbook is to provide you with tasks that relate to the general operating environment of business. The work that you do on these tasks enables you to develop your BTEC common skills and a skills chart is provided at the end of this introduction for you to note your practice of each skill. One sheet is probably not enough, so cut this sheet out and photocopy it when you require new sheets.

Aims of the workbook

This workbook examines approaches to enhancing personal and organisational effectiveness through focusing on the internal nature of organisations, identifying alternative structures and common patterns of behaviour. It provides a framework for examining the varied and dynamic nature of organisations' structure and internal relations.

The book has four sections which are designed to cover the learning outcomes (as shown in bold in the boxes below) for this core module. These are as given in the BTEC publication (code 02–104–4) on the Higher National programmes in Business Studies. Where appropriate, BTEC's suggested content may be reordered within the sections of this book.

SECTION ONE: IDENTIFYING STRUCTURES

On completion of this section, you should be able to:

> **▶ Identify and describe different organisational structures**

> **▶ evalute the appropriateness of different organisational structures**

> **▶ participate in the design of different structures to meet identified needs**

Content

Nature of organisations: the boundaries, goals and formal structures of organisations; the key issues and importance of organisation structures; organisational classification and theory; hierarchies and how tasks are grouped into jobs; understanding organisational goals and missions; measures of performance.

Designing an organisation's structure: analysing work specialisation and the importance of job enrichment; how organisation charts reflect the balance between hierarchical levels and spans of control; the appropriateness of groupings to the task at hand; identifying and analysing an organisation's integrative processes and forms of management control.

Section two: Changing structures

On completion of this section, you should be able to:

> ▶ **identify different organisational environments**

> ▶ **analyse the relationship between different structures and an organisation's performance and development**

> ▶ **participate in the management of organisational change**

Content

Organisational environments: how an organisation's size, strategy, technology and environment influence its structure and the specific effects of each of these contingency factors; structures tailored to environmental uncertainty; the role of technological complexity in change and stability.

Organisation structures: the six key parts of an organisation identified by Mintzberg and how they influence its structure; the seven basic structures of organisations; stages in an organisation's life cycle and how its structure adapts to changing organisational needs; the differences between power, control and authority; future trends in organisation structures.

Organisational change and its management: the main forces that make change inevitable; change through restructuring human resources, functional resources, technological capabilities and organisational capabilities; analysing the management and control of change; evolutionary and revolutionary change; the effects of technology on change.

SECTION THREE: COMMUNICATING IN ORGANISATIONS

On completion of this section, you should be able to:

> ▶ evaluate the effectiveness of different communication systems

> ▶ identify and evaluate relationships between organisation type and communication systems

> ▶ examine and evaluate the impact and implications of technology on communication and administrative systems

> ▶ communicate through formal and informal organisation channels using a variety of appropriate media

> ▶ make recommendations for improved organisational communication

Content

Communications systems: communication as a tool to control, motivate, inform and express emotions; models of communication; choosing appropriate communication channels; principal communications media; feedback and control mechanisms; information technology in communications.

Communication and the organisation: relaying information within an organisation; the relationship between communication systems and organisation structures; the role of communications in organisational change and culture; ways of improving communication and information transfer.

SECTION FOUR: IDENTIFYING AND CHANGING ORGANISATIONAL CULTURE

On completion of this section, you should be able to:

> ▶ **identify organisational cultures, rules and norms**

> ▶ **identify and analyse the factors which influence changing organisational cultures, rules and norms**

> ▶ **identify and evaluate the relationship between organisational cultures, structures and performance**

> ▶ **influence and adapt to organisational change**

Content

Organisational culture: the meaning and relevance of culture; the characteristics of organisational culture and the internal and external environments that shape it; how values and beliefs are learnt from the culture; the different types of organisational culture and how they operate.

Culture in action: the impact of founders, environment, management and national values on an organisation's culture; the functions and importance of culture in facilitating internal integration and external adaptability; organisational culture and social responsibility; planning cultural diversity.

Culture and change: the contribution of culture to organisational efficiency and performance; the task of altering shared and individual values and attitudes; understanding and managing organisational culture change; the importance of human resource management and leadership in the implementation of change.

In working through the BTEC Higher National programme in Business Studies, you will practice the following BTEC common skills:

Managing and developing self ✔

Working with and relating to others ✔

Communicating ✔

Managing tasks and solving problems ✔

Applying numeracy ✔

Applying technology ✔

Applying design and creativity ✔

You will practise most of these skills in working through this module.

Recommended reading

SECTION ONE

Huczynski, A. and Buchanan, D., 1991, Organizational Behavior: An Introductory Text, 2nd edition, Englewood Cliffs, NJ, Prentice Hall.

Jones, G.R., 1995, Organization Theory: Text and Cases, Reading, MA, Addison-Wesley.

Mullins L., 1993, Management and Organisational Behaviour, 3rd edition, London, Pitman.

Robbins, S.P., 1991 Organizational Behavior: Concepts, Controversies and Applications, 5th edition, Englewood Cliffs, NJ, Prentice Hall.

Stoner, J.A.F. and Freeman, R.E., 1989, Management, 4th edition, Englewood Cliffs, NJ, Prentice Hall.

SECTION TWO

Galbraith, J.R., 1974, 'Organisation design: an information processing view', Interfaces, 4(3), May, pp. 28–36.

Handy, C., 1993, Understanding Organisations, 4th edition, London, Penguin.

Huczynski, A. and Buchanan, D., 1991, Organizational Behavior: An Introductory Text, 2nd edition, Englewood Cliffs, NJ, Prentice Hall.

Jones, G.R., 1995, Organization Theory: Text and Cases, Reading, MA, Addison-Wesley.

Mintzberg, H. and Quinn, J.B., 1991, The Strategy Process: Concepts, Contexts, Cases, 2nd edition, Englewood Cliffs, NJ, Prentice Hall.

Pugh, D.S., 1990, Organization Theory: Selected Readings, 3rd edition, London, Penguin Books.

Robbins, S.P., 1991, Organizational Behavior: Concepts, Controversies and Applications, 5th edition, Englewood Cliffs, NJ, Prentice Hall.

Stoner, J.A.F. and Freeman, R.E., 1989, Management, 4th edition, Englewood Cliffs, NJ, Prentice Hall.

SECTION THREE

Clampitt, P.G., 1991, Communicating for Managerial Effectiveness, London, Sage.

Evans, D.W., 1990, People, Communication and Organisations, 2nd edition, London. Pitman.

Huczynski, A. and Buchanan, D., 1991, Organizational Behavior: An Introductory Text, 2nd edition, Englewood Cliffs, NJ, Prentice Hall.

Robbins, S.P. 1991, Organizational Behavior: Concepts, Controversies and Applications, 5th edition, Englewood Cliffs, NJ, Prentice Hall.

Frenzel, C.W., 1992, Management of Information Technology, Boston, MA, Boyd & Fraser.

SECTION FOUR

Brown, A., 1995, Organisational Culture, London: Pitman.

Handy, C., 1993, Understanding Organizations, 4th edition, London, Penguin.

Name

Module

BTEC SKILL	ACTIVITY No./DATE	ACTIVITY No./DATE	ACTIVITY No./DATE	ACTIVITY No./DATE	ACTIVITY No./DATE
Managing and developing self					
Working with and relating to others					
Communicating					
Managing tasks and solving problems					
Applying numeracy					
Applying technology					
Applying design and creativity					

Identifying Structures

Nature of organisations

Objectives

After participating in this session, you should be able to:

> ▶ describe the main characteristics of organisations

> ▶ understand the important organisation structures

> ▶ identify the key issues that must be considered in structuring an organisation

> ▶ relate your learning to a real organisation through a research exercise

> ▶ understand the nature of organisational missions and goals

> ▶ describe measures of organisational performance.

In working through this session, you will practise the following BTEC common skills:

Managing and developing self	✔
Working with and relating to others	✔
Communicating	✔
Managing tasks and solving problems	✔
Applying numeracy	
Applying technology	
Applying design and creativity	

What is an organisation?

We see examples of organisations around us everyday: schools, universities, churches, football teams, youth clubs, supermarkets, bus companies, garages and so on. All of these are organisations whose goods and services we might purchase, for whom we may work, or of which we are members. What do they have in common that makes them organisations and which distinguishes them from other forms of social entity? Let's look at a definition.

!?! An organisation is a clearly bounded group (or groups) of people interacting together to achieve a particular goal (or goals) in a formally structured and co-ordinated way.

This definition picks out certain key features of organisations, which distinguish them from other social groupings, such as a crowd or a group of friends.

An organisation has clear boundaries. We can tell, for example, who is a member of the army, the police, a football team. Employees are clearly members of the organisation for which they work, whether they be supermarket employees, post office staff or customs officials.

An organisation involves people collaborating with one another. For example, a detective may collaborate with a uniformed police officer to investigate a crime.

An organisation has a defined goal (or goals). It exists to achieve a particular purpose (or purposes). For example, the police exist to protect the public from crime, among other reasons. A company may exist to make profits.

An organisation has a formal structure. Its various tasks are clearly defined and grouped together into jobs and departments. In a police force, for example, the Criminal Investigation Department (CID) is separate from the Traffic Department.

An organisation's activities are formally co-ordinated. An organisation has rules and procedures. These set out when and how the people working for an organisation will collaborate to ensure that its purposes are achieved. For example, if a bomb explodes in a city centre, the local police force has procedures setting out how to deal with the emergency. These include both the duties of the CID – to investigate the causes of the blast – and of the Traffic Department - to minimise the disruption to traffic.

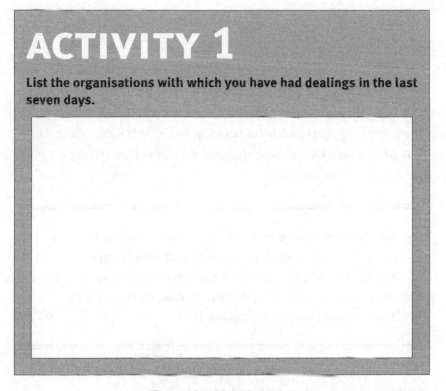

ACTIVITY 1

List the organisations with which you have had dealings in the last seven days.

Commentary...

Your list might include the college where you study, or the company where you work. It might include a supermarket, newsagent, bank, post office, Inland Revenue, petrol station, farm shop, cinema, hardware store or library. It would be surprising if you cannot find at least seven to ten examples. Organisations are part of your daily life.

FORMALITY AND INFORMALITY

Our definition of an organisation indicates that certain of its key features are not left to chance. There are rules about who is and who is not a member. When you join a college as a student you must enrol. When you join a firm as an employee you sign a contract of employment.

The key purposes of the organisation will have been agreed and written down by its senior management. This becomes the organisation's mission statement. For example, your college, university or company almost certainly has a mission statement. Your particular department may have one too.

The people who work for an organisation are likely to have their tasks defined in written job descriptions. This can apply even when the tasks are performed on an unpaid, voluntary basis. For example, the secretary of a youth football team may have a list of duties he or she is expected to undertake.

Anybody working for an organisation should know the rules and procedures that they must follow, and when and how they should report on their activities. These rules and procedures, formally laid down by those responsible for running an organisation, make it clear that an organisation can be distinguished from other social groupings because it is a formal entity.

> **⁉** Formality in an organisation means that it has been created with a declared and agreed purpose (or purposes), that its membership can be clearly defined, and that its tasks are defined and co-ordinated according to rules and procedures set out by those responsible for its management.

This does not mean, however, that organisations are only formal entities. When people meet together at work, or in other organisations, much interaction takes place that is outside the formal rules and procedures of the organisation. Some people like one another and form friendships. Some people bring common experiences to the organisation and so may share a particular outlook towards their work. Some may share a common background, perhaps having qualified through taking the same training course at a university. There is great scope within an organisation for informal patterns of behaviour – for activity and interaction that takes place without reference to the formal aspects of the organisation's purpose and mission.

> **⁉** Informality within an organisation refers to those behaviours that take place without direct reference to its declared purposes, rules and procedures, but which arise from the spontaneous social interactions of its members.

It is possible for the formal and informal aspects of an organisation's life to be in conflict. For example, different sections or departments may develop animosities or feuds that prevent people working together effectively. Nevertheless, the informal parts of organisation can also be very beneficial and help the organisation to achieve its mission. The friendships that people form in organisations help them to enjoy their work and encourage them to collaborate closely with colleagues. Working groups that share a common training and professional pride may well set informal norms or standards for their work that are higher than those formally required by the organisation. When new and unique problems arise, for which no formal rules or procedures exist, informal processes and collaboration can often solve or ameliorate them in the short term, while highlighting the need for new formal steps to be taken to resolve them in the longer term.

It is important for managers to take into account both the formal and informal aspects of organisational life. It is by no means easy to ensure that the informal aspects are at least compatible with the organisation's formal purpose and goals.

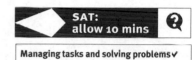

SAT:
allow 10 mins

Managing tasks and solving problems ✔

ACTIVITY 2

Consider your student life and, if you are working, the organisation in which you work.

First, list the key formal rules and procedures that you are subject to as a student (and as an employee).

Then, note the informal behaviour that you engage in as a student or an employee.

Commentary...

As a student, you are subject to rules and procedures concerning matters such as enrolment, attendance, library use, handing in assignments, and so on. As a worker you will have agreed your working hours and job description.

It may be harder to be precise about your informal behaviour. You will almost certainly socialise. You may discuss your work with others. You may organise social events.

TYPES OF ORGANISATIONS

Organisations vary greatly. Some are large; some are small. Some are very formal; others are more informal. Some serve their members; some serve others; and some serve both. Some are in the public sector (i.e. they are owned by the state); others are in the private sector (i.e. they are owned by individuals and groups in society). Some have voluntary membership, like a university; others do not, like a prison.

This variety means that there is not a single, universally accepted, way of grouping or classifying organisations into their different types. Mullins (Management and Organisational Behaviour, 3rd edition, 1993, Pitman, London) classifies organisations on the basis of their primary purposes, distinguishing:

- economic organisations, whose primary purpose is to sell goods and services in a market

- protective organisations, whose primary purpose is to defend the interests of a particular social group or groups or society at large (such as a police force, or trade union, or some charities)

- associative organisations, whose primary purpose is to bring people together to pursue some common leisure interest or purpose (such as a youth club or sports club)

- public service organisations which provide a government service (such as hospitals or roads)

- religious organisations (such as specific church or mosque congregations).

An alternative typology, proposed by Blau and Scott (Formal Organisations, 1966, Routledge and Kegan Paul, London), divides organisations into different types according to who is intended to be the primary beneficiary of their activities. They distinguish four types of organisation:

- mutual benefit associations, intended primarily to benefit their own members, like a trade union

- business concerns, intended primarily to benefit their owners, like a company

- service organisations, intended primarily to meet the needs of an external client group, like many charities

- Commonwealth organisation, intended primarily to meet the needs of the public at large, like many public services, such as the police or the army.

ACTIVITY 3

Taking the list of organisations with whom you have dealt in the last seven days, classify them first using Mullins' five categories and then Blau and Scott's four categories.

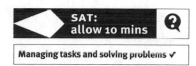

SAT:
allow 10 mins

Managing tasks and solving problems ✓

Commentary...

If you cannot classify each organisation clearly into one of the categories, do not worry too much. One of the problems with almost any system of classification is that not all organisations will fit neatly into it!

ORGANISATIONAL THEORY DEVELOPMENT

Another way of attempting to understand and classify organisations is through looking at how they work. Organisational theory attempts to explain the factors that influence the way organisations are structured and operate. It helps to create a better understanding of how organisations work.

Like all theories, the aim is to describe a set of relationships that allows predictions to be made about the effects of changes in circumstances. (There are many well-known theories in physics, chemistry and engineering such as Einstein's Theory of Relativity.) However, the relationships within an organisation and its relationships with its environment are so complex that it is not easy to make predictions with any degree of confidence. This means that often 'theories' are in fact a set of principles built up from observed activity.

In this century, the thinking about organisations has developed through three main approaches:

- classical theory

- human relations theories

- systems theory.

Classical theory was the first body of principles to develop in the early part of this century. It is typified by the work of Urwick, Taylor and Fayol. They were concerned with authority, responsibility, delegation, span of control, specialisation and hierarchical structures. As a theory of organisational development, classical theory assumes that:

- once a decision has been made it will be implemented

- the environment is stable

- the major influence on man is economic.

The theory assumes that man maximises – that people will work as hard and as long as possible in order to earn as much as possible.

The next approach to develop was human relations theories. These arose out of the work of theorists such as Mayo, McGregor, Argyris and Likert. Unlike classical theory which is primarily concerned with structure, this school of thought is concerned with people. It suggests that:

- the motivation of individuals and groups is not, in general, specifically directed at organisational goals

- an organisation's operating structure tends to be informal rather than formal

- acceptable authority is not necessarily structural authority.

Human relationalists were consequently interested in inter-relationships and their effect on motivation.

Systems theory can be seen as the bringing together of both the classical and the human relations approaches. The exponents of this theory include Katz and Kohn, Emery and Trist and Herbert Simon. They were concerned with the interaction of the variables which are actually influencing the organisations. Internal variables include, for example, competition for resources by individuals or departments, while the external variables are usually grouped under four main headings: economic, technological, social and political.

The theory tends to centre on three elements: the interdependence of parts, the process and the dynamics of organisations. We have illustrated these elements very simply (figures 1.1, 1.2, 1.3), but you must understand they are much more complex.

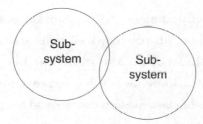

FIGURE 1.1: Interdependence of parts.

These different subsystems may, for example, be departments within a company.

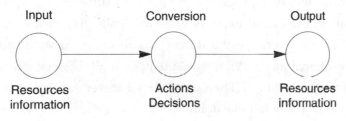

FIGURE 1.2: Process.

An example of a process is the way that materials and components enter a car producing plant and are converted to a finished product which is then sold to a customer.

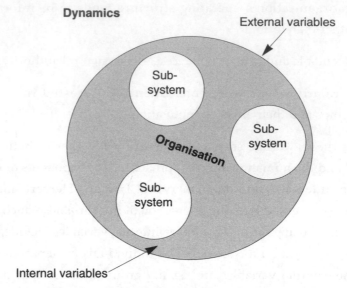

FIGURE 1.3: Dynamics.

The external variables which impinge on an organisation may include laws and business regulations, the availability of capital, and the impact and potential of new technology. Internal variables include power struggles and the availability of resources for carrying out defined tasks.

We have only briefly summarised the main issues that concerned the three schools of thought. You may well come across these theories as you take your study of organisations further. For the present, however, you need to be aware that organisations vary and that different methods of classification can be used to emphasise different aspects of their variety.

Organisation structures

Organisations bring together people with different backgrounds, education, skills and experiences. Their collective task is to work together, doing a range of different jobs, to achieve a set of common, organisational goals. What would happen if all these people simply 'did their own thing'? They could do whatever work they felt like doing, when they felt like doing it, in the way they thought best. The result might well be chaos. Structures attempt to impose order and purpose.

SAT:
allow 10 mins

Managing tasks and solving problems ✓

ACTIVITY 4

Imagine you were allowed to 'do your own thing' at work or college.

	Yes	No
1. Would you still arrive as early and go home as late?	☐	☐
2. Would you spend as much time on the less pleasant aspects of your work or study as you do presently?	☐	☐
3. Would all aspects of your work or study be done to the same standard as they are now?	☐	☐
4. Even if you can answer 'Yes' to the first three questions, do you think that everyone in your workplace (employees and managers) or college (students and lecturers) would do the same?	☐	☐

List three things you would like to do differently at work or at college if you were allowed to 'do your own thing'. Now suggest reasons why organisations need a structure.

Commentary...

If you are very well motivated – and have a high opinion of your colleagues – and are able to act independently, then you could answer 'yes' to the four questions above. Most organisations might question such a response. They need a structure which:

- creates a hierarchy, giving someone (or some people) the duty of setting out rules about time-keeping

- allocates both pleasant and unpleasant tasks to various people within the organisation according to their job descriptions

- allocates to some people the task of checking that work or study is carried out to a sufficiently high standard.

An organisation structure plays an important part in ensuring that rules and procedures exist (and are obeyed) that are necessary for the smooth running (and even the continued existence) of the whole organisation. Unless you and everyone else in your organisation can behave in a self-disciplined way, then its structure provides an essential framework for the efficient running of your organisation.

An organisation's structure sets out formally:

- how tasks are grouped together into jobs, e.g. a counter clerk in a bank or building society may deal with initial customer queries, take in and pay out cash, make up accounts for customers, and make up till balances

- how jobs are grouped together into sections, departments and divisions, e.g. an organisation may decide to group together all its typists and word processor operators

- who reports to whom, e.g. at the end of their beat police constables report to a sergeant at the station any significant events that have occurred

- who has authority over whom, e.g. at the beginning of each shift, the same police sergeant may instruct the constables who is to take which beat.

The organisation's structure does not tell us anything about the informal (or unofficial) side of the organisation.

> !?! An organisation structure sets out the formal framework of relationships within an organisation: the grouping together of its activities; its lines of communication; and its hierarchy. Within this framework the co-ordination and control of the organisation's activities can take place.

DIFFERENTIATION AND INTEGRATION

To create an organisation structure two key processes must take place: differentiation and integration. As part of the management team, it is the organisation designer's role to make decisions about these two processes.

> !?! Differentiation is the process of allocating the tasks that need to be done within an organisation to a series of sets or groups (which we call jobs, teams, sections and departments). This might be done because they contain a range of tasks that have important elements in common (such as common knowledge, common skills, or the same type of customers).

Differentiation can be horizontal. People are divided into groups who are at the same level in the organisation. For example, a college may have departments of business studies, engineering and humanities. Each department has lecturers – grouped according to their ability to teach different subjects – of broadly equal status within the college. Similarly a large car show room may have a department that deals with sales and a department that deals with car spares and servicing.

Differentiation can also be vertical. People (who may share similar skills, knowledge, etc.) are divided into different managerial levels in the organisation's hierarchy. For example, the business studies department in your college may contain a head, a deputy head, a number of course managers and, below them in the hierarchy, the remainder of the lecturers. Similarly, in the car show room, the sales department may have a sales manager in charge of a group of salespersons.

> **!?!** Integration is the process of ensuring that the activities of the various work groups in the organisation are linked together harmoniously, so that each group can maximise its contribution to the achievement of the organisation's goals.

Like differentiation, integration can be both horizontal or vertical. Horizontal integration concerns the activities that go on at the same hierarchical level within an organisation to ensure that members of staff co-ordinate their activities. For example, at an electricity company, customer account staff dealing with telephone enquiries from customers share a common computer database so that they can deal with any customer who happens to telephone. Similarly, in a college, a group of lecturers who teach a BTEC module jointly will meet periodically to discuss how it is progressing and to consider any changes that need to be made.

Vertical integration concerns the activities that go on at different hierarchical levels within an organisation to ensure that members of staff co-ordinate their activities. For example, at the end of each day at the regional office of a bank, information will be collated and presented electronically to allow regional managers to assess the business that has been done by each branch. Similarly, the national head office of the bank will send out sets of standard operating procedures to tell branches how they should deal with particular kinds of transaction, such as the exchange of foreign currency or the selling of traveller's cheques.

THE COMFORTABLE SHOE COMPANY

It is 8.45 a.m. on a Monday. Mark Green, a salesperson with the Comfortable Shoe Company is setting out to visit a number of stores that stock his company's shoes in the nearby market town of Mapplethorpe. Mark is a member of the Comfortable Shoe Company's North West regional sales team. The other members are Bill Battersby (the North West regional sales manager), Sue Long and Jane Sutcliffe. Bill has divided the region into three districts. Mark, Sue and Jane are each responsible for one of them.

Before leaving home, Mark had telephoned Bill to say that he would call into the regional sales office on his way home from Mapplethorpe to let Bill have a detailed break-down of his district's sales figures for last month. This pleased Bill because he is about to compile the North West regional sales report for last month and send it to head office in London. It will be compared with other regions' sales figures for the month. Bill is anxious that the North West's performance compares well against that of other regions.

Just before Mark rang off Bill had said, "Good luck at Campbell's, and don't go offering them more than the company's standard discounts. You know it drives head office wild." Mark is worried about visiting Campbell's. It is

Mapplethorpe's largest department store and had been the North West's biggest outlet for Comfortable Shoes. Over the past year, however, it had begun to stock fewer and fewer of Comfortable's shoes, and had replaced them with imported shoes from South America. Mark believed that the problem lay in his company's introduction of a standard discount policy. A new memorandum from head office instructs regional sales teams on what levels of discount they are allowed to offer to customers. Previously, the sales staff had been free to determine what discounts they offered, and major customers had often obtained much larger discounts than are possible under the new standard discounts policy.

Mark cheered up as he thought of lunch. He had agreed to eat with Sue Long. She had promised to bring with her some samples of the company's latest shoe designs which Mark thought would be of particular interest to Campbell's. Campbell's customers are especially fashion conscious. He reflected that working in the North West sales team is not really so bad. They really are a team and their monthly team meetings are one of the best parts of the job.

ACTIVITY 5

SAT:
allow 30 mins

Managing tasks and solving problems ✓

Read the case study on the Comfortable Shoe Company, and list all the examples of:

- horizontal differentiation

- vertical differentiation

- horizontal integration

- vertical integration.

Commentary...

This case illustrates a number of examples of each form of differentiation and integration.

Horizontal differentiation can be seen in the way that Mark, Sue and Jane each take responsibility for a separate district and in the division of the country into regions.

Vertical differentiation is reflected in the different roles of Bill, as regional sales manager, with those of his team. Bill's job is office-based and managerial, Mark, Sue and Jane are highly mobile and deal directly with potential customers.

Horizontal integration can be found in Bill's wish to compare his region's sales with those of other regions, in Mark and Sue's lunchtime meeting to co-ordinate the sales drive on Campbell's, and in the North West sales team's monthly meetings.

Vertical integration can be seen in Mark's delivery of sales figures to Bill, in Bill's preparation of a monthly regional sales report for Head Office, and in Head Office's comparisons of regional performance. It can be seen very clearly in the company's standard discounts policy, which amounts to a standard operating procedure. Bill's participation in his region's monthly team meetings provide a further occasion for vertical integration.

Understanding an organisation's design

Designing an organisation involves two processes: differentiating the various aspects of the organisation, and then integrating them. John Child (Organisation: A Guide to Problems and Practice, 2nd edition, 1988, Paul Chapman, London) draws the organisation designer's attention to five key questions that need to be answered if an organisation is to be well structured.

1. To what extent should the work of an organisation be broken down into small parts, creating rather narrow specialised jobs?

Such jobs can then be combined to form rather narrow, specialist departments. For example, should a production worker perform the same task on a production line perhaps thousands of times per day or be moved to other tasks periodically?

2. How many levels should an organisation have in its hierarchy and how wide should be the spans of control of its managers?

For example, at the Comfortable Shoe Company Bill Battersby manages a staff of three and reports to a sales director at head office, who in turn reports to the managing director. Does Bill manage too many, too few or the right number of staff? Are there too many steps between the managing director and the ordinary salespersons, like Mark Green?

3. How should jobs and departments be grouped together?

At the Comfortable Shoe Company, the North West sales team has been created partly because the staff concerned perform the same task and partly because they work in the same region.

4. How closely do the various parts of an organisation need to be integrated?

For example, in a hospital, it is sometimes very important for the catering staff to know about the medical condition of patients, so that they can offer the patients an appropriate diet. This involves a high level of co-ordination between medical staff and those who prepare patients' meals.

5. How much control should management exercise over the activities of an organisation?

At the Comfortable Shoe Company, the standard discounts policy allows sales staff little flexibility in the amount of discount they can offer a customer. In the past, sales staff were given more opportunity to use their own initiative in negotiating deals with their customers.

These are the key questions: providing answers is rather more difficult, because there are no 'right' answers. The organisation structure of your workplace or college may be completely different from that of other seemingly similar organisations. This does not mean that your organisation is right and the others are wrong, or vice versa. What it shows is that even apparently similar organisations can be markedly different and, quite possibly, equally successful. The appropriate structure for a particular organisation depends both upon the characteristics of the organisation itself and upon its relationship to its environment.

If it is not possible to provide 'right' answers, nevertheless it is important to explore each question to see what choices are faced by an organisation designer in trying to answer it. A thorough understanding of these choices will enable you to know your organisation better and, if you are in a senior management position, allow you to make more informed decisions about its structure.

UNDERSTANDING AN
ORGANISATION'S DESIGN

In session two, we analyse each of Child's questions in detail. However, to achieve the learning objectives of this module, you will need to be able to apply what you learn to real organisations. So, before proceeding to look for answers to Child's five questions, it would be helpful if you found out more about an organisation with which you are already familiar. This we will call your chosen organisation.

The next activity asks you to conduct interviews to find out some information about your chosen organisation. In the next session, you will then analyse this information as we consider Child's questions. The data that you collect will form the basis of an assignment at the end of this section. In addition you will use your chosen organisation in other sections of the workbook and, even though you may not understand the questions completely, you may combine the following exercise with activity 2 (page 265) in session one, section four in which you are asked to gather information on cultural issues.

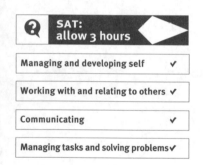

SAT: allow 3 hours	
Managing and developing self	✔
Working with and relating to others	✔
Communicating	✔
Managing tasks and solving problems	✔

ACTIVITY 6

First, you must decide upon your chosen organisation. If you are in full-time employment, you will probably find it most beneficial to choose the organisation for which you work. You will already possess much useful information about it, and a well-developed knowledge of your employing organisation is likely to be of value both to you and to your employer.

If you are not in full-time employment, choose an organisation with which you are already familiar. This will help you to understand what you find out and to put it in context. You could, for example, choose a place where you work part-time, or have worked in the fairly recent past. You could choose an organisation whose services you use regularly (such as a supermarket, a leisure centre or a bus company). The choice is your own.

(If you have a serious problem in finding an organisation, the college at which you are studying for this BTEC award may be willing to help you, either by finding you an organisation which will allow you to conduct the necessary interviews, or by allowing you to conduct interviews with members of the college's own staff.)

You should check your choice of organisation with your tutor to make sure that it is appropriate for our purposes here. You may work for a very small or very unusual company, that would not have any or many of the characteristics that you need to investigate.

You will need to contact the organisation and obtain its approval to conduct the interviews.

Within your chosen organisation you need to select two persons to interview. Choose two persons whom you think will be knowledgeable about the organisation and who will each be willing to give up an hour or so of their time to speak to you. You will need to conduct a further short interview with these persons at a later time, to be agreed (see activity 2, page 265). If this is not possible you will need to add those questions to your initial interviews. You should interview them on the basis of the questionnaire below. Select people who work in different parts of the organisation and who do different jobs, so that you obtain varied points of view in answer to your questions. At least one of your interviewees should be in a supervisory or managerial position, as some questions relate to the interviewee's supervisory responsibilities.

The questionnaire below asks your interviewees a number of key questions about their work and their organisation. Before your two interviews, test the questions on yourself first and make sure you understand them. Check with your tutor if the questions do not seem to fit your organisation at all, because you may need to reconsider your choice of organisation.

Treat the interview schedule as a whole and use the questions themselves as guidelines. You may be able to think of more precise ways to phrase particular questions, to suit your chosen organisation. The aim is to obtain the most informative and accurate answers to the questions. Do not worry if your interviewees' replies do not seem consistent. If possible ask extra, supplementary, questions to clarify matters whenever it seems beneficial.

Before you undertake the interviews, think through how you are going to record your interviewees' responses. You may tape record your interview and/or take detailed notes. Space has been left after each question to allow you to summarise your interviewees' answers. Having completed each interview, read your answers carefully both to refresh your memory as to what you have discovered, and to make sure that what you have written accurately and completely reflects what you were told.

Remember at the beginning of each interview, to:

- explain why you are conducting the interview

- reassure the interviewee that everything he/she says during the interview will be treated as confidential

- explain that you will return to give the interviewee a report on your findings

- if the interviewee agrees this is acceptable, confirm that he or she will also be able to answer a few further questions at a later date

- thank the interviewee for giving their time to see you.

INTERVIEW SCHEDULE

Part 1. Your organisation

1. What is the name of the organisation?

2. How many staff does your organisation employ?

3. How many sites or branches does your organisation operate from?

4. At which site or branch do you work?

Part 2. Your job

5. What is your job title?

6. What are the major responsibilities of your job?

7. Does your organisation require that persons doing your job possess any particular qualifications or undertake any particular training? (If your answer is 'yes' please specify the requirement(s).)

8. Are the requirements of your job set out in a formal written job specification?

9. Does your organisation have rules or procedures which lay down how you should perform particular tasks, (e.g. standard operating procedures), or are you free to choose how you go about your work? (Please give examples of any rules or procedures you have in mind.)

10. Is the output of your work measured in any particular way to see if it is up to the standard your organisation expects? (Again please give examples of any forms of measurement you have in mind and identify who is responsible for the monitoring process.)

11. On the site or at the branch where you work is your job unique, or are there other people with the same or very similar title and job description, or who perform the same or very similar tasks?

If the interviewee answered that his/her job is unique, go directly to question 13.

12. Do you work independently from the other person(s) on your site or at your branch who have the same or very similar job to you, or do you work as a team with them, sharing tasks and responsibilities?

13. In carrying out your work to what extent are you dependent upon the work of other colleagues doing different jobs to your own?

14. In carrying out their jobs to what extent are other people in your workplace dependent upon the way in which you do your job?

Part 3. Supervision at work

15. Do you supervise the work of anyone else in your organisation?

If the interviewee answered 'no' to question 15, please go directly to question 22.

16. How many members of staff report directly to you?

17. What jobs are done by the staff who report to you?

18. Are the staff who report to you responsible to you for all of their work, or do they report to another supervisor for some aspects of their work?

19. Is your supervision of your staff's work mainly a matter of your instructing them what tasks to perform and how to perform them, or it is more a matter of discussion and negotiation as to how tasks should best be performed?

20. Do you feel that you are able to give adequate support and attention to the staff whose work you supervise? (If your answer is 'no' please try to identify reasons why this may be so.)

21. Where do the persons who report to you fit into your organisation's management system? Do they also supervise staff? If so, how many staff, doing what jobs, are they responsible for?

22. To whom are you directly responsible for your work in your organisation's management system?

23. How many other people, doing what jobs, does this person supervise?

24. In ascending order of seniority, what are the job titles of the managers who have direct authority over you? Start with your own supervisor and finish with the chief executive.

25. Do you feel that your supervisor instructs you how to do your work or discusses with you the best way to do it?

26. Do you feel that your supervisor has the knowledge and time to assist you as fully as you would like in your work?

27. Many organisations have attempted to reduce their numbers and levels of managers in recent years. Has yours done so?

If your interviewee's answer is 'no' to this question, go directly to question 30.

28. Why did your organisation attempt to reduce its levels of management?

29. What do you believe the consequences have been of your organisation's attempts to reduce its levels of management?

Part 4. The departments at your organisation

30. What are the key tasks performed at your site or branch?

31. Are these various tasks performed in separate departments? If so, which?

32. Are other key tasks for your organisation performed at other sites or at other branches? If so, please specify which and where they are performed.

33. Does your organisation produce different products at different sites? If so, please specify which and where they are produced.

34. Does your organisation have a regional or district structure? If so, which are the regions or districts?

35. Does your organisation serve different types of customer (e.g. wholesale and retail) on different sites or branches? If so, please specify which types of customers are dealt with at which places.

The questions from activity 2 on page 265 will have to be asked at this point if it is not possible to arrange a further short interview.

Organisational goals and effectiveness

In any discussion of organisations and their structures, we implicitly assume that they want to achieve certain things and not others. We regard structures as being good if they help an organisation to achieve its aims. To do that, we must have an understanding of an organisation's goals and the measures which allow us to assess whether these goals are being achieved.

> **\?!** An organisational goal is a state of affairs that an organisation wishes to achieve and in pursuit of which it directs its efforts.

Without goals, an organisation will tend to drift. It has no particular targets to aim at. Senior managers will tend to take decisions in an inconsistent way, following whatever course seems to be appropriate at the time and changing course whenever a new piece of information, or even a change of mood, makes a change seem desirable. This is likely to confuse or unsettle those lower down in the organisation's hierarchy. They will not know what they are expected to achieve. For some, the lack of clear guidance from the top may be taken as an opportunity to go their own way, and do what is good for them personally or for their particular part of the organisation.

CAMPBELL'S DEPARTMENT STORE

Campbell's store in Mapplethorpe is a family-owned business. It was run for 50 years by Tobias Campbell until his death seven years ago. Tobias Campbell was a somewhat autocratic man who liked to give firm, clear leadership. He had declared that the store's motto would be: "The best store with the best selection of quality merchandise available in Mapplethorpe, in every department." Under his leadership, departmental managers and the store's buyers knew that they had to stock a very full range of articles from the best known manufacturers. If they did not do so they would be severely reprimanded by Tobias Campbell and possibly lose their annual bonus. Campbell's prices were not the lowest in Mapplethorpe, but under Tobias Campbell's leadership it certainly became the premier store in Mapplethorpe. It was consistently profitable, and when the town's two other department stores were taken over by national chain-stores, Campbell's remained proud and independent.

After Tobias Campbell's death, the managing directorship was taken over by his nephew, Cecil Campbell. Cecil had, up to then, taken relatively little interest in the business, preferring to spend his time on his country estate 50 miles away. He and his uncle, Tobias, had heartily disliked everything about the other. On the day he became managing director, he was asked if he wished the company still to follow Tobias Campbell's motto. He had replied, "Definitely not." When asked what the store's new motto should be, he said, "I haven't thought of one yet, but I'll let you know."

ORGANISATIONAL GOALS
AND EFFECTIVENESS

Seven years on, he still had not announced what the new motto would be. During this time departmental managers and store buyers had begun to go their own ways. Most no longer stocked a full range of the best lines from well-known manufacturers. Some even filled their departments with cheap, rather shoddy items sold at discount prices. Campbell's traditional customers have become disgruntled, new customers have not been attracted in large numbers and the company's profits have fallen. During the last three years, it has recorded losses for the first time in its history.

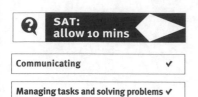

SAT:
allow 10 mins

| Communicating | ✔ |
| Managing tasks and solving problems | ✔ |

ACTIVITY 7

Read the case study on Campbell's Department Store, then answer the following questions.

1. **What was Campbell's organisational goal under Tobias Campbell's leadership?**

2. **Does the store have an organisational goal under Cecil Campbell's leadership?**

3. **How did Campbell's benefit from having Tobias Campbell's organisational goal?**

Commentary...

Under Tobias Campbell's leadership the organisation's goal was to be the best quality departmental store in town. This can be summarised in the words of his motto: "The best store with the best selection of quality merchandise available in Mapplethorpe, in every department." By contrast, there is no apparent or clearly-defined organisational goal under Cecil Campbell's leadership.

By setting a clear goal, departmental managers and buyers knew clearly what was expected of them. They knew that their performance would be judged on their success in establishing their departments as the best in Mapplethorpe in its particular field. One might also expect that a determination to be the best in town might act as a motivator both for managers and their staff, and attract people to want to work at the store.

As the Campbell's case illustrates, goals can be very useful for an organisation. Tobias Campbell's motto is, in fact, a particular kind of organisational goal. It is what is called a mission statement or mission.

> **!?!** An organisational mission is the long-term or overall goal of an organisation. It is a statement that sets out why the organisation exists and what it is trying to achieve.

Today, many organisations have mission statements. For a mission statement to be of real value as a guide and motivator for staff and for it to be of value in informing the organisation's customers or clients, it must be both relevant to their needs and readily accessible.

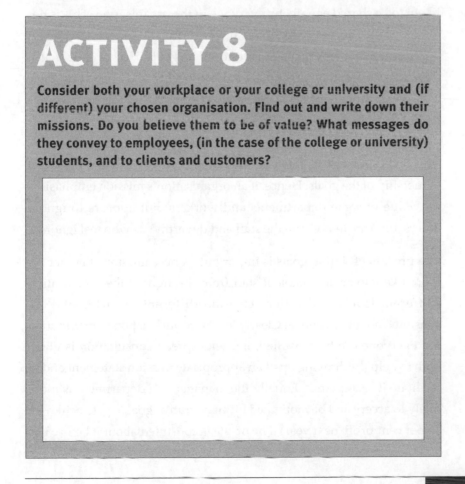

ACTIVITY 8

Consider both your workplace or your college or university and (if different) your chosen organisation. Find out and write down their missions. Do you believe them to be of value? What messages do they convey to employees, (in the case of the college or university) students, and to clients and customers?

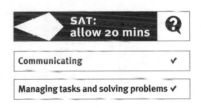

SAT: allow 20 mins	?
Communicating	✓
Managing tasks and solving problems	✓

ORGANISATIONAL GOALS
AND EFFECTIVENESS

Usually an organisation does not find it enough simply to have a mission statement. Mission statements tend to be rather broad and general, and concerned with long-term aims. An organisation needs shorter-term goals which can be related to its various key activities and which can be measured to be sure that the organisation is performing satisfactorily. Richard Daft (Organization Theory and Design, 1992, West, St. Paul) refers to the longer-term, broader goals included in a mission statement as an organisation's official goals. He refers to the shorter-term, more task-related goals that serve as way-stations to achieving an organisation's mission as an organisation's operative goals. Examples of operative goals are profitability, market share, development of a new product within a particular time period.

> **!?!** An organisation's operative goals are specific measures of achievement, usually covering particular key organisational tasks. Successive organisational goals over time act as steps towards the achievement of an organisation's mission.

WHOSE GOALS?

So far we have tended to assume that an organisation's formal goals are likely to be shared equally by everyone in the organisation. This is not necessarily the case. In general, it is the responsibility of an organisation's senior management to set its goals. However, it is also their task to see that such goals are achievable and shared by their colleagues throughout the organisation. If goals are set that staff feel are not achievable then, rather than motivating them to try harder, this is likely to demoralise them. Equally, it is important that an organisation's staff feel that its goals relate to them and their work. They must feel ownership of the goals. Hence, if an organisation's mission emphasises the value of some departments and workers, but appears to ignore others, this can demotivate the staff and departments who feel ignored.

The process of setting goals is important. A new mission statement is more likely to be acceptable if staff from throughout the organisation (different levels in the hierarchy and different departments) are consulted about its content. Clearly in a large, international organisation not everyone can be consulted, but widespread consultation is likely both to help the drawing up of an appropriate mission statement and to facilitate its acceptance. Equally the manager of a department is more likely to accept and be motivated by an operative goal (e.g. to achieve a 15 per cent profit next year) if he or she is consulted about it before it is set. Finally, however, it is for senior management to take responsibility for the organisational goals they set, whatever the process of consultation that has taken place. In practice the key influence upon an organisation's goals is that of a dominant group of its senior managers.

The organisation's goals tend to be espoused with different degrees of enthusiasm in different parts of the organisation. One of the consequences of the process of differentiation is that separate departments, divisions or groups of staff, in an organisation develop goals and values of their own; goals which are not officially approved by the organisation. These are informal goals.

> \?\/ Informal goals are measures of achievement which are developed by groups of staff within an organisation without the formal approval of its senior management.

Informal goals can even be at complete variance with the officially approved goals of an organisation. For example, an organisation may specifically declare itself to be an equal opportunities employer in its mission statement, but a group of staff in a particular department may decide it does not want to work with women or with members of racial minorities. It could then develop informal processes to prevent their appointment or could make working in the department so unpleasant that such persons do not stay long even if appointed. Of course, informal goals need not always be bad for the organisation. For example, a group of craftsmen may, from pride in their craft, agree among themselves to work at higher standards than the organisation normally requires.

The process in which an organisation's formal goals are set aside by informal ones is called goal displacement. This process of goal displacement should alert us to the need for organisations to keep their formal goals under review, to see that they remain relevant and are not being replaced.

EFFECTIVENESS

An effective organisation is an organisation that achieves its goals. The Brazilian soccer team which won the 1994 World Cup was, therefore, an effective organisation. It achieved what it set out to do.

> \?\/ Organisational effectiveness is the extent to which an organisation is able to achieve the goals which have been set for it or which it has set itself.

ORGANISATIONAL GOALS
AND EFFECTIVENESS

Effectiveness is the broadest and most significant measure of an organisation's performance. It exemplifies the importance of goals to an organisation and reminds managers of an organisation of their duty to achieve its goals.

If an organisation's goals are set with insufficient care then an organisation could achieve both its operative goals and even its mission, and yet not make the best use of its resources and its people. It could underachieve because the organisation's goals are insufficiently ambitious (so that staff are not encouraged to try hard enough), or over ambitious (so that staff become demoralised).

Equally an organisation's goals may simply be misguided or misplaced, so that they lead an organisation into markets or products to which its resources and capacities are not entirely suited. As a result, the organisation may not fully utilise its capacities. For example, returning to Campbell's stores, consider what might happen if Cecil Campbell (the new managing director) decides to set a revised mission for the organisation to stock a narrower range of cheaper products that appeal to a wider range of Mapplethorpe shoppers. This might not secure the company's future. It may well be that the two national chain stores operating in the town are better able to pursue such an approach, as they can buy in bulk (and hence more cheaply) and use national marketing to publicise their bargains. It will be very difficult for Campbell's to compete effectively and for their staff to achieve the goals set for them. Even if they do so, it might be argued that Campbell's is not making the best use of the company's resources and is wasting its long-established reputation for high quality.

Apart from effectiveness, there are two other (though narrower) measures of an organisation's achievements: efficiency and economy.

> **!?!** Organisational efficiency concerns the capacity of an organisation to produce goods or services at the lowest possible cost per unit of output, i.e. with the lowest possible amount of its resources (human and material) going into each unit of output.

Efficiency is usually measured by putting a cash value upon each organisational resource used in the production of a particular item or the provision of a service and then aggregating them to arrive at a unit cost.

Consider for example, Eco-Pumps which manufactures water pumps. The company rents a factory for £100,000 per annum, employs 20 staff at cost of £400,000 per annum and uses materials at a cost of £500,000 per annum; its total costs are £1,000,000 per annum. The company produces £2,000 pumps per annum, so the unit cost of each pump is £500. If Eco-Pumps expands its production to 2,500 pumps per annum, but manages to keep rent and staff costs the same and only increases material costs by £100,000, then its total costs would be £1,100,000. The unit cost of each pump would fall to £440 per pump. Eco-Pumps would have become markedly more efficient.

Organisations are concerned about efficiency. Most include efficiency targets in their operative goals. Many make some mention of efficiency-related matters in their mission statements. Nevertheless, efficiency goals are essentially internally focused upon the organisation's use of its resources; they do not tell us about what an organisation's customers think of its products. For example, Eco-Pumps will not have improved its market position if its customers find that, when production rises to 2,500 pumps per annum, quality falls and that pumps break down more often. Sales will quickly decrease.

> !?! Organisational economy is the total value of the resources used by an organisation. Hence to become more economical an organisation must use fewer resources than it used formerly.

Note that economy is an even narrower internal measure of an organisation's use of its resources. If Eco-Pumps expanded its production to 2,500 pumps per annum, its total costs would grow from £1,000,000 to £1,100,000. Therefore, it would become a less economical organisation (by £100,000 per annum) even though it might become a more efficient one.

Effectiveness, efficiency and economy – sometimes called the three Es of value for money – are all important measures. However, as has been shown, they have a potential to conflict with one another. It is quite possible for organisations to become more economical and even more efficient, but less effective. Effectiveness is the key measure: it is the only measure that directly relates an organisation's activities to the needs of its customers or clients. However, if an organisation is to be effective and to make the best potential use of its resources, much depends upon the care with which its goals are set.

summary

This session has looked at the nature of organisations and their structures.

> ▶ Organisations have clear boundaries, defined goals, formal structures, are formally co-ordinated and involve people working together.

> ▶ Organisations may be classified in different ways. In this session, we reviewed Mullins' classification based on primary purpose and Blau and Scott's based on primary beneficiaries.

> ▶ Organisational theory helps to create a better understanding of how organisations work. We identified three broad movements: classical, human relations and system theory.

> ▶ Organisation structure sets out how tasks are grouped into jobs, how jobs are grouped, who reports to whom and who has authority over whom.

> ▶ John Child's five key questions about organisation design concern specialisation (or differentiation), hierarchy, grouping, integration and management control.

> ▶ Without goals, organisations tend to drift. A mission is a long-term overall goal. Operative goals are specific short-term performance measures.

> ▶ Goals should be set after a consultation process so staff feel ownership of them. Informal goals of individuals or groups may correspond with, or be at variance with, official goals.

> ▶ Effectiveness, efficiency and economy are three measures of an organisation's performance.

Designing an organisation's structure

DIFFERENTIATION

HIERARCHY

GROUPING ACTIVITIES

INTEGRATION

CONTROL

Objectives

After participating in this session, you should be able to:

- analyse the extent to which particular jobs or departments within an organisation are specialised

- use organisation charts to describe the management hierarchy

- analyse the ways in which an organisation's jobs and departments are grouped together, and to evaluate the appropriateness of those groupings

- identify and evaluate the integrative processes at work within an organisation

- identify and evaluate the forms of managerial control used within an organisation.

In working through this session, you will practise the following BTEC common skills:

Managing and developing self	✔
Working with and relating to others	✔
Communicating	✔
Managing tasks and solving problems	✔
Applying numeracy	
Applying technology	
Applying design and creativity	

Differentiation

In session one, we introduced John Child's five key questions on organisation structure:

1. To what extent should the work of an organisation be broken down into small parts, creating rather narrow specialised jobs?

2. How many levels should an organisation have in its hierarchy and for how many people should each manager be responsible?

3. How should jobs and departments be grouped together?

4. How closely do the various parts of an organisation need to be integrated?

5. How much control should management exercise over the activities of an organisation?

Now we are going to examine them in some depth and see how they relate to the overall design of the organisation.

1. To what extent should the work of the organisation be broken down into small parts, creating rather narrow specialised jobs?

Any organisation has a number of tasks that need to be performed if its work is going to be properly accomplished and its objectives achieved. These might range from deciding whether or not to build a new factory, to controlling a piece of machinery on a production line, to answering customer complaints, to making the tea. In a very large organisation there may be many thousands of such tasks. So, for example, a major engineering company such as GEC manufactures a wide range of products from simple electrical fuses to complex, advanced radar for jet aircraft. It is a key part of the management process – and, specifically, it is the organisation designer's role – to group these tasks into the sets or collections that we call jobs.

This process of 'designing' jobs or grouping tasks into jobs is a very important one because:

- it tells each of the organisation's employees what they are expected to do at work, i.e. what their responsibilities are

- it tells each employee how and where they fit into the organisation as a whole, e.g. to whom they report and, if they have managerial responsibilities, who reports to them

- it helps to let outsiders, e.g. customers and suppliers, know from whom they should seek help or advice if they want to have a task performed by the organisation.

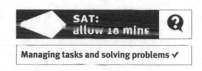

Managing tasks and solving problems ✓

ACTIVITY 1

Refer to the interview schedules with your chosen organisation, and for each of your interviewees in turn, answer the following questions:

1. To whom is each interviewee responsible for the quality of his or her work?

2. If you are a customer or client of your chosen organisation, in what ways might your interviewees offer assistance, either by performing a task for you, or giving you advice?

Commentary...

If one of your interviewees is a shop assistant in a supermarket, he or she might be able to assist customers by telling them where a particular product is kept in the store or by advising them of the price of an item, and so on.

If you cannot think of any ways in which your interviewees could be of assistance to a customer, it is likely that their jobs are so defined that they have little regular contact with the public. In this case, you could have suggested how their work might help colleagues who do deal directly with customers.

When dividing an organisation's tasks into a series of jobs for its employees to perform, two key choices have to be made.

1. To what extent should each particular job consist of a small number of similar tasks which the employee performs repeatedly so increasing his or her expertise (through work specialisation)? To what extent should each job consist of a wide range of varied tasks so that each employee has increased interest in their work and a broader range of skills (through job enrichment)?

2. Should each employee in the organisation be given a discrete job description, which is exclusive to each of them, so that the work overlaps as little as possible with that of any colleagues? Should the organisation deliberately define each person's job so that it overlaps significantly with that of his or her colleagues?

WORK SPECIALISATION VERSUS JOB ENRICHMENT

The concepts of work specialisation and job enrichment are important. Work specialisation involves dividing the organisation's tasks into narrowly defined jobs. Job enrichment is the process of designing jobs so that the employee has increased levels of interest, achievement and recognition. The aim of job enrichment is to generate greater employee motivation.

The case for specialisation in job design was recognised as early as 1776 by the economist Adam Smith in his book The Wealth of Nations. He argued that if workers are able to concentrate on one or a small number of specific tasks then, through repeated practice, they would become more knowledgeable, dexterous and efficient, working faster and making fewer mistakes.

However, there are dangers if specialisation is taken to extremes. Workers may become bored, performing repetitive tasks; they may work less hard, pay less attention and make more mistakes. Also jobs involving only a few repetitive tasks tend to be lowly valued and carry low status in organisations; this can demotivate those who perform them.

SPECIALISATION AND JOB ENRICHMENT IN THE MOTOR INDUSTRY

The British motor industry has recently seen major changes in the ways in which the jobs of production workers are defined. Traditionally, cars were made on a long production-line. This involved a series of small individual steps, starting with a basic chassis or subframe and ending with a painted, polished car. Each step in the process would be carried out by one or a few workers, performing a task that might last seconds or at most a few minutes. The workers would perform these repetitive tasks all day, as each new car came down the production line. Workers certainly knew their jobs well, but also sometimes became bored and demotivated and did not always work efficiently. They required close supervision, not least to avoid substandard work.

By the late 1980s, it was clear that British motor manufacturers faced a major competitive threat from Japanese car manufacturers such as Nissan, Toyota and Honda. Japanese cars were generally being built to higher standards and were often cheaper, not least because Japanese motor industry workers were more productive. In response, firms such as Rover and Vauxhall (part of General Motors) have taken a radical look at production workers' jobs. They are engaged in a process of multi-skilling, i.e. they are trying to give production workers a range of skills. This means that workers can perform several tasks upon a car as it passes their workstation on the production line and that they can be moved from one workstation to another on the production line. This has required a great deal of investment in new training but it is beginning to pay dividends. The car companies have found that workers are better motivated; they have raised their productivity, they make fewer mistakes and they require less supervision.

DISCRETE JOB VERSUS OVERLAPPING

Now consider, the options under choice two. Clear, discrete job descriptions are beneficial in that they ensure that each person knows clearly what his or her job is, and for what he or she is responsible. People have a tendency to become demotivated if they do not know what is expected of them. Equally other people inside and outside the organisation need to find out who is responsible for what. It can also avoid the kind of squabbling and disagreements that can occur when colleagues in an organisation disagree about who is responsible for what tasks. So, for example, in a bank, a customer account manager might only be allowed to approve loans up to £10,000; all other loans require the branch manager's approval. The job is clear and disputes are unlikely to occur.

However, such tight job descriptions can lead individuals only to take an interest in their own job, to ignore its impact upon colleagues and their work, and not to feel a responsibility for the work of the organisation as a whole. So, for example, the bank's customer account manager may take great care advising a customer requiring a loan of £8,000, because it is 'his (or her) customer', but spend less time trying to advise or help a customer who visits the bank seeking a £150,000 loan, knowing that the latter customer's case will eventually have to be dealt with by the branch manager. Yet the customer requiring the larger loan may need more advice and may prove a more profitable customer for the bank as a whole.

Issues of this sort have led some organisations to conclude that while their employees do need to know clearly what their jobs are, at the same time there can be value in seeing that groups of workers performing related tasks have overlapping job descriptions. In other words, there is an argument in some cases for shared responsibilities.

Such overlapping needs to be designed with great care to avoid duplication of work and squabbles over responsibilities. It needs to be accompanied by team-building activities, in which groups of colleagues working on a series of related tasks are encouraged to work together harmoniously, and to recognise that their responsibility is for the work of the group as a whole, not just for the particular task they happen to be performing at the moment. Such team-building can improve employee motivation and cut costs. In an effective team, individuals will see to it that their work is done in harmony with that of their colleagues and will take time to help a colleague who has a problem.

OVERLAPPING JOBS AND TEAM-BUILDING IN THE MOTOR INDUSTRY

Complementing the introduction of multi-skilling, British motor manufacturers have reorganised production. Workers now operate in teams who share overlapping job descriptions.

Previously, the British motor industry was notorious for tight lines of demarcation which laid down precisely what each production worker was expected to do. Workers were very reluctant to do anything outside their particular narrowly defined job. As a consequence if a piece of machinery had a simple breakdown on a production line, the whole line might have to stop until a maintenance person could be brought in to repair it, yet the production worker might have been quite capable of repairing the machine in seconds.

Today great strides have been made to set such restrictions aside. A production worker whose machine breaks down can recognise that, as a team member, he or she has shared responsibility for repairing breakdowns with the team member specifically appointed to do maintenance work. A simple breakdown can be repaired on the spot without calling in a maintenance worker and with the minimum halt to production.

In this case, the planned overlapping of jobs is closely integrated with the process of job enrichment. Simple maintenance is part of the production workers' wider and more interesting responsibilities.

Hierarchy

Child's second question referred to the hierarchy in an organisation.

> **\?/** The hierarchy describes the levels of seniority within an organisation from its chief executive to its least experienced operative. It sets out who reports to whom and who is responsible for whose work. It is a rigid structure.

2. How many levels should an organisation have in its hierarchy and how wide should be the spans of control of its managers?

Organisations often attempt to present their hierarchies pictorially using an organisation chart. These charts present certain aspects of an organisation's structure, such as its hierarchy, the jobs that have been defined within it and its department structure. It is quite common to see such diagrams displayed at the entrance to buildings or departments, including the names and pictures of the members of staff who hold various posts. There may well be such a chart in your college or workplace. Look at it and see if it tells you anything important about the organisation's structure.

Organisation charts can be very useful. They provide a quick and sharp impression of the key elements of an organisation's structure. However, like maps, they are abstractions from reality, which exclude much information about the organisation's structure. For example, they commonly include job titles but not job descriptions. Equally, they tell you about the formal side of the organisation, not its informal side, so they can give a misleading impression of how things really work. Their value should be recognised, but they should be used with care. Several organisation charts are illustrated in this section. They do not cover the whole of the organisation depicted, but those parts of it about which you need to know.

Figure 2.1 shows an extract of the organisation chart of Acme Manufacturing. The company works a 24-hour day and operates a three-shift system. The chart illustrates the number of steps in the hierarchy from the managing director to the operatives who make the company's products in its factory. Normally, the steps in an organisation's hierarchy are presented diagrammatically by vertical divisions and linked by vertical lines. As a consequence hierarchical relationships (relationships which indicate seniority) in an organisation are frequently referred to as its vertical relationships.

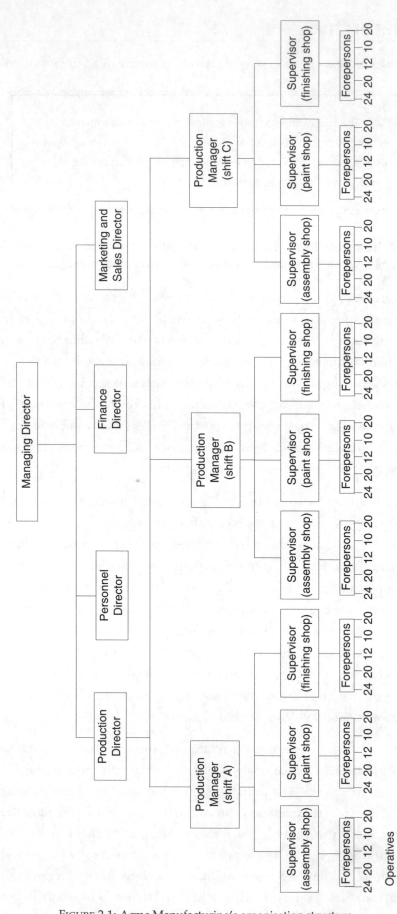

FIGURE 2.1: Acme Manufacturing's organisation structure.

Acme Manufacturing has five steps in the management chain, from managing director (most senior) to production director (first step), from production director to production manager (second step), from production manager to supervisor (third step), from supervisor to foreperson (fourth step) and from foreperson to operative (the least senior employee, fifth step).

Organisations need hierarchy because of the range of tasks that they have to perform and the variety of different people with varying skills that they employ. Acme Manufacturing needs skilled operatives to assemble, paint and finish its products, but it also needs a production manager to ensure that the flow of work proceeds smoothly on each shift, a production director to ensure that factory is equipped with modern machinery and a managing director to ensure that the whole operation runs smoothly and that plans are drawn up for its future development.

It is generally thought that it is more efficient for organisations to have as few levels as possible in their hierarchies. The more levels there are in a hierarchy, the more steps are needed for information (orders, directives or reports) to pass from top to bottom (or vice versa). At Acme Manufacturing, a message from the managing director must pass through five stages to reach the operatives. Each stage is likely to add to the time the message takes to reach its destination. There is also the danger that it will be distorted through differing interpretations at each stage, so that the operatives will not receive the precise message intended by the managing director.

The more steps there are in an organisation's hierarchy, the taller it is said to be; the fewer stages there are in an organisation's hierarchy, the flatter it is said to be.

HIERARCHY

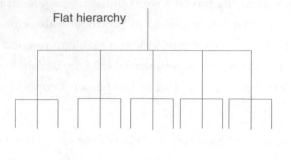

Flat hierarchy

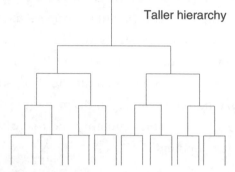

Taller hierarchy

FIGURE 2.2: Organisational hierarchies.

SAT:
allow 10 mins

Managing tasks and solving problems ✔

ACTIVITY 2

Refer to the interviews with your chosen organisation, and determine how many levels it has in its hierarchy. If your chosen organisation is a large one, your interviewees may not be aware of the full extent of the hierarchy or you may not have captured all the information you need. However, describe the hierarchy as fully as you can.

To have an adequate understanding of an organisation's structure we need to understand how many levels there are in its hierarchy (i.e. whether it is tall or flat); but also we need information about the extent of the supervisory responsibilities of its employees. The width of a person's supervisory responsibilities is called his or her span of control.

> **\?/** The span of control is the number of subordinates who report to an employee and for whose work that employee is responsible.

At Acme Manufacturing, each production manager has a span of control of three supervisors. Note that each production manager's span of control does not include all of the 94 people below him or her in the hierarchy. The five forepersons and 860 operatives do not report directly to the production managers and so they are not part of their span of control.

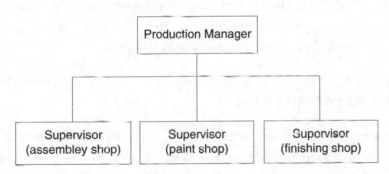

FIGURE 2.3: Production manager's span of control.

It is a difficult judgement to decide what is an appropriate span of control. If a supervisor's span of control is too wide then he or she may be unable to devote sufficient time to the various subordinates in the span. The supervisor may be unable to co-ordinate the subordinates' activities thoroughly, or to advise them when they face difficult problems. Early organisation theorists (e.g. Graicunas V., 'Relationship in organization', in Papers on the Science of Administration, 1937, University of Columbia Press, New York) concluded that spans of control should generally be quite narrow, generally not more than ten people.

However, organisations frequently expect supervisors to manage more than ten people. For example, at Acme Manufacturing forepersons in the assembly shop are responsible for 24 operatives. It is argued that narrow spans of control can lead to 'over-supervision'; subordinates' work is overseen so closely that they have insufficient scope to use their own judgement and initiative, they might feel under-utilised and so become demotivated. Equally, if supervisors are responsible only for a narrow body of work, then there may be inadequate attention paid to the need to co-ordinate the work of the organisation as a whole. Finally, there is a cost involved. It follows logically that the narrower spans of control in an organisation, the taller its hierarchy will be.

In practice, spans of control vary according to several considerations:

- The complexity and variety of the jobs performed by the subordinates – at Acme Manufacturing the managing director has only a four-person span, but in the assembly shop forepersons have a 24-person span.

- The abilities of the supervisor and the subordinates – good supervisors and subordinates can both operate in broad spans of control.

- The range of the supervisor's own responsibilities – at Acme Manufacturing the finishing shop supervisor only has a five-person span, but this is because he or she also acts as a quality inspector and this is a time-consuming task.

THE FLAT ORGANISATION

In recent years, many organisations have devoted attention to shortening their hierarchies. For example, in 1994, the government asked police forces in Britain to reduce the length of their hierarchies by removing one rank from among their senior officers (probably Chief Inspector). The reasons put forward for creating flatter organisations have to do with cutting costs and enriching the jobs of employees. Costs are cut because, as hierarchies are shortened, fewer people are employed as managers and supervisors. Jobs are enriched because the fewer managers who remain have wider spans of control and greater responsibilities. This means that they supervise their subordinates less closely, so that the subordinates are expected to do more for themselves and show greater initiative.

If Acme Manufacturing decides to remove the grade of supervisor, the production manager for each shift would have a span of control of five, instead of only three. The forepersons might be expected to take decisions and responsibilities previously taken by a supervisor. Given the broader remit of the foreperson, the operatives might well be expected to take more responsibility for the quality of their work without having it so closely inspected, tasks that previously would have been done for them by the foreperson. Taking on broader responsibilities means giving employees a more varied and richer job. It can help to make them better motivated.

However, it is a mistake to believe that simply cutting the length of a hierarchy will produce beneficial effects. Those who take on increased responsibilities need to be trained to do so, or they may become overworked and suffer from stress, and the overall quality of their work may fall. They may also become demotivated as their promotion opportunities diminish. For example, at Acme Manufacturing, an ambitious foreperson no longer has nine supervisors' jobs to aspire to, but only three, much more senior, production managers' jobs. Finally, wider spans of control can mean that the supervisor has less time to spend with subordinates, so that the organisation's communications will deteriorate.

You may wish to look back at the interviews with your chosen organisation, to see if it has attempted to introduce a flatter hierarchy in recent years. If so, did your interviewees report any benefits or drawbacks from this change?

Grouping activities

Child's third question is:

3. How should jobs and departments be grouped together?

The way in which an organisation chooses to group together its activities to form units, sections, teams, departments or divisions (the names may vary from organisation to organisation) should reflect its strategic (or fundamental) goals, and the ways in which it expects those goals to be achieved. For example, during the 1980s, many pharmaceutical companies created biotechnology research teams or departments to reflect the major changes they expected to take place in their product ranges as a consequence of the development of genetic engineering techniques. Similarly, many colleges and universities, having identified business and management courses as a potential growth area, formed business schools to link together a range of business-related disciplines, such as economics and accounting.

The choice that an organisation makes when grouping its activities together is also important for its staff. It determines which colleagues are to be supervised by a particular manager, to share a common set of objectives and to draw upon a common pool of resources. Staff in a particular department tend to identify with one another and to build up bonds of loyalty, common purpose and achievement with one another.

Organisations can foster loyalties between team colleagues in this way. They can also encourage competition between teams to achieve the best results. Such rivalries can be constructive for the team and for the organisation as a whole, provided they are carefully managed and do not lead team members to hinder the performance of rival teams.

When deciding how to group jobs together to form departments, an organisation needs to decide precisely what common characteristics or logical links between its activities it regards as being paramount. In other words, it needs to decide the basis upon which it wishes to form its departments. There are three common ways in which organisations build their teams, units, departments and so on.

1. The activities, processes or functions that jobs share in common might lead to their being grouped together. This is called the functional principle and it creates a functional structure.

2. The outputs, products, goods or services that groups of colleagues work together to produce might be used to decide. This is called the product principle, and it creates a product structure

3. The customers that groups of colleagues work together to serve might be used. This is called the customer principle and it creates a customer structure.

We now look at each of these three structures in turn: to see what they look like; to find out when they are used; and to find out what advantages and disadvantages they may have. In addition, we look at other structures – hybrid, matrix and project teams – where particular structural characteristics are combined, or completely discarded.

FUNCTIONAL STRUCTURE

This is the most common form of structure. Using the functional principle, jobs are grouped together to form departments because they involve similar or related sets of activities or skills which provide a key service to the organisation and to the achievement of its goals.

The Acme Manufacturing Company has a functional structure. It has four functional departments: a production department; a personnel department; a finance department; and a marketing and sales department. Each department has its own director who reports directly to the managing director.

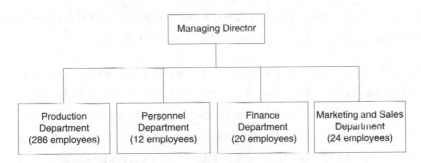

FIGURE 2.4: Functional structure – Acme Manufacturing.

Each department provides an essential service for Acme Manufacturing.

- The production department assembles and paints its products and then checks them to ensure that they are manufactured to the standard that customers expect.

- The personnel department ensures that the company has the right staff with the right skills throughout all four departments to do all the jobs that need to be done. It also ensures that those staff are appropriately rewarded, that they are trained and that their legal rights as employees are respected.

- The finance department ensures that Acme Manufacturing has the funds necessary to carry on its activities, that its bills are paid, that staff wages are paid in the correct amounts and on time, that proper accounts are kept, and so on.

- The marketing and sales department ensures that the company knows what is happening in its markets, that potential customers are kept informed about the company's products, that salespersons visit customers to take orders, and that those orders are delivered on time.

Notice that the departments do not have to be of equal size. The production department is considerably larger than the other three. What is important is that each department has an important, coherent and logically related set of tasks to perform.

A functional structure has generally been found to be effective for small and medium-sized companies because it helps to ensure that each of the key functions in the company is performed by specialists who concentrate on performing their particular tasks, so gaining experience and utilising their particular skills (in marketing, bookkeeping and so on). It can help to cut costs by enabling organisations to make the best use of expensive equipment (notice that Acme Manufacturing has three shifts to maximise the use of its production machinery) and of expensively trained staff (by allowing them to concentrate upon their particular specialisms).

Functional structures, however, do pose problems of horizontal co-ordination between the various functional departments. In relatively small organisations, like Acme Manufacturing, such problems can be overcome because managers often know one another well, see one another frequently and so have sufficient opportunities to deal with common problems. As organisations grow larger such possibilities are likely to become fewer, because there are more managers, perhaps working on different sites, and so a functional structure may come to be less satisfactory. Then the organisation will need to consider restructuring itself.

A similar problem may occur if the environment outside the organisation is changing in ways that require new responses and ways of working from several departments at once. For example, Acme Manufacturing might find that technological changes require it to make and market new products. This would require close collaboration between the production and marketing departments. Companies with functional structures have often found it difficult to organise the necessary horizontal collaboration. Again, a reorganisation may be necessary if the company is to solve its problem.

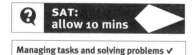

SAT:
allow 10 mins

Managing tasks and solving problems ✔

ACTIVITY 3

Refer to the interviews with your chosen organisation, and identify and list the key functions that it has to perform.

Are these key functions located in separate departments or are closely related functions such as research and development, marketing and sales or sales and distribution banded together? If so, list the functional departments you can identify.

Commentary...

Although you may have identified some functional departments, this does not necessarily mean that your chosen organisation has a functional structure. It may use another of the three organising principles, as well as the functional principle.

PRODUCT STRUCTURE

The product principle implies grouping all the jobs necessary to the development, manufacture, marketing and sales of a particular good or service or closely related group of goods or services. So, a product structure brings together all of the functions (marketing, production, and so on) that are necessary to bring a particular product to the consumer.

Product structures tend to be particularly well suited to meeting the needs of consumers. The focus for everyone, no matter what their specific function and training, is on the needs of the product. If consumers indicate that they wish to see the product changed in some way then the attention of everyone in the department can be brought to bear on bringing about the necessary changes.

Large organisations producing a variety of different products or providing a variety of services often favour a product structure. It enables them to focus their efforts upon the changing needs of consumers in a variety of markets.

FIGURE 2.5: Product structure – PFM Leisure plc.

Take as an example PFM Leisure plc. The company is quite large, with over 6,000 employees. It has three distinctive product lines, a small group of 12 luxury hotels, a chain of betting shops and six Happy Hols Holiday Camps.

The management of each product line involves different considerations. Each is catering for different customers and different patterns of consumption. The luxury hotels provide a year-round service, including conference facilities, largely to businesses and senior business executives. The holiday camps offer a wide range of entertainment facilities for children and are targeted at families on tight budgets. It is a seasonal business, the camps are closed from October to March. In the betting shops, customers usually drop in for only a short while, to place a bet, then leave.

These are not static businesses. PFM Leisure must respond to new trends and seek to exploit new opportunities. For example, in 1994 the law was changed to allow betting shops to be made more attractive and comfortable. PFM Leisure will need to respond to this change or their betting shops will lose custom to those of other companies who do begin to offer greater comfort to customers placing bets.

Given PFM Leisure's structure it is relatively well placed to meet this challenge. Responsibility for the betting shops lies completely in the gaming division. Here staff, no matter what their specialism, will be aware of the implications of the legal changes. The finance staff know that money will have to be found to upgrade the betting shops. The personnel staff know that betting shop managers may have to be trained to manage a wider range of services (such as catering services to offer meals to customers) and new staff may need to be employed to provide them. The marketing staff know that they will need a new strategy to market and advertise the improved facilities.

The need for such changes might be missed in a solely functional structure. Here, for example, marketing staff have to monitor changes in every company market, and they might miss significant changes in particular small or unusual markets. Furthermore, once the need for a change has been identified, it may be difficult to bring together all the staff with the required skills and to focus their attention upon the activities needed to implement a new approach.

Although a product structure is good at identifying changes in existing markets, it is less good both at identifying the development of new markets and of related changes taking place in more than one company market at once. The result can be missed opportunities, as new products are not developed; and duplicated efforts, as two departments attempt to deal with the same change in each of their markets. Even where changing market needs can be identified, it can be difficult to make two or more different product departments work together effectively in order to meet them.

For example, an engineering company with product divisions might waste time, effort and money developing two very similar components to go into products manufactured by each of two of its divisions, when a single component might have been developed that was suitable for both products.

A major fashion retailer with divisions specialising in mail-order retailing and high-street retailing in stores, might easily miss the growth of tele-shopping (where consumers purchase items seen on television using the latest communications technologies) because neither of them is directly involved in the market already. Yet, some years hence, a failure to enter this market might seriously affect the company's prospects.

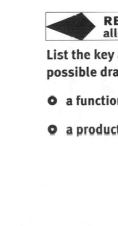

RECALL:
allow 10 mins

List the key advantages and possible drawbacks of:

○ a functional structure

○ a product structure.

CUSTOMER STRUCTURE

The customer principle implies grouping all the jobs necessary to service the needs of a particular group of clients or customers. A customer structure brings together all of the functions (marketing, sales, production and so on) necessary to serve a particular group of customers.

When deciding to operate a customer structure, an organisation must decide what is the key feature (or characteristic) of its customers, so that they can be grouped together sensibly. One commonly used criterion for grouping customers is geographical, i.e. on the basis of where they live or work. This leads organisations to adopt local or regional structures or, if they are international, to have national structures.

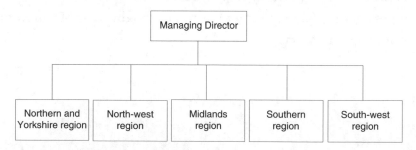

FIGURE 2.6: Customer structure – Union Dairies.

Union Dairies is a national manufacturer and distributor of dairy products. Because customers' demands for dairy products vary from place to place and because bulky raw materials, such as milk, are expensive to transport over long distances, the company has adopted a regional structure. Each region has all the functional specialisms necessary to serve its market, so that it can meet its particular needs e.g. for local cheeses.

Some local authorities, such as Middlesborough and Tower Hamlets, though they do not have an entirely geographically based customer structure, have moved a long way towards one. They run most council services through a series of local offices. This allows them to co-ordinate services at a local level and vary them to meet the needs of particular localities.

It is not necessary to base a customer structure on geography; an organisation can choose some other criterion for grouping customers. Age can be a criterion; political parties usually organise separate sections for young people and older members, such as the Young Conservatives. Hospitals frequently are divided into departments, each treating patients with a different kind of illness.

This kind of structure has many of the advantages of a product structure. It allows all the staff in a district or region, for example, to focus their attentions upon the needs of a particular group of customers. Again, it is a structure of particular value to large organisations with a variety of different client groups, in different countries, and so on. But like a product structure, the customer structure can lead to missed opportunities, if they arise among a previously unserved group of customers; and it can lead to duplication of effort if different departments both attempt to solve the same problem which has occurred in different customer groups.

HYBRID STRUCTURE

Sometimes an organisation may choose not to organise itself according to one of these three principles (the function, product and customer principles). Instead, it might develop a structure by combining two of them together. Doing so gives rise to one of two other forms of organisation structure, a hybrid structure or a matrix structure. A hybrid structure occurs when an organisation adopts a structure which uses two of the functional, product and customer principles as a basis for its design.

In Merritt Chemicals, a functional principle is adopted at the corporate level. There are four directors (of research, human resources, finance and marketing), each of whom manages a key function and reports to the managing director. In addition, there are four directors each of whom manages a particular product division (plastics, pharmaceuticals, fibres and speciality chemicals). They are each responsible for all aspects of the development, production and marketing of their particular product ranges, but within the constraints of any company-wide policies set by the four corporate functional directors. For example, it may be that Merritt Chemicals decides to introduce a company-wide system of staff appraisal. The human resources director and his staff at corporate level would devise an appraisal system to be introduced across the whole company, including in both the four product divisions and the other three functional divisions.

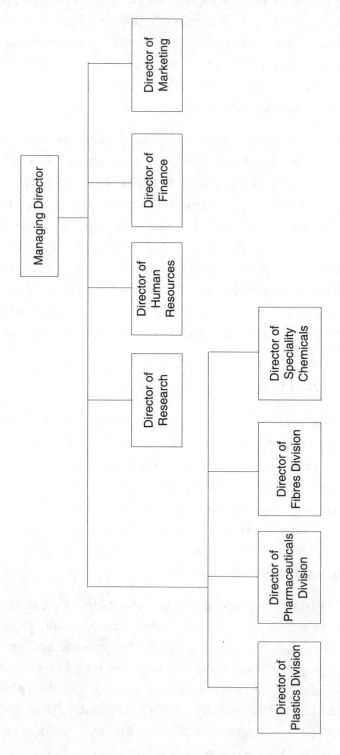

FIGURE 2.7: Hybrid structure – Merritt Chemicals plc.

THE TASTY BUN AND BISCUIT COMPANY

The Tasty Bun and Biscuit Company is on the verge of a major expansion. At present it has a single factory at Tiptown in the Midlands. This factory produces biscuits and cakes, and employs 600 staff. The company's current organisation structure is shown in figure 2.8.

FIGURE 2.8: Tasty Bun and Biscuit's organisation structure.

Now Tasty Bun is faced with major decisions. It has recently won two major new contracts, each with a national supermarket chain. These will necessitate a 200 per cent growth in the company's production of both cakes and biscuits. The company will have to make daily deliveries of its products all over the country each day.

To cope with the growth the company has decided to open two new factories, each as large as the Tiptown site and each employing 600 staff. It has purchased two suitable sites for these factories, one near Plymouth and the other near Manchester. It has now to decide how to organise itself to cope with expansion.

Biscuits and cakes have always been produced using different production lines, processes and machinery at the Tiptown factory. Some economies could be gained by having one of the new factories concentrate on biscuits and the other one on cakes. This would allow each factory to develop a very large production line and a high level of expertise in producing one of the two product-lines. The company feels that the gains of so doing would be beneficial but small, as it has been able to develop its two smaller existing production lines at Tiptown to a very high level of efficiency already.

The problem with this approach would be that some products would have to be shipped very long distances daily from Plymouth and Manchester to meet the supermarkets' national requirements. The alternative would be to build production lines for biscuits and cakes at each of the new factories and divide the country into three regional markets each served by a single factory. This would also have the advantage of allowing each factory to deal with the variations in regional demand that exist (e.g. for Eccles cakes in the North-west), which are significant, though not overriding.

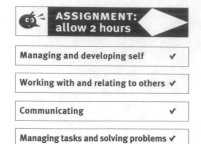

ASSIGNMENT:
allow 2 hours

Managing and developing self	✓
Working with and relating to others	✓
Communicating	✓
Managing tasks and solving problems	✓

ACTIVITY 4

Read the case study about the Tasty Bun and Biscuit Company. Working in a small group, discuss how you would advise the Tasty Bun and Biscuit Company about how to organise its production. Consider the production of individual lines at each factory, and how this affects the overall management structure and how the control of supply and distribution are carried out. You should highlight how different structures would affect the organisation as a whole.

Following your group discussions, write a 750-word report containing your recommendations. You should explain why you are offering the particular advice. Your report should contain an organisation chart illustrating your suggested new structure. Prepare your report on separate sheets of paper to submit to your tutor. You may wish to summarise the key points made in the group discussion in the box below.

The hybrid structure at Merritt Chemicals is a common one in large corporations. Large organisations also frequently adopt a structure combining functional departments or divisions at corporate level with a customer-based structure for providing its goods or services to customers.

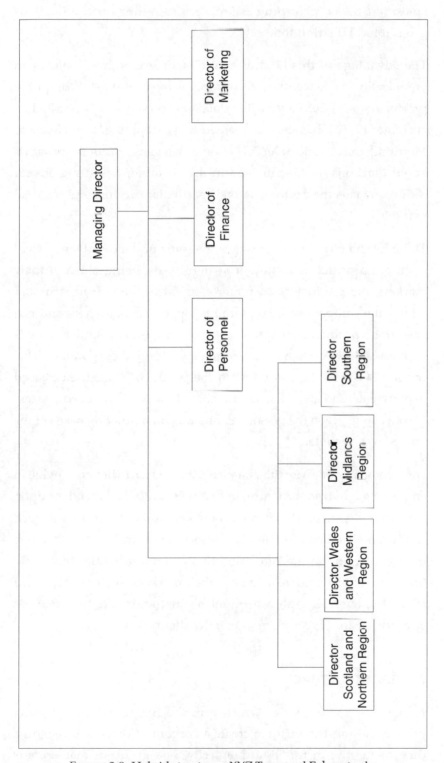

FIGURE 2.9: Hybrid structure – XYZ Tyres and Exhausts plc.

XYZ Tyres and Exhausts plc is a national company with over 100 service centres which supply and fit a variety of car parts such as exhausts, tyres, batteries and brake linings. There are three functional directors at corporate level (for personnel, finance and marketing) and four directors at regional level. The latter are organised on a customer basis, grouping customers together on the basis of geographical distribution.

The advantage of this kind of hybrid structure is that it allows an organisation to concentrate the efforts of most of its staff upon the production and delivery of its goods and services on a product or customer basis whichever is deemed most advantageous. Hence at Merritt Chemicals and at XYZ Tyres and Exhausts staff in the product-based divisions (at Merritt) and in the customer-based regions (at XYZ) can focus their efforts on their particular product and regional markets.

These hybrid structures can overcome some of the disadvantages of a simple product or customer structure. By being close to their markets, the product or customer element of the hybrid structure allows the companies to be more responsive to customers and can encourage product innovation. At the same time, each company's structure allows certain functions to be performed corporately. This can avoid duplication of effort in the product- or customer-based departments, and allow the best functional specialists, at headquarters to concentrate upon the personnel, finance and marketing needs of the business as a whole.

For a company like Merritt Chemicals there is a further advantage in employing a hybrid structure, in that its success is dependent upon expensive research. This is both too costly to be duplicated in each product division and frequently relates to the work of more than one division. Organisations often find that certain important but costly functions, of relevance to a range of their markets, are best performed centrally, even though a product or customer function may be appropriate to serve each market individually.

MATRIX STRUCTURE

A matrix structure is one which uses the functional and product principles simultaneously to create an organisation structure with a dual hierarchy. In this dual hierarchy, one group of managers is responsible primarily for functional-related issues and the second group is responsible primarily for product-related issues. In a matrix structure many staff will be responsible to and report to two managers, one in each hierarchy. This is a complex form of structure often used when an organisation is trying to provide a range of products in changing markets. The organisation perceives itself as being under a number of conflicting pressures, so that neither the functional, nor product, nor customer principles can be applied satisfactorily across the whole organisation.

You may well be familiar with this kind of organisation, as it has frequently been adopted in universities and colleges to manage large departments and modular course programmes. This is illustrated in figure 2.10 which shows the organisation structure of Brightpool Business School.

Management group	Head of Human Resource Group	Head of Accounting and Finance Strategy	Head of Marketing and Business Group	Head of Information Management Group
BTEC courses manager				
Undergraduate degrees manager				
Professional courses manager				
Postgraduate degrees manager				
Short courses manager				

FIGURE 2.10: Matrix structure – Brightpool Business School.

At Brightpool Business School there are two hierarchies: one with four heads responsible for managing groups of staff who teach the same subjects (the vertical hierarchy); and one with five managers each responsible for controlling a group of related courses (the horizontal hierarchy). The vertical hierarchy is based upon the functional principle as each of the staff groupings reflects the particular academic expertise of its members. The horizontal hierarchy is based upon the product principle as each manager is responsible for a group of closely related products.

In a matrix structure like this, the teaching staff are responsible to two managers. For example, a lecturer in accounting and finance teaching on the BTEC programme is responsible to the BTEC courses manager for various aspects of his or her work such as teaching to the agreed syllabus, marking assignments on time and so on. However, he or she is also responsible to the head of accounting and finance for seeing that lectures are up to date and that course hand-outs are of an acceptable quality. The head of accounting and finance is responsible for deciding which staff from the accounting and finance group teach on the BTEC programmes. The BTEC courses manager is responsible for ensuring that all of the lecturers on BTEC courses work together as a team to provide a good service for students.

In all the other organisation structures we have considered, authority lies in the vertical hierarchy and any horizontal links represent co-ordination between people of the same rank. In an matrix structure, the horizontal links represent a horizontal hierarchy of equal authority to that of the vertical hierarchy.

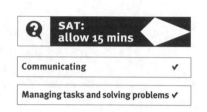

SAT:
allow 15 mins

Communicating	✔
Managing tasks and solving problems	✔

ACTIVITY 5

Look back over the material on the hybrid and matrix organisations. Make two lists:

1. the features that hybrid and matrix organisations have in common

2. the ways in which hybrid and matrix organisations differ.

Commentary...

Hybrid and matrix organisations are each based upon the application of two structural principles in the same organisation. They differ in that matrix structures involve the application of both principles to the same parts of the organisation at the same time, and hence give rise to a dual hierarchy as in the Brightpool Business School. In a hybrid structure, each principle is applied to different parts of the organisation at the same time. For example, in XYZ Tyres and Exhausts plc the functional principle is applied to the senior and head office staff, and a geographically based customer principle is applied to the remainder of the staff.

A matrix structure can provide very high levels of horizontal co-ordination, because the organisation's horizontal linkages (as well as its vertical ones) are represented within its own hierarchy. It also provides for a high degree of flexibility which is valuable when serving very varied markets. At Brightpool Business School, the needs of a full-time BTEC HND student on a two-year full-time programme are likely to be quite different from those of a senior manager attending a one-day short-course on the latest management thinking in a particular field. The BTEC courses manager and the short courses manager can ensure that each student receives a properly designed programme, while the heads of each staff group can see that capable staff are appointed to teach each programme.

The matrix structure is closely associated with the idea of the project team. This is when a group of staff are brought together from both hierarchies to deal with a particular project or problem. The flexibility of the matrix structure allows the organisation to call upon a team of people with the right mix of skills to handle the project successfully. For example, if Brightpool Business School decided to set up a new undergraduate degree in accounting and information management, then the undergraduate degrees manager could lead a team of appropriately qualified colleagues from the accounting and finance group and the information management group to set it up.

A number of large organisations have adopted, at least in part, a matrix structure. Examples include Monsanto Chemicals, ICI and Prudential Assurance. However, matrix structures do pose problems for organisations: it can take a long time to arrive at decisions because staff from two hierarchies have to agree them; disputes can arise between the two hierarchies, as each has different priorities and concerns; and employees can become confused as they have to respond to the (sometimes inconsistent) wishes of two different managers.

Given these difficulties, and the extra costs of employing two sets of managers, an organisation will only find it worthwhile to set up a matrix structure in quite specific circumstances:

- when it faces varied external pressures, to run courses of high quality (to satisfy students and awarding bodies such as BTEC) and to run them at low cost (to satisfy central government which provides the funds to run most courses)

- when it serves a variety of changing markets, so that it constantly has to adjust its services to meet their needs

- where the organisation lacks the resources to provide for each of its markets separately, so that resources have to be shared between the various markets. For example, the lecturers teaching on Brightpool Business School's BTEC courses are likely also to be teaching on a range of other courses as well.

Even if these conditions are met, the organisation needs to put considerable effort into making sure that managers in each hierarchy are clear about their responsibilities and those of their colleagues in the other hierarchy, in order to avoid disputes and confusion. It also needs to ensure that its organisational culture emphasises teamwork so that its staff will work together closely in an effective way.

PROJECT TEAMS

Task forces or project teams are set up within existing organisations to deal with specific problems or tasks. They are usually temporary arrangements. Teams usually include representatives or key decision-makers from sub-units and technical experts. They exist until the task or problem is completed. They can achieve results by:

- making recommendations to the executive to whom they are responsible

- reaching decisions in the group when the appropriate executive is the formal leader

- the representatives of the sub-units taking back recommendations to their sub-units.

In a matrix structure, the project team may be autonomous. It may have the authority and expertise to implement decisions.

Within some organisations, project teams may be set up to undertake product development. Ultimately, as the new product takes shape, the team may become an integral part of the organisation structure. A product team structure is something of a halfway house between the product division structure where support functions are centralised and the multi-divisional structure where each division is responsible for its own support functions. Each team is self-contained and managed by a product team manager. Specialists from the support functions are combined into product development teams to serve the needs of particular product divisions. The team focuses on, and is responsible for, one product or a small group of related products. This empowers individuals to take control of their activities and means that a synergy is created with the sum of the group or team being more than the individuals.

For example, when Lee Iacocca took over Chrysler, the company changed its approach to product development by establishing a product team structure. This is more decentralised than a product or a functional structure and allows specialists within the team to act. He calls it a 'platform team' and it consists of engineers, planners, buyers, designers, financial analysts, sales and marketing personnel brought together to develop particular models of car. He set up four major teams: large car, small car, van and jeep/trucks.

MAKING CHOICES

As we have emphasised, the grouping of jobs into departments and departments into divisions and regions (or whatever an organisation may choose to call them) is a key choice that has to be made about the structuring of an organisation. This choice can be made using the functional, product or customer principles, or by using two of them to form a hybrid or matrix structure. Whatever the choice that is made about how to group an organisation's activities it is usually not an easy one, with costs as well as benefits for the organisation and its staff. The departmental structure chosen should be that which best reflects the objectives and purposes of the organisation.

Here, we have looked at some of the internal operating factors that affect structure. In section two, we shall review the different factors that affect an organisation's structure, some of these are internal and some external, some the organisation can control and others it cannot.

Integration

So far, in answering the first three of Child's five questions, we have discovered that organisations need to divide their various tasks up into jobs, that jobs are bound together into divisions and departments, and that organisations normally create hierarchies in which some employees are responsible for (i.e. manage) the work of others.

We have also discussed the need for co-ordination.

> **!?!** Co-ordination is the process which integrates the different tasks of individuals and departments so that the organisation can work smoothly and its objectives be efficiently achieved.

Co-ordination is a key issue for organisations for, having divided employees' tasks up into various separate and specialist jobs, which tend to be grouped into specialist departments (whether by function, product or customer), the organisation then needs to ensure that these employees and departments work together efficiently for the good of the organisation as a whole. This is the essence of Child's fourth question:

4. How closely do the various parts of an organisation need to be integrated?

Henry Mintzberg (The Structuring of Organizations, 1979, Prentice Hall, New York), the American writer on management and organisations, has written that co-ordination occurs in three key ways: mutual adjustment, direct supervision and standardisation.

> **!?!** Mutual adjustment is the essentially informal process in which individuals adapt their understanding of a particular issue and their behaviour with regard to that issue in light of others' understandings, reactions or proposed reactions to that issue.

Consider for example, a maintenance worker on a factory assembly line, who if faced with a new and particularly difficult machine breakdown might ask advice from a number of people before attempting to repair it. These might include fellow maintenance workers and the maintenance supervisor. It might also involve asking the production workers familiar with the machinery, and their supervisor, to see if they have useful suggestions. The maintenance worker might also want to assess the possible consequences on production of any steps he or she proposes to take to repair the machine.

The maintenance worker's final decision about what to do will reflect his or her 'adjustment' to all the pieces of information and advice received. Notice though that the process of adjustment is mutual. The production line workers and their supervisor are likely to approach their work differently as a consequence of the maintenance worker's decision about how to tackle this problem.

In this case, co-ordination has taken place as well as mutual adjustment. Co-ordination has been both horizontal (between the maintenance worker and production workers) and vertical (between the maintenance worker and the production and maintenance supervisors).

An organisation can generally only rely upon this kind of mutual adjustment if it is small. It is an informal approach and often relies significantly upon people's social relationships. Larger organisations can utilise mutual adjustment within small working groups, but need to supplement it with other mechanisms for larger-scale co-ordination.

> **!?!** Direct supervision occurs when one person is given formal responsibility for the work of another. This responsibility is defined, so that the person being supervised has a clear job description setting out his or her work and the supervisor is held responsible for the work that falls within that description.

Direct supervision tends to be increasingly used in organisations as they grow larger. They can no longer rely solely on the informal co-ordination provided by mutual adjustment. As jobs are created, some people are required to undertake supervisory tasks as part or all of their job descriptions. So, the creation of a system of direct supervision can be related to the process of specialisation and the division of work. It also involves the creation of a hierarchy in the organisation, and those in the supervisory positions are superior in the hierarchy to those whom they supervise, and those being supervised report to those supervising them. The organisation chart of Acme Manufacturing (figure 2.1) shows that the managing director supervises the work of the production director (among others), who supervises the work of the production managers, and so on.

> **\?/** Standardisation is the process of defining a set of perfor-
> mance criteria to which some persons, things or processes are
> required to conform. It involves both determining what are the
> important features to which the item to be measured must conform
> and the level of performance to be expected for each feature.

Mintzberg suggests that organisations co-ordinate their activities by
standardising skills, output and work processes. According to
Mintzberg, when an organisation grows too large and complex to be
adequately co-ordinated using both mutual adjustment and direct
supervision, then it needs to standardise. This both allows employees
to know clearly what the organisation expects of them, and allows
those in supervisory positions easily to identify divergences from the
organisation's agreed standards.

Using direct supervision and mutual adjustment, a supervisor in a
craft workshop making high quality wooden furniture might
reasonably oversee the work of, say, ten experienced carpenters, each
of whom makes whole pieces of furniture individually and
approaches each job in his or her own way. The supervisor may
proceed partly through giving advice (mutual adjustment) and partly
by instruction, e.g. instructing a carpenter which job to do first to
meet part of an urgent order awaiting delivery (direct supervision).

This approach is not possible at Acme Manufacturing, where a
foreperson may supervise as many as 24 operatives. Their work must
be closely co-ordinated with that of other workers in the
manufacturing process, if production is to proceed smoothly, and if
products are to be made to consistent quality standards demanded by
consumers. Here:

- skills need to be standardised, so that employees in a particular
  job can reasonably expect to work at a particular speed and to
  a particular standard

- output needs to be standardised, so that those responsible for
  quality inspections in the finishing shop are able to tell by
  performing a few speedy tasks whether or not an item or batch
  of items conforms to the performance criteria laid down

- the work process needs to be standardised, so that each
  performs an agreed task or set of tasks in an agreed way.

In this way, each operative's work when completed will be precisely ready for the next operative in the production process to undertake his or her work and will be ready at the right time so that the next operative does not have to stand idle waiting for work to do.

SAT:
allow 15 mins

Managing tasks and solving problems ✓

ACTIVITY 6

Refer to the interviews with your chosen organisation and determine to what extent the interviewees' activities are co-ordinated by mutual adjustment, direct supervision and standardisation. You may find the answers to Questions 9, 10, 11, 12, 13, 14, 15 and 19 helpful. Note down the ways in which your two interviewees' work is co-ordinated.

Commentary...

Unless your chosen organisation is a small one, it is likely that you should be able to identify all three forms of co-ordinating activity in their answers.

STAFF AND LINE RELATIONSHIPS

One further aspect of co-ordination is worth noting. The form of vertical hierarchy associated with direct supervision (as at Acme Manufacturing) is sometimes called a line relationship. Here there is a chain of command from the managing director to the operatives concerned with one of Acme Manufacturing's primary purposes, i.e. making its products.

However, many organisations are complex and have functions performed within them which are subsidiary to the organisation's primary purposes. People performing such secondary tasks usually have their own hierarchy and are often only able to advise rather than to instruct colleagues performing the primary functions.

These secondary functions are often called staff functions and people performing them are said to have a staff relationship to those in the line management of the organisation. For example, at Acme Manufacturing the personnel director and the employees in the personnel department may well perform a staff role for the company, giving advice about employment issues to managers (but not instructing) production and sales and marketing.

Finally, it is worth noting that the concept of staff and line, though sometimes valuable in helping us to understand organisations, is not always easy to apply in practice. It can sometimes be difficult to determine whether a particular department, or everyone in it, is staff or line.

Control

> !?! Organisational control is the process in which management regulates the behaviour of employees so that their work activities are consistent with the organisation's objectives.

We now consider Child's fifth and final question:

5. How much control should management exercise over the activities of an organisation?

As we have just discovered, organisations need to ensure that their employees' activities are co-ordinated so that one person's work is dovetailed with that of those colleagues whose work is dependent upon his or her efforts. However, organisations need also to ensure that employee's behaviour is controlled in a more general sense, to see that what they do and how they do it meets the needs of the organisation.

All organisations need to control the activities of their workers, but the key issue here is the extent to which such control should be exercised. This is the balance between centralisation and decentralisation.

\?/ Centralisation occurs when all, or nearly all, of the significant decisions in an organisation's life are taken at or near the top by senior managers.

Decentralisation occurs when many of the significant decisions in an organisation's life are taken by more junior staff in the organisation's hierarchy.

Much of modern management theory tends to stress the benefits of decentralisation. For example, Rosabeth Moss Kanter (The Change Masters, 1984, Allen and Unwin, London) emphasises the benefits of empowering employees to enable them to take more control over their work and to take more decisions themselves. It gives employees direct responsibility and ownership of their actions. Such decentralisation enriches people's work and improves their motivation and commitment to the organisation. It is an essential step if the organisation is to develop a flatter structure.

The current management theorists view is that many layers of hierarchy should be removed by cutting out many of the middle management roles and reducing the hierarchy to a maximum of five layers of management. Giving relatively junior staff more control over their work can also give them experience of managing tasks and of taking decisions, so training them to take on more senior posts and responsibilities.

Decentralisation also allows decisions to be taken close to the point where operations are being carried out, so that they are more likely to be influenced by the practical problems faced by the staff who have to carry them out, and the customers whose needs are to be served. This closeness to the customer and to the supplier provides its own control mechanism, as personnel who are directly dealing with situations also have the authority and responsibility to make decisions that have an immediate effect on their everyday life and effectiveness.

Despite the current emphasis on decentralisation, all organisations must exercise a measure of control over their employees. They must strike a balance between centralisation and decentralisation. Centralisation has its merits. It ensures that employees carry out a common policy and do not go their own way. It allows for quick decision making as decisions are taken by a few senior managers, rather than through negotiation with a larger group and control is retained by this top management team. Centralisation can also reduce costs and increase specialisation as employees can work in more specialist units reporting to top management, rather than having to spread expertise more widely through the organisation to serve a larger group of decision-makers.

GREATWEAR PLC

Greatwear plc, is a world-wide chain which specialises in fashionable clothes for young women. It has some 200 branches. It began in the 1970s as a single store run by an entrepreneurial retailer, Geoff Smith, who made all decisions himself. By 1985, Geoff Smith had expanded the business; he had 20 stores in Britain and decided to go public. Greatwear became a public limited company.

Smith still preferred to back his own judgement, rather than trust his managers to take any but the least important decisions. Among his decisions in that year was one to expand into the European market with 20 more stores in France, the Netherlands and Germany. In the short-run this proved disastrous, as Smith's judgement about the kinds of clothes young French, Dutch and German women would buy proved very wide of the mark. Greatwear made a loss for the first time in 1986.

As a consequence, at the end of the year, the shareholders voted to replace Smith as managing director with Arthur Brown, a less flamboyant figure with a long career in fashion retailing. Brown vowed to continue the company's international expansion and it grew rapidly. He said its style and philosophy must change to put its people first. Decision making must be devolved so far as possible to store managers. New communications technologies would be introduced to keep them fully informed about what stock was available and which fashion lines were selling well or badly in which markets.

This strategy worked well in the late 1980s. However, during the early 1990s, as world recession took hold, expansion slowed and new investments became much more risky. Even well-established branches lost money. As a consequence, Arthur Brown decided to use the company's advanced information technology system to monitor weekly sales in each branch and take greater control over what lines were stocked in each store.

ACTIVITY 7

In striking the right balance for an organisation between centralisation and decentralisation, a number of factors are likely to be influential.

Read the case study about Greatwear plc.

1. What key decisions were made at Greatwear plc about centralising and decentralising control at particular stages in the company's life?

2. What factors influenced these decisions?

3. Who were the decision makers at each stage?

Write a short report of 250 words, summarising your findings in the box below.

Commentary...

In the 1970s, Geoff Smith began as an entrepreneur with a single store. As the company grew and he opened more stores, he still retained control and made all the decisions. In 1985 Smith went public, relinquishing some control to his shareholders and board of directors but still continued to make management decisions about opening stores in Europe by himself. However, in 1986 Smith was forced out of the decision-making managing director role. The company was decentralised as it had grown too large and varied to be controlled by a single person.

This decentralisation was made possible by the use of new communications technology, which enabled branch managers to be kept better informed. The new managing director, Arthur Brown, had a policy of putting staff first to motivate them and this reflected a need to change the company's culture. The company was centralised in 1991 with changes in the world's fashion markets, again with the assistance of new technologies. This reduced risks and cut the costs of loss-making branches.

The Greatwear plc case illustrates a number of the key influences that lead companies to centralise and decentralise. It also illustrates the very important point that the best balance between centralisation and decentralisation is likely to vary with circumstances over time as the company and its environment change.

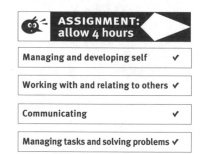

ASSIGNMENT:
allow 4 hours

Managing and developing self	✔
Working with and relating to others	✔
Communicating	✔
Managing tasks and solving problems	✔

ACTIVITY 8

You now are aware of the key questions and issues that arise in designing an organisation. Drawing on what you have learned about organisation design, this activity requires you to analyse the interview data you collected on your chosen organisation in session one.

1. Write a 750-word report describing the key elements in the design of your chosen organisation. Your report should contain an organisation chart. (If you are unable to construct an organisation chart for the whole organisation do not worry, simply make it clear that your information did not allow you to cover the whole organisation and explain which part of the organisation – for example a department, a division, a factory – your chart covers.) Your report should also include issues such as job design, hierarchy, spans of control, the departmental structure, co-ordination, the balance of centralisation and decentralisation, and management control.

2. Analyse the structure of the company and make recommendations for any changes you believe to be necessary.

3. Return to each of your interviewees and, using your description and chart, give them a 10-minute oral presentation on their organisation as you see it. Make notes on their reactions, so that you can correct any errors you have made, and record any new information they give you.

4. Amend your description and organisation chart in the light of what you have discovered. Prepare a best copy of your revised report for submission to your tutor. Use the box below for notes and to summarise key points.

summary

This session has looked at the key decisions involved in designing an organisation's structure.

▶ Work specialisation and job enrichment are key considerations when designing jobs.

▶ There must be a balance between the number of hierarchical levels and the extent of spans of control.

▶ Organisation charts provide a quick and sharp impression of the key elements of an organisation's structure but exclude much information such as job description.

▶ Jobs and departments can be organised by function, by product or by consumer base.

▶ Many organisations comprise a mix of these basic structures operating hybrid, matrix or product team structures.

▶ Organisations need to co-ordinate the activities of their members and this can be done by mutual adjustment, direct supervision and standardisation.

▶ In seeking to exercise management control, senior managers must decide between centralised and decentralised approaches.

Changing Structures

Organisational environments

Objectives

After participating in this session, you should be able to:

> describe different environments and their effects on organisational structure

> explain the role of contingency factors in an organisation's structure

> identify the effects of technology, and its role in change and stability.

In working through this session, you will practise the following BTEC common skills:

Managing and developing self	
Working with and relating to others	✔
Communicating	✔
Managing tasks and solving problems	✔
Applying numeracy	
Applying technology	
Applying design and creativity	

The environment

In today's world, organisations need to respond quickly and effectively to the changing environment if they are to succeed. It is important to understand the environment in which the organisation operates and how this affects its structure.

Organisations do not exist in isolation. Every organisation exists in an environment with which it interacts in order to survive and prosper. Organisation theorists often find it helpful to think of organisations as open systems. In this concept, an organisation is a set of interacting elements which takes inputs from its environment, transforms or changes them in some way, and produces outputs (goods or services) which are used by individuals or other organisations in its environment.

An organisation consists of structures and processes. It draws on people, technologies, machinery, raw materials and so on and uses them to produce goods and services. An organisation is influenced both by the provision of inputs from its environment and by its need to produce goods or services required within its environment. So, the age profile of the population, and their education, skills, and values, has an influence on the kind of people an organisation can employ. Similarly, the capabilities of the labour force in turn influences both the quality and quantity of products an organisation can produce.

From the late 1950s, a new approach to organisation theory was developed which became known as contingency theory. This argues that there is no single best way to structure an organisation. An organisation will face a range of choices when determining how it should be structured. Successful organisations adopt structures that are an appropriate response to a number of variables (or contingencies) which influence both the needs of the organisation and how it works. Four variables or contingencies are particularly important in influencing an organisation's structure: its size, its strategy, the technology it uses, and its environment.

The environment is a major 'contingency factor'. An organisation must take its environment into account in its planning and in managing its activities. In building a picture of the environment, it is useful to distinguish between the immediate specific environment in which an organisation operates and the more general environment which impacts on its affairs.

> !?! The specific environment includes customers, producers, suppliers and distributors, competitors, shareholders, unions, banks, government bodies and regulatory agencies.
>
> The general environment includes economic forces, international forces, technology, demographic and cultural forces, and political forces.

Consider, as an example, the environment of a local supermarket. Its specific environment includes:

- the customers and their tastes, habits and income

- a vast array of suppliers, distributors and producers who provide the stock

- companies which provide supplies and services to maintain the store's infrastructure (heat, light, shelving, freezers, etc.)

- staff from cleaners, shelf stackers and check-out personnel to supervisors and store managers.

The supermarket's managers must take into account a whole range of factors in its specific environment:

- It is affected by government and EU regulations covering the production, display and sale of food.

- Its personnel policies and freedom to hire and dismiss staff are influenced by unions and governed by legislation.

- Its pricing policies are affected by the action of its direct competitors.

- Its shareholders expect a return on their investment.

- It is reliant to some extent on banks for providing funding and cash flow.

- Its sales are affected by how much money its customers have to spend and their lifestyle.

The general environment affects the specific environments of all organisations. The specific environments are shaped by:

- economic forces

- international forces

- technology

- demographic and cultural forces

- political forces.

Economic forces impact on interest rates, unemployment, and the state of the national economy. Your local supermarket is affected, as any business would be, by a change in interest rates. This directly affects the cost of any borrowing from the bank or the return on any investments. It also affects the price of property and investors' expectations of their return on investment. The change in interest rates also impacts on a supermarket's customers. People with mortgages and interest-linked credit may have less or more to spend on groceries and other purchases each week if interest rates change.

International forces impact on foreign exchange rates. The state of other countries' national economies affect organisations involved in import and export markets. The supermarket would stock a wide range of imported goods such as wine from Europe, Chile and Australia and dates from the Middle East. Changes in the host country's economy would affect internal production costs; these together with any changes in the exchange rate, directly affect prices of imported products.

Technology directly impacts on most aspects of an organisation's activities. The development of computer-aided manufacturing technology can increase productivity. Advances in communications and information technology can improve decision making and enables routine tasks to be computerised. Computer systems lead to new and improved distribution networks. Air transport supports a global economy.

In your supermarket, for example, the development of bar coding and its effective use in warehousing and stock control has made retailing much more efficient. Note when you are next in the supermarket, the check-out person does not need to key in any information, the bar code is read, and the price is automatically included in your sales receipt and the stock number is also automatically deducted. When there are special offers, the computer can be instructed to recognise specific items and automatically discount them. This makes the whole check-out procedure much quicker, more accurate and more useful as stock figures are instantly available.

Demographic and cultural forces shape the age profile of the population, their education attainments, people's taste and attitudes, and trends in consumer spending. They impact on an organisation's customers and its staff. Changes in the culture of the marketplace affect the demand for different products and services. In the supermarket, demand for particular products change as the public wants more fat-free products, or products with less fancy packaging, or a particular product that is connected with a television series or a movie. Other products become fashionable; for example, as people have become 'environmentally aware' there has been a greater demand for cosmetic products that are 'not tested on animals'.

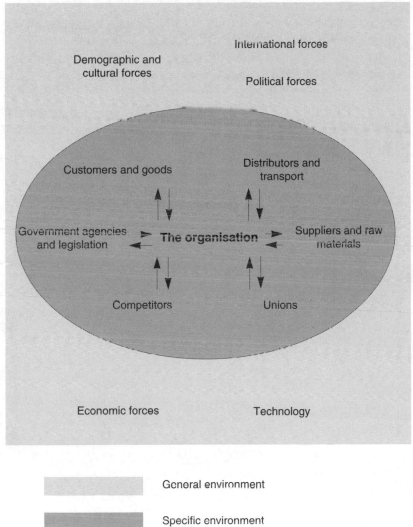

FIGURE 1.1: The organisational environment.

Political forces shape both the legislative and regulatory framework and the political climate in which organisations must operate. Governments might place import or export restrictions on particular raw materials and products. Some governments provide subsidies or erect trade barriers to protect their own industries. The EU farm support system directly intervenes and shapes the agricultural industry.

In both environments – specific and general – the organisation may have little or no control over the particular environmental factors. However, it can respond to minimise the impact of any detrimental environmental changes or to use them to its benefit. Figure 1.1 illustrates these interactions.

SAT:
allow 30 mins

Managing tasks and solving problems ✓

ACTIVITY 1

Review your chosen organisation drawing on your interview notes (from activity 6 in section one, session one). Describe the environment in which it operates. List the factors that are involved in both its specific and general environment.

Commentary...

If you have chosen a large organisation, then you should be able to list numerous factors. Smaller organisations may be subject to a narrower range of environmental factors. Our example of the supermarket shows the wide range of factors in its specific and general environments. These factors are not only numerous but can have a significant impact on the supermarket's business. You only have to look at the advertisements on the television and in the newspapers to see the intensity of competition between the supermarket chains. And competition is just one factor in the specific environment.

The key to understanding the influence of an organisation's environment upon its structure is to analyse the level of uncertainty or unpredictability in that environment. An environment can be uncertain because it is complex and varied, making it difficult to predict trends. It may also be uncertain because it is unstable, i.e. it is subject to rapid and major changes. This environmental uncertainty impacts on an organisation's structure.

Some organisations operate in relatively static environments. There may be no new competitors, no technological advances, and no new government regulations. For example, your local church or primary school has functioned in much the same way for many years, its chief 'environment' concern will be to obtain continued funding. However, even the Church of England is restructuring. It is moving the power base and decision-making centre; this may not affect your local church too much, but it will affect the hierarchies above it.

Other organisations operate in very dynamic conditions with rapidly changing technology, many new competitors in an expanding field, political instability or world-wide changes. For example, any company involved in technology itself, software or hardware, or in products that have a relatively short life span – fashion, cars – will need to make fast adjustments to its operations and its products. If a company is involved in armaments then it operates in an environment of world-wide political turmoil. These are both opportunities – to sell more weapons – and threats; there may be trading restrictions with countries that are seen to be the 'enemy'. For example, British companies are not allowed to supply arms to Iraq.

How quickly and effectively an organisation successfully can respond to environmental changes depends on its structure and what adjustments it can make in its structure to reduce environmental uncertainty. Environmental uncertainty is affected by:

- the complexity of the environment

- the dynamism of the environment

- the richness of the environment.

Environmental complexity is a function of the strength, number and relatedness of the factors within an organisation's specific and general environments. Obviously, the more factors that there are and the more diverse they are, the more difficult they are to manage. If many factors interrelate then the effect on the organisation becomes even more unpredictable.

A supermarket has many consumers, staff and suppliers. It is caught up in the economic worlds of its own locality in Britain, it is reliant on local labour and customers, but equally it is subject to national tastes and trends. Its supplies and its operations can be affected by local, national and international political decisions. As we discussed, a change in interest rates affects direct funding, investor expectations, consumer spending power and capital investment.

Environmental dynamism concerns the size and speed of changes in both the specific and general environment. An environment is stable if the forces act predictably. An environment is unstable and dynamic if the forces are not acting predictably and are changing rapidly. The computer industry is having to respond to rapidly changing technology, so its environment is dynamic. An organisation in this environment will look for ways of making it more predictable and lessening the uncertainty. Airline companies, for example, are currently experiencing environmental uncertainty with increased capacity and increased competition exacerbated by the world recession which has reduced the number of travellers. In 1995, British Airways launched a campaign with new specially designed seats to tempt lucrative first class passengers to travel with them. Our supermarket continually has to respond to its main competitors' actions, whether it is the establishment of a new store, or a publicity campaign, or reductions in prices, or the creation of an own brand line.

Environmental richness concerns the amount of resources available to an organisation. These resources may be staff, raw materials or funds. In poor environments, resources are scarce. This may be due to non-availability or fierce competition for the resources that are available. In an environment that is poor, unstable and complex, resources are more difficult to obtain and the organisation faces the greatest uncertainty. In a rich, stable and simple environment, resources are readily available and uncertainty is low. Our supermarket may wish to hire a highly trained pharmacist for its new pharmacy counter. The right person may not be available locally, it may need to recruit someone from another town and have to offer incentives to induce the person to take the job. Or it may wish to import saffron from Sri Lanka. This spice is only available in very small quantities from a sole supplier, so the supermarket needs to make sure that it has ordered sufficient supplies for this season. Otherwise it will be competing with other distributors who are buying up supplies. The political situation in Sri Lanka may also affect supply.

As the environment becomes more complex, less stable, and poorer rather than richer, the level of uncertainty rises.

ACTIVITY 2

Review the kind of environmental uncertainty faced by your chosen organisation. Are there many variables in its environment? Consider whether its environment can be described as:

- **simple or complex**
- **stable or unstable**
- **resource rich or resource poor.**

Commentary...

In the supermarket example, we have seen that it operates in a specific and general environment with many variables. The environment is complex because there are so many interrelating variables. It is relatively stable because the store's products have a reasonable life cycle; supermarkets provide people's basic living requirements and not just luxury, faddish, or technology-based products. It operates mainly in a resource rich environment; there is a vast array of products it could sell and, in general, there is no problem recruiting staff in the current environment.

Figure 1.2 summarises the interaction between the environment and an organisation's transactions. The more links the organisation has with its specific environment, and the more linkages there are between these specific environmental factors and the general environment, the more complex the environment becomes. With the increase in the complexity, comes an increase in uncertainty.

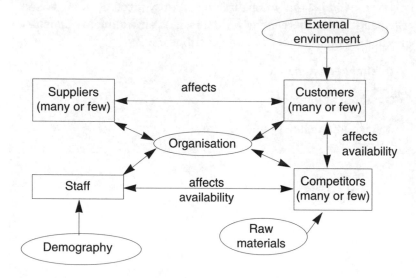

FIGURE 1.2: Analysing the environment.

ACTIVITY 3

EXERCISE:
allow 20 mins

Working with and relating to others ✔

Managing tasks and solving problems ✔

In small groups, discuss whether an organisation can affect its environment or whether it is totally subject to it. Suggest ways and strategies which organisations might adopt to reduce environmental uncertainty. You might want to draw on examples from your respective chosen organisations. Summarise your group's findings in the box below.

Commentary...

Organisations do try to reduce environmental uncertainty. Some of the strategies they adopt include:

- choosing to operate in more favourable environments
- competitor analysis
- forecasting trends
- contingency planning
- relocating
- reducing risk by joint ventures
- lobbying government to lift unfavourable regulations.

These strategies and tactics are explained in more detail below.

THE ENVIRONMENT

An organisation can have some effect on its environment in reducing environmental uncertainty. Here, we review some of the ways organisations try to reduce its impact.

First, organisations aim to choose a favourable environment in which to operate. If an organisation already exists in one environment, it may find it hard to move out of it into another. However, it can be achieved; for example, supermarkets are now competing with petrol stations for sales of petrol, so extending and changing their operating environment. Supermarkets now also include bakeries, flower shops, butchers, coffee shops, pharmacies. They have extended from their traditional grocery role to 'one-shop' shopping.

Organisations respond to competition by analysing their competitors. They try to anticipate their competitors' future plans. They might try to recruit staff from competitors. Our supermarket could hire a top manager from another supermarket chain who is well known for his or her innovative ideas.

Forecasting is a key activity. Organisations scan the environment for activity and changes. They want to anticipate what is happening in countries that control the supply of raw materials, what developments are likely in technology and information technology, and what competitors are planning. They need to understand trends in the national economy, trends in fashion and consumer tastes, and how the demographic changes are affecting consumer wants and needs.

Current demographic forecasts predict that there will be an increasingly ageing population. Older people will become an more important market segment. Our supermarket may choose to offer particular incentives for older people as Tesco's has done, allowing senior citizens to benefit from its Clubcard scheme even though they make smaller purchases than most families. Our supermarket may look to the future by developing new lines that are more appropriate for older people, by packaging more goods in ones and twos rather than in bulk packs for larger families, or by offering transport to their out of town shops for pensioners.

Organisations also take steps to minimise uncertainty by contingency planning. They ensure supplies or sales in uncertain times by stockpiling materials, using multiple suppliers, and creating finished-goods inventories. They try to protect themselves against inflation by using fixed-priced contracts for supplies. Our supermarket could find a back-up supplier of saffron in France if the Sri Lankan sole supplier has no (or low) stock.

If the local environment is very uncertain, one option is relocation. An organisation could move to a different location if staffing or the customer base would be improved. An out-of-town location with ample parking may be appropriate, even if our supermarket retains a smaller branch in the town centre.

Some organisations aim to improve their competitive position through mergers or joint ventures with competitors. British Airways has recently bought some small regional airlines including Manx Airlines and Brynon Airways. In 1995, Tesco took over the Scottish retailer William Low, and converted all the stores into a Tesco format. BMW, the German car manufacturer bought the UK car manufacturer Rover in 1994.

Finally, organisations seek to improve the regulatory environment by lobbying government agencies. For example, with the privatisation of the utility companies in the UK, there have been a spate of takeovers and buy-outs. However, these sales and purchases need authorisation by the Monopolies and Mergers Commission. The relevant parties will often lobby both the government directly and the Commission. For other types of transaction, the industry regulatory body may need to give approval so the individual companies may lobby for support. A company may lobby the government directly. For example, in 1995 Bernard Matthews, the turkey farming group, lobbied the government to prevent grain being exported from the EU. The company feared that poor harvests would force up the price of feed, raising the cost of farming turkeys.

We have reviewed here some of the ways our supermarket can respond to changes in its environment in a positive way and can exercise some control. However, other organisations may be much more subject to outside influences and some will struggle to survive. If we look at any selection of organisations in a particular industry, we can see that a variety of structural forms exist. Those that fit the environment will survive and others will fail or need to change. There is a competitive arena in any field and the fittest – and best suited – organisations will survive.

Consider some failed products. Afternoon newspapers have failed in most regions because the news is readily available from other sources. Typewriters have been replaced by word processors; vinyl records have been largely replaced by cassettes and CDs; Betamax video-recorders lost out to VHS machines. Failure is attributed to the changing environment; improvements in technology has driven all these changes, not any specific action or failure on the part of management. Of course, management is not entirely absolved of responsibility; it could be argued that the companies should have identified the advances and taken alternative routes in developing new products.

We now consider ways of characterising environments. Emery and Trist ('The causal texture of organizational environments', Human Relations, February 1965, pp. 21–32) identified four kinds of environments with increasing complexity that an organisation might meet:

- placid-randomised
- placid-clustered
- disturbed-reactive
- turbulent-field.

The placid-randomised environment does not change very much over time and so presents little threat to an organisation. Demands are randomly distributed. Environmental uncertainty is low. Few organisations, except perhaps government agencies, religious bodies or some traditional educational institutions, are in this situation.

The placid-clustered environment also does not change very much over time, but threats do occur in clusters, not randomly. For example, suppliers or customers may join forces and present a consolidated threat. Organisations in this environment need long-range strategic planning and centralised decision making. Our supermarket is likely to come into this category.

The disturbed-reactive environment is more complex. It is typified by environments dominated by one or more large organisations that, for example, can control prices in a particular industry. IBM is central to the computer industry and its activities cannot be ignored by competitors. Organisations in this environment need to behave tactically and be responsive to counteractions, so they must have a flexible operation. Our supermarket might even come into this category if it is competing with one of the large chains like Sainsburys, Tesco or Safeways. These are sufficiently large and dominant to affect other competitors. Smaller chains and franchises such as Spar and Londis will be affected by the actions of the major chains such as the location of their large stores and their range of products and pricing policies.

The turbulent-field environment is dynamic and has a high level of uncertainty. It is always changing and elements within it are interrelated. An organisation in this environment needs to be continually changing and developing new products and services to survive. Examples are manufacturers of microchips, software programmers and companies involved in the advertising or media business or the fashion trade; they are all highly subject to quickly changing fads and trends.

SAT:
allow 20 mins ❓

Managing tasks and solving problems ✓

ACTIVITY 4

Review the types of organisational structure you met in section one, session two. List the types of structure that you think will fit each of these different environments.

Commentary...

Organisations having placid-randomised or placid clustered environments will operate better with a mechanistic structure. They can operate with high differentiation, formalisation, integration and communication, and centralised decision making as they are stable and do not need to make rapid changes.

However, organisations with disturbed-reactive and turbulent-field environments will operate better with an organic structure. This requires less differentiation, low formalisation and integration, informal communication, and decentralised decision making. We review these structures later in the session.

Contingency theory

Contingency theory agues that there is no best way to structure an organisation. An organisation needs to respond to some key variables or contingencies and make the best choice for the organisation at any given time.

There are two significant implications of contingency theory:

1. If there is no 'one best way' then even apparently quite similar organisations (e.g. two nearby colleges) may choose significantly different structures and still be reasonably successful in achieving their missions.

2. If different parts of the same organisation are influenced in different ways by the contingencies affecting them, then it may be appropriate for them to be structured differently, e.g. one college department may have a functional structure, while another may have a matrix structure.

Paul Lawrence and Jay Lorsch did much research work in this area. They looked at the relationship between the environment and effective organisational structure (Organization and Environment, 1967, Harvard University Press). They considered how the forces in the environment affect the detail of the internal organisational structuring by investigating two different measures of structure:

1. the ways in which staff in different functional departments vary in goals and values (differentiation)

2. the ways in which these staff share a unity of effort (integration).

They looked at successful companies within three industries – plastics, food and container – with different levels of environmental uncertainty.

Lawrence and Lorsch found that even within companies, different departments might well face different environmental conditions, so that a department facing a stable environment might need a mechanistic structure, and a department facing a changing environment might require an organic structure. This means that the company might need to emphasise differentiation in its structural decisions. However, such an organisation will also require a high level of integration, as the various departments will need to work closely together in a flexible way if the organisation is to meet the changing needs of its clients or customers.

Figure 1.3 summarises Lawrence and Lorsch's findings. As you can see, a complex uncertain environment like the plastics industry requires the functional departments to develop different approaches to their tasks; this involves a high level of differentiation. The organisation requires a lot of co-ordination between the departments to achieve unity of effort, so there is a high level of integration. By contrast, in the stable container industry, there was low differentiation.

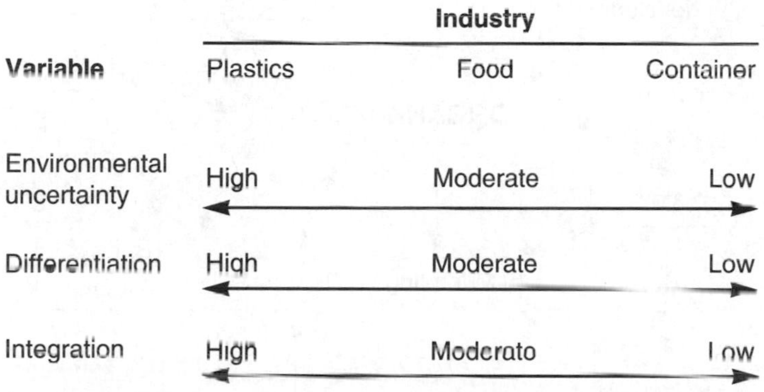

	Industry		
Variable	Plastics	Food	Container
Environmental uncertainty	High	Moderate	Low
Differentiation	High	Moderate	Low
Integration	High	Moderate	Low

FIGURE 1.3: Lawrence and Lorsch's research on the relationship between environment and organisation structure.

The number and size of an organisation's functional departments reflect the number and size of transactions with its environment. It might have a purchasing department to deal with suppliers, a sales department to deal with customers, and a public relations department to deal with its public, so a functional structure is built up to deal with the demands from the environment; see figure 1.4.

As the functional departments increase, there is increased differentiation as specific tasks and problems are tackled; this requires increased integration so the whole organisation acts as a cohesive team. The key to success for an organisation is to balance the two opposing forces of integration and differentiation by matching internal sub-units to external sub-environments.

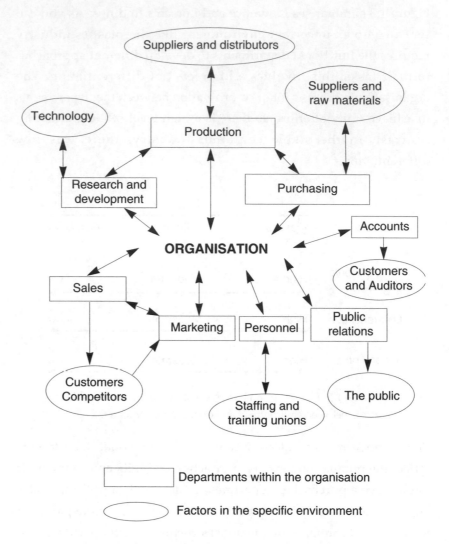

Departments within the organisation

Factors in the specific environment

FIGURE 1.4: Developing a functional structure to respond to external factors.

The idea that an organisation can design its structure to fit into the environment in which it operates forms the contingency theory. The closer the fit between structure and the environment the more chance there is of success. Burns and Stalker (The Management of Innovation, 1961, Tavistock) supported this approach. They found that companies with a complex organic structure, i.e. with high differentiation and integration, and a team approach, survive better in an unstable, changing environment; low-level staff can make rapid decisions and there is rapid communication and information sharing. And the reverse is true; in a stable environment, a simple mechanistic structure with low differentiation and integration, is more successful with no need for complex decision making and with authority centralised at the top (see figure 1.5).

Organisations in stable environments tend to adopt what Burns and Stalker called a mechanistic structure. This is characterised by the following features:

- jobs are clearly defined and specialised

- there is a clear hierarchy

- communications tend to be vertical, up and down the hierarchy

- decisions are made near the top of the hierarchy and issued as instructions and rules.

There is a similarity between a mechanistic structure and some of the prescriptions of early writers on management and organisations such as Fayol and Weber.

Burns and Stalker also found that organisations in more unstable and unpredictable environments tended to adopt a less rigid approach, which they called an organic structure. This is characterised by the following features:

- authority tends to be based upon knowledge and expertise, not upon rank in the hierarchy

- jobs are not clearly or permanently defined, but allowed to develop and change with circumstances

- communication tend to be horizontal, across the hierarchy

- few instructions are given; rather colleagues gave one another advice.

This kind of structure enables the organisation to respond more quickly and flexibly to changes in its environment.

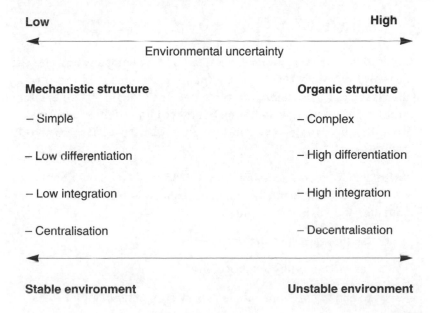

Low	High
←	→
	Environmental uncertainty	
Mechanistic structure	**Organic structure**
− Simple	− Complex
− Low differentiation	− High differentiation
− Low integration	− High integration
− Centralisation	− Decentralisation
←	→
Stable environment	**Unstable environment**

FIGURE 1.5: Burns and Stalker's relationship between environmental uncertainty and organisational structure.

Jonathan's Pizza Company

Jonathan Pescatore set up a wholesale pizza business in 1979. He worked from a small factory unit on an industrial estate and, by 1985, he employed ten craft bakers and two drivers. Jonathan personally undertook all management roles including sales and marketing. The dough for the bases of his pizzas was mixed in a mixing machine, but the remainder of the production process was carried out by hand, each craftsman baker making, baking and wrapping batches of pizzas using the skills learned during their apprenticeship. The pizzas were sold in 20 delicatessens in neighbouring towns.

By the late 1980s, demand had grown markedly. Jonathan Pescatore had been approached by a number of supermarket chains to see if he could make a brand of luxury pizzas for their stores. To meet this demand, production would need to rise from about 2,000 pizzas per day to some 20,000 per day, and delivery would be required to two or three central depots at some distance form the factory. Jonathan was attracted by the potential growth in the business, but he was concerned that the supermarkets were unwilling to order only one or two types of pizza; they wanted to order large batches of new flavours of pizza, often at short notice to maintain a mass public interest in the product.

He quickly realised that he would require not only a larger factory but a totally different method of production. Batches would need to be much larger, and each stage of the production process would need to be mechanised. The dough bases would need not only to be mixed, but also formed (into circles) by machine. Tomato sauce would need to be extended by a machine onto the bases, and grated cheese sprinkled over them by another machine. Only the final decorating with ingredients such as ham, mushrooms, anchovies might be done by hand to give the final article a hand-finished appearance that would justify a premium price.

Jonathan calculated that he would need 80 workers in the new factory. Most would not need to be highly skilled bakers but semi-skilled machine operators. His drivers' jobs would also need to be adjusted; instead of making local deliveries, they would be undertaking more long-distance routes.

? SAT:
allow 25 mins

Communicating ✔

Managing tasks and solving problems ✔

ACTIVITY 5

Refer to the case study above. Jonathan's Pizza Company now has to consider how to structure the expanded company. In the terms discussed in this session, the company must consider the need for greater differentiation and formalisation of its activities and how it intends to manage the change in stability of its external environment.

Write a short report advising Jonathan's Pizza Company about the issues it must consider in planning its expansion. Your report should consider and advise on the need:

- for clear job specifications

- for written rules and procedures

- to employ other people in supervisory or managerial roles

- to employ a marketing specialist.

Commentary...

Jonathan's Pizza Company is moving from craft-based, small batch production, to much larger batch, more mechanised production, and from a rather stable to a more unstable environment. This tends to dictate the need for clear job specifications and for written rules and procedures. This formalisation helps to create a more mechanistic structure in which the larger numbers of semi-skilled workers will know clearly what their jobs are and how to do them.

Jonathan Pescatore is unlikely to be able to manage and supervise all 80 workers directly himself. So, he will need to lengthen the hierarchy and create supervisory and junior managerial jobs (e.g. a production manager) within the factory. The move into a larger, more unstable market is likely to require the employment of a marketing specialist, so that the company continues to win orders to utilise its new capacity. A process of differentiation will take place.

The next case study looks at how McDonald's is having to respond to changes in its environment.

McDonald's

McDonald's environment is changing as consumer tastes change; put simply, people are eating less beef and fat. It faces other challenges: environmentalists are looking at the packaging and competitors are still coming into the market. McDonald's had operated on the basis of a completely standard world-wide product, but customers in new areas are demanding different foods. The organisation is having to be flexible and is now offering different foods in different locations. It is allowing franchisees to design their own menus and decors to suit local tastes.

This new flexibility creates strains within McDonald's current mechanistic structure, and the company still needs to maintain the standards and centralised control on which it has built its reputation. McDonald's is likely to survive; it has probably not become too large to respond quickly enough to changes in its environment. However, it may need some restructuring to a more organic structure. It uses a franchising approach, but this is now only an effective part-franchise as it allows franchisees more scope and, as a consequence, the company is more dependent on their individual successes.

At the start of this session we listed four contingencies that are important in influencing an organisation's structure. We have studied one – the environment – in some detail. Now, we look briefly at the other three contingency factors: strategy, size and technology.

Strategy

An organisation's structure is designed to achieve its overall objectives, and hence it is linked to its strategy. Chandler's work in the 1960s on the relationship of strategy and structure concluded that structure derives from strategy (Strategy and Structure: Chapters in the History of the Industrial Enterprise, 1962, MIT Press). Companies start out with simple strategies that can be executed through simple organisational structures. As the strategies become more complicated and the organisation moves from a single product or service to product diversification, so the structure becomes more complicated with more differentiation.

To illustrate this point, consider some examples. NCR first made calculators and then diversified into many different types of computer. It is now part of the giant AT&T telecommunications company but, in 1995, is due to be changed again in AT&T's restructuring plans. Many supermarkets may have started as grocery stores but now the large stores include a florist, a newsagent, a bakery, a butchery, a delicatessen, a pharmacy, an off-licence and a petrol station. In the Greatwear case study (section one, session two), Geoff

Smith developed from a one-store retailer to the owner of a chain with 200 stores throughout Europe. Organisational changes were forces upon him by his shareholders after his unsuccessful strategic expansion into Europe.

There are three main strategic options:

1. innovation strategy involves introduction of major new products and services

2. cost-minimisation strategy involves tight cost controls and price cutting

3. imitation strategy involves moving into already established products or markets.

Introduction of a new service might mean, for example, that your local supermarket sets up a carry-out pizza service, which will involve, among other things, new staffing requirements, meeting health regulations and a driver delivery service. In adopting a cost-minimisation strategy, the supermarket may have to tighten internal budgetary controls, not stock some unprofitable products and cut margins on some products that their competitors are offering at lower prices. And the move into petrol sales is imitating the success of petrol stations.

Although strategy affects structure at the top of an organisation's hierarchy where the key decisions are made, it has less potential impact on the organisation at lower levels. Obviously if an organisation is innovative, then it needs a flexible organic structure. Cost-minimisers need the efficiency and stability of a mechanistic structure. Imitators combine the two structures with the need for tight controls and low costs through mechanistic structures, and innovation through discrete organic sub-units.

Size

Organisations can grow in two ways:

- they can simply grow larger, employing more people, using more machinery, utilising more buildings in different locations, and so on

- they can grow more complex, i.e. more varied, in the work they do, the types of people they employ, the goods and services they provide, and so on.

Of course, the two kinds of growth usually go together.

GROWING IN SIZE

We have already shown that simple growth in size often leads both to a need for increased formalisation and decentralisation. In looking at the need for integration in organisations we concluded that, as organisations grow, they tend to rely on different forms of integrative activity. When they are small they can rely on mutual adjustment, as they grow they will adopt direct supervision and, finally, as they grow larger still they will adopt standardisation.

Formalisation is a closely related concept to standardisation. It involves the setting of rules, procedures and instructions in writing and formal written reporting procedures. As an organisation grows it needs written procedures, if its managers are to retain effective control and if its activities are to be well integrated. The use of rules and written communications are a key feature of bureaucracy. Child (Organisation: A Guide to Problems and Practice, 2nd edition, 1988, Paul Chapman, London) found that as successful organisations grew they tended to adopt greater formalisation.

> **\?/** Formalisation involves the setting down by management of rules and procedures to govern important aspects of an organisation's activities. It further involves the use of written media in order to communicate significant rules, procedures or instructions, and for the presentation of reports.

Decentralisation occurs when many of the significant decisions in an organisation's life are taken by more junior staff in the organisation's life. Look again at the Greatwear case study. As the company grew larger up to 1986, it became more difficult to control by a single leader. It was necessary to decentralise many important decisions to store managers, rather than retaining authority at the top of the organisation's hierarchy.

It is common for organisations to decentralise as they grow larger, because those at the top cannot know about all of an organisation's activities in sufficient detail, nor can they respond quickly enough to the many issues requiring a decision. However, you should not believe that organisational growth is accompanied by an inevitable and inexorable process of decentralisation. Circumstances can arise when large organisations may choose to re-centralise aspects of their decision making.

GROWING IN COMPLEXITY

The Greatwear case study also serves to illustrate that increased organisational size is frequently accompanied by increased complexity. The company's expansion into France, the Netherlands and Germany meant that it had to meet the fashion needs of a much wider range of potential customers.

Complexity also arises because as an organisation grows, its departments and divisions enlarge. As they grow, they become too difficult to manage as single entities, so they divide into more specialist units. Specialist units may acquire great expertise, but their work may also become less familiar and more difficult to understand than before. Equally, when a unit splits, its two parts may require a specialist unit to co-ordinate them. Hence growth can mean that the organisation's hierarchy becomes both wider and longer.

FIGURE 1.6: Greatwear's pre-1986 structure.

Figures 1.6 and 1.7 illustrate how Greatwear's organisation structure changed as the company expanded. Notice that the more complex, wider and longer post-1986 hierarchy does not, of itself, preclude Arthur Brown's declared intention to increase decentralisation. If the new national divisional directors and the store managers are able to take decisions that in the past would have been taken at headquarters, and possibly by Geoff Smith personally, then decentralisation will have taken place.

Nearly 75 years ago, Du Pont was probably the first modern divisionalised organisation structure with separate functional units – R&D, engineering, purchasing, manufacturing, distribution and sales. It has been estimated that between 1945 and 1970, 90 per cent of the top 500 US companies decentralised into divisional structures.

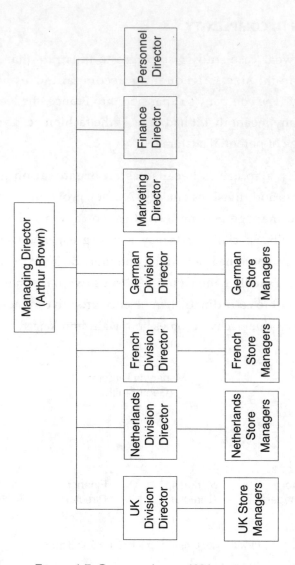

FIGURE 1.7: Greatwear's post-1986 structure.

The trend was for each function to increase its importance through new marketing theories, new environmental pressures, technology changes, transport and communication developments, and emphasis on the individual. Each development required more centralised staff to manage the company, with the increased need for more reporting and co-ordinating and, as a consequence, structures became more complicated.

This culminated in the 'matrix' structure, with everyone being linked to everyone else through a complicated structure. The idea was to develop synergies that would be achieved from co-ordinating everything. In the mid-1970s, new marketing themes developed based on the matrix structure. Global branding led to international organisations taking authority back from local divisions into head office, thereby re-centralising. Organisations became larger with increased centralisation and increased layering leading to totally dysfunctional monoliths.

We would expect to see that the larger the organisation, the more likely it is to be a complex mechanistic structure. This is not necessarily the case, as the next case study on W L Gore & Associates shows.

W L Gore & Associates

The American company, W L Gore & Associates, has annual sales of over $200 million. Its most famous and highly successful product is GORE-TEX, the strong waterproof fabric that is used in outdoor clothing, tents, skiing and mountaineering gear. The company employs over 3,000 people but has no formal hierarchy or structure. There are no job titles, bosses or chains of command. No one is an employee, everyone is an 'associate'. The company is formed into work groups of 200 people and operates as a number of small plants. It considers that it achieves double the productivity of an average manufacturer and keeps its workforce happy.

Source: S.W. Angrist, 'Classless capitalists', Forbes, May 9 1983, pp. 122–4.

Gore uses a team approach. This can be very hard to achieve, especially with a company of this size and given that the work groups are so large. However, the company's culture supports this management approach and makes it successful. We consider how culture can help an organisation later in this workbook.

Size has a significant influence on some but not all parts of structure. As organisations increase in size, more levels are added but at a decreasing rate. There is a strong link between formalisation and size, as organisations increase in size they become more formalised. And as size increases and management becomes unable to exercise control centrally; it is forced to decentralise. Direct supervision becomes more difficult, and needs to be replaced by standardisation and mutual adjustment.

Technology

> **!?!** An organisation's technology consists of the knowledge, equipment, techniques and processes that it uses to transform its various inputs into goods and/or services.

Every organisation produces some goods or services that its clients or customers value, or it could not obtain the funds necessary to buy the resources it needs (such as staff, buildings, machinery) to continue to exist. Technology is the means by which an organisation transforms its inputs to outputs.

ACTIVITY 6

List the goods or services provided by the following organisations:

- Arsenal Football Club

- The Church of England

- The Coca Cola Company

- a university.

Commentary...

Arsenal Football Club provides entertainment, and a sense of identity which is enhanced by merchandising. Its basic resource is the football player.

The Church of England provides teaching (about Christianity), reinforcement of faith, various forms of social service, a location for public and private prayer, and so on. Its basic resource is people and their faith.

The Coca Cola Company provides soft drinks and an image and identity for young people. Its basic resource is the raw material to make the product.

A university provides education, as well as research and consultancy. Its basic resource is well-educated people.

To provide such goods and services, an organisation employs a technology, or a range of technologies. Every organisation has at least one technology for converting its human, financial and physical resources into products or services. Two key dimensions of an organisation's technology can influence its structure significantly:

1. the complexity of the technology employed

2. the predictability of the technology employed and its susceptibility to analysis.

TECHNOLOGICAL COMPLEXITY

In a famous study of 100 manufacturing companies in South East Essex, Joan Woodward (Industrial Organisation: Theory and Practice, 1965, Oxford University Press) concluded that between them they employed three types of technology:

1. Unit and small batch production
    Goods are produced singly or a few at a time. Each unit or small batch is unique and is made to meet the needs of a particular client. Such production involves high levels of skills to make goods such as made-to-measure clothing and space satellites.

2. Mass production
    Large volumes of identical goods are produced and are sold in a mass market to customers expecting a standardised product such as boxes of washing powder or cars. Here machinery does most of the work, with employees in a subordinate role.

3. Continuous process production
    The manufacturing process never stops and is conducted entirely by machines. Here the human beings do not make the product (the machines do) but simply monitor and control it. Examples are the chemical and oil-refining industries.

Woodward concluded that each type of technology sets different challenges for the organisation. For example, different steps will need to be taken to control the flow of work and motivate the staff in a craft furniture workshop than in an oil refinery. This, in turn, has consequences for the organisation's structure. In particular, as the technology employed became more complex, so the organisation structure became more complex:

- the hierarchy grows longer, not least because of the need for managers in integrative roles

- the chief executive's span of control widens

- the numbers employed in indirect, staff roles increase

- the number of managers increases to supervise and integrate the more complex processes involved.

Unit and process production fits best with an organic structure and mass production fits best with a mechanistic structure. Figure 1.8 summarises Woodward's findings.

Unit production	Mass production	Process production
Low vertical, low horizontal differentiation	Moderate vertical, high horizontal differentiation	High vertical, low horizontal differentiation
Low formalisation	High formalisation	Low formalisation
Organic	Mechanistic	Organic

FIGURE 1.8: Woodward's classification of technology and its links with structure.

TECHNOLOGICAL PREDICTABILITY

In another study, Charles Perrow ('A framework for the comparative analysis of organisations', American Sociological Review, April, 1967, pp. 194–208) concluded that the key features of a technology are:

- the extent to which it behaves predictably, so that few problems arise and those that did are familiar

- the extent to which the technology can be analysed, divided up into a series of steps and standard procedures (especially when dealing with problems).

Thus, he identified task variability – the number of exceptions that an individual meets in work tasks – and problem analysis – the type of search procedures that are required to deal with these exceptions.

He found that organisations using predictable and easily analysed technologies (where there tended to be few exceptions and few breakdowns, and those that occurred could be solved using standardised procedures) tended to:

- have discrete job descriptions

- have little interdependence between different groups of workers

- lay down many precise rules

- set out precise procedures for dealing with problems

- set out precise plans, so that activities are co-ordinated

- allow little discretion to people lower down in the hierarchy.

These rather bureaucratic organisations, he called routine organisations.

In organisations where the technology behaved unpredictably, with many exceptions, variations and breakdowns, Perrow found that:

- job descriptions were not discrete, but overlapped

- there were high levels of interdependence between different groups of workers

- high levels of discretion were allowed, even at quite low levels in the organisation

- co-ordination took place through good co-ordination and feedback between different groups of workers.

Charles Perrow's two factors together provide a way of classifying technologies:

- Routine technologies have few exceptions and the problems are easy to analyse. Examples include assembly-line manufacture of cars, or pizzas, or anything that is mass produced.

- Engineering technologies have many exceptions but the problems are simple to analyse. Examples include building, bridge and road construction.

- Craft technologies have few exceptions but the problems are difficult to analyse. Examples include furniture making, pizza making individually by hand, dressmaking and tailoring.

- Non-routine technologies have many exceptions and the problems are difficult to analyse. Examples include management consultancy and advertising.

Perrow suggested that mechanistic structures are best suited to routine and engineering technologies, while organic structures are best suited to craft and non-routine technologies. Taking the Woodward and Perrow studies together, we can see that the technology employed within an organisation is likely to have a significant effect upon the choice of an appropriate structure.

Another approach to technology classification based on the type of tasks performed was proposed by Thompson (Organisations in Action, McGraw-Hill, 1967). He defines technologies as:

- **long-linked**, if the tasks have to be performed sequentially as in mass production assembly, one task has to be completed before the next one is started so the tasks are sequential

- **mediating**, if units inputting and outputting to the organisation are linked as for example in the transactions between a building society and its lenders and borrowers, money is required from one to go out to the other

- **intensive**, if there is a customised response to many contingencies as in hospitals and universities – parties need to be aware of what the other parties are doing, and they are all interdependent and linked.

(a)

(b)
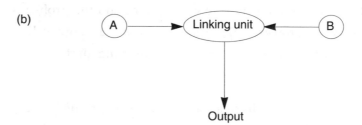

(c)
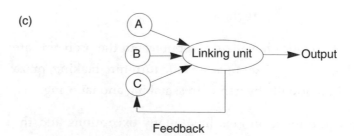

FIGURE 1.9: Thompson's technology classification: (a) long-linked; (b) mediating; and (c) intensive.

Thompson proposed that technology determines the selection of a strategy for reducing uncertainty and in designing a specific structure. Long-linked and mediating technologies are likely to fit better with mechanistic structures, and intensive technology is likely to fit better with an organic structure.

SAT:
allow 15 mins ❓

Managing tasks and solving problems ✓

ACTIVITY 7

Classify the following into long-linked, mediating or intensive technologies using Thompson's classification:

1. members of Arsenal football team

2. members of a British 100 metres relay team

3. members of a Davis Cup tennis team

4. the relationship between individuals receiving, processing, dispatching and invoicing orders in a automotive parts factory

5. the relationship between engineering and design departments in a manufacturing company.

Commentary...

Members of a football team need to be aware of what other members of the team are doing at all times, so this is intensive. Members of a relay team act in sequence, one after the other, so this is long-linked. Members of a tennis team generally play individually against the opposition, so their interdependence is pooled for the final result, so this is mediating.

In the sales department of the automotive parts factory, orders are sequentially processed, despatched and invoiced at the end of the operation, so this is long-linked. In the manufacturing company, design and engineering are interlinked, with the output of one affecting the other and feeding back to the other, so they are interdependent and intensive.

TECHNOLOGY AND CHANGE

Thompson's classification of technology emphasises how organisational tasks are linked and are dependent on each other. Any changes in how individual tasks are carried out will affect other departments in the organisation and can act as a destabilising force. Any change in technology necessitates change elsewhere in the organisation. This change needs to be processed and managed well; otherwise it may severely affect the organisation's effectiveness.

Consider the case of a mass-produced item like a clock radio. Marketing decides that the product needs redesigning to keep it up to date. The design department proposes fresh ideas which involve changes on the assembly line. A new feature is added which involves more work for the assembly line workers. This will affect their output and end-of-month productivity bonus. This change will need managing, otherwise the assembly line workers will become dissatisfied and demotivated; management may have to offer a different incentive scheme for the assembly line.

Similarly, the expansion at Jonathan's Pizza Company meant that the craft bakers no longer had individual responsibility for making their own batch of pizzas; instead their jobs changed to overseeing and putting the final touches to the thousands of pizzas that are produced mechanically. Their motivation is likely to have changed markedly. The management structure would need to change to manage the increased number of semi-skilled machine operators, rather than a few craft bakers. In Perrow's classification, the technology changed from craft to routine, with implications for the organisation's structure.

Technology is also a factor in an organisation's environment. For example, new technologies reduce the costs, and change the operation, of transportation and communication. With good communication and transportation links and the increase in supplies required, Jonathan's Pizza Company may decide to order ingredients for the pizzas directly from international producers rather than through a distributor. This may increase the amount and type of work that has to be done internally in purchasing, and the company may need to hire an experienced person to handle it. The change in technology in one area causes a change in another quite different one.

The change of technology also affects the organisation's relationship with its specific environment, so changing the environmental uncertainty. By ordering its pizza supplies directly, Jonathan's Pizza Company is now subject to different factors. Though cheaper, the tomato sauce producer in Italy may be more unreliable than the UK distributor. The distributor held back-up stocks, warehoused in the UK, and met any shortfall in supply from the original producer; so Jonathan must stock extra quantities or risk running out.

We have emphasised that any changes in 'technology' can have a direct bearing on the organisation structure. Technology is linked with the complexity and the formalisation of an organisation and its level of centralisation. But, again, note that new technologies are having an impact. Sophisticated computer information systems can allow management to make organisations more organic and flatter without losing control. Formalisation can be reduced and the organisation more decentralised. A manager can now call up information on his desk top terminal to find out what is going on in other functional areas and then make appropriate decisions. This enables management control over many more employees, reduces the number of managers and levels in the hierarchy required and makes decision making more effective.

summary

▶ Contingency theory argues that there is no single best way to structure an organisation. An organisation will face a range of choices when determining how it should be structured.

▶ Four variables or contingencies are particularly important in influencing an organisation's structure: its size, its strategy, the technology it uses and its environment.

▶ An organisation must take into account its specific environment: customers, producers, suppliers and distributors, competitors, shareholders, unions, banks, government bodies and regulatory agencies.

▶ An organisation is also affected by its general environment: economic forces, international forces, technology, demographic and cultural forces, and political forces.

▶ The level of environmental uncertainty impacts on an organisation's structure. Environmental uncertainty is affected by the complexity, dynamism and richness of the environment. Environments can be characterised as placid-randomised, placid-clustered, disturbed-reactive and turbulent-field.

▶ Organisations in stable environments tend to adopt a mechanistic structure characterised by clearly defined jobs, a clear hierarchy, vertical communications structure and centralised decision making.

▶ Organisations in more unstable and unpredictable environments tend to adopt a more flexible, organic structure, characterised by jobs which change with circumstances, authority based on knowledge not upon rank, horizontal communications structure and few top-down instructions.

▶ An organisation's technology can influence its structure significantly, depending on the complexity of the technology employed and the predictability of that technology.

Organisation structures

Objectives

After participating in this session, you should be able to:

▶ describe different types of organisational structure

▶ describe the phases of an organisation's life cycle

▶ relate developmental change in the organisation to
different structures

▶ identify the differences between power, control and
authorIty

▶ identify some future trends in organisational
structures.

in working through this session, you will practise the following
BTEC common skills:

Managing and developing self	✔
Working with and relating to others	✔
Communicating	✔
Managing tasks and solving problems	✔
Applying numeracy	
Applying technology	
Applying design and creativity	

Types of organisation structure

In this session, we first look at the types of organisational structure that exist, and consider then how they relate to different stages in the organisation's life cycle. The last session introduced mechanistic and organic structures, two very general structures that describe a general response to different types of environment. Here we look at structures in more detail and particularly from the perspective of what is happening inside, rather than outside, the organisation.

MINTZBERG'S ELEMENTS OF ORGANISATIONS

The contingency approach argues that there is no single best way to structure an organisation. A structure should adjust to a number of variables or contingency factors. We can take this a stage further by looking at a configuration approach. In this approach, we look at all the different parts of an organisation and the key structural issues like decentralisation, integration, span of control, decision making, control and planning, and see how they configure into an internal organisation structure.

First, we look at the elements that make up an organisation, then at how they are co-ordinated, and finally at different levels of decentralisation. Mintzberg, a well-known American writer on organisations, initially proposed five basic parts to an organisation: the operating core, the strategic apex, the middle line, the technostructure and the support staff. He then added a sixth part: the organisation's ideology or culture ('The structuring of organizations', The Strategy Process: Concepts, Contexts, Cases, edited by Mintzberg, H. and Quinn, J. B., 2nd edition, 1991, Prentice Hall, pp. 330–50). He also concluded that an organisation might still exist and have none of these six parts.

1. The operating core comprises the employees who carry out the basic work of producing the products or supplying the services of the organisation. It might include assembly line workers, the check-out and counter personnel in a supermarket, or the machine operators and craft bakers making pizzas in Jonathan's Pizza Company.

2. The strategic apex comprises the top-level managers who oversee the complete operation. Even a very simple organisation requires at least one manager. Top management makes overall decisions and might include a managing director,

a chief executive officer, and a board of directors. Jonathan is the strategic apex in Jonathan's Pizza Company.

3. The middle line are managers who connect the operating core to the strategic apex. These might be the managers who supervise the assembly line workers or all the check-out and counter staff in the supermarket. This will include Jonathan's new production manager who oversees the machine operators making the pizzas.

4. The technostructure comprises the analysts who plan, control and standardise the work of others. They are outside the main line of authority. This might include a quality control manager or department in a manufacturing plant. Jonathan may employ someone to check the quality, consistency, packaging and scheduling of his pizza manufacture.

5. The support staff fill the staff units and provide support services. They are outside the main line of authority. The accounting staff grouped in a separate department provide accounting services for the entire organisation; or a canteen might provide catering services for all personnel. Jonathan's new marketing manager will provide marketing and sales support services for the new company.

6. Ideology is the culture of the organisation and includes its traditions and beliefs. Jonathan's Pizza Company will have to work at generating a new culture that will support the larger company with its new focus. The product has changed from a handmade craft product to a mass-produced one; and the craft bakers, who would have worked as apprentices for the company and grown up with it, are now just semi-skilled operators who could be hired without any particular experience.

**TYPES OF ORGANISATION
STRUCTURE**

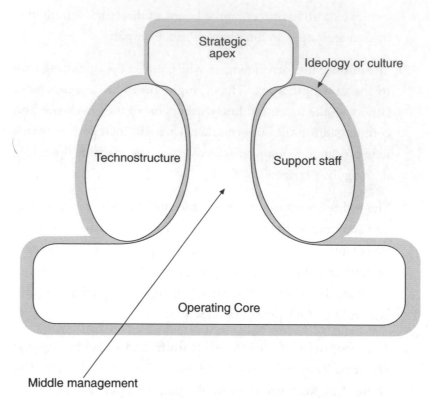

FIGURE 2.1: Mintzberg's six basic parts of an organisation.
SOURCE: Mintzberg, H., 'The structuring of organizations',
The Strategy Process: Concepts, Contexts, Cases, edited by Mintzberg, H.
and Quinn, J.B., 2nd edition, 1991, Prentice Hall.

Any of these six constituent parts can dominate an organisation. Six different structures or 'structural configurations' arise depending on which part dominates and has control of the organisation.

If control is in the operating core, then decisions are decentralised and we have a professional bureaucracy. If the strategic apex is dominant, we have a simple or entrepreneurial structure. If middle management is in control, we have autonomous units operating in a diversified or divisional structure. If the technostructure dominates through standardisation, we have a machine bureaucracy. And if the support staff dominates, and control is by mutual adjustment, we have an adhocracy. If ideology is dominant, then we have a missionary structure where the beliefs of the individuals take over. If none of these forces dominate, then they pull against each other in a political structure.

We shall look at each of these structures in turn. First though, we need to introduce Mintzberg's co-ordinating mechanisms and basic types of decentralisation. In section one, we reviewed three co-ordinating mechanisms: mutual adjustment, direct supervision and standardisation.

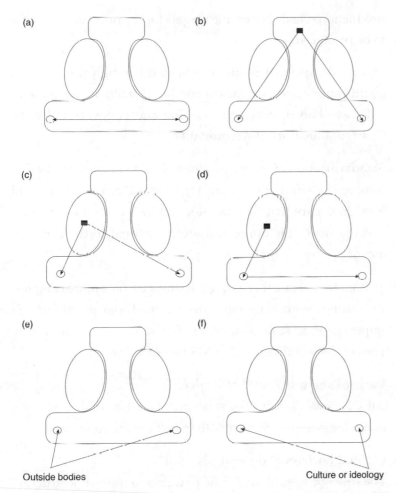

FIGURE 2.2: Mintzberg's six basic mechanisms of co-ordination: (a) mutual adjustment; (b) direct supervision; (c) standardisation of work; (d) standardisation of outputs; (e) standardisation of skills; and (f) standardisation of norms
SOURCE: Mintzberg, H., 'The structuring of organizations', The Strategy Process: Concepts, Contexts, Cases, edited by Mintzberg, H. and Quinn, J.B., 2nd edition, 1991, Prentice Hall.

Mintzberg expanded this classification into six basic mechanisms that co-ordinate the different tasks of the organisation:

1. Mutual adjustment is by informal communication between members of the operating core. For example, the pizza operators might help out with each other's scheduling problems.

2. Direct supervision is carried out by a manager or leader and involves direct instruction. For example, the production manager will tell each of the pizza operators what to do.

3. Standardisation of work is carried out by strict procedures and instructions. Jonathan issues instructions about what to do in making the pizzas.

4. Standardisation of outputs is carried out by setting out what results are required. Jonathan sets quality guidelines and

production schedules, giving targets for the numbers of pizzas to be produced.

5. Standardisation of skills is achieved through professional qualifications and by codes of conduct. Jonathan's accountant will have had professional training and is governed by the Chartered Institute of Accountants.

6. Standardisation of norms is achieved through workers sharing common beliefs. For example, Jonathan's Pizza Company will want to ensure that the operators all believe in the company and the work it is doing and are committed to the common aim of producing high quality pizzas.

It is important to reiterate that as organisations become more complex, the co-ordinating mechanisms move from mutual adjustment through direct supervision to standardisation. The same applies to the six basic types of decentralisation that Mintzberg considered:

1. Vertical and horizontal centralisation
   All the power is with the strategic apex. Jonathan is still the main decision maker even with growth in the company.

2. Limited horizontal decentralisation
   The strategic apex shares some power with the technostructure that standardises work. In Jonathan's case, if he sets up a quality control department to monitor the output then he will give some of his control away.

3. Limited vertical decentralisation
   Managers exercise control in their line units. By employing a production manager to control the operators making the pizzas, again Jonathan will relinquish some direct control.

4. Horizontal decentralisation
   The power is with the operating core. If the operators making the pizzas are given responsibility for their own output, quality control, etc. then more power would be in the operating core.

5. Selective vertical and horizontal decentralisation
   Control is dispersed at various levels and the organisation works as teams at these levels. Jonathan might structure the staff into teams of operators, each with a quality controller and packager, on particular varieties of pizza. Each team would then be responsible for their particular product, and make decisions to ensure supply, quality, etc.

6. Pure decentralisation

Power is shared by all members of the organisation. This would be difficult for Jonathan to do as he requires staffing and job tasks at differing levels of skills and responsibilities. It would only really work in, say, a partnership of doctors.

Table 2.1 summarises the different configurations, their chief co-ordinating mechanism, the key or dominant part of the organisation and type of decentralisation.

Configuration	Prime co-ordinating mechanism	Key part of organisation	Type of decentralisation
Entrepreneurial structure	Direct supervision	Strategic apex	Vertical and horizontal centralisation
Machine bureaucracy	Standardisation of work processes	Technostructure	Limited horizontal decentralisation
Professional bureaucracy	Standardisation of skills	Operating core	Horizontal decentralisation
Diversified structure	Standardisation of outputs	Middle line	Limited vertical decentralisation
Innovative structure	Mutual adjustment	Support staff	Selected decentralisation
Missionary structure	Standardisation of norms	Ideology	Decentralisation
Political organisation	None	None	Varies

TABLE 2.1: Mintzberg's configurations

SOURCE: Mintzberg, H., 'The structuring of organizations', The Strategy Process: Concepts, Contexts, Cases, edited by Mintzberg, H. and Quinn, J.B., 2nd edition, 1991, Prentice Hall.

Now let us look in more detail at specific structures.

THE SIMPLE OR ENTREPRENEURIAL STRUCTURE

The simple structure is flat, not complex, has little formalisation and authority is centralised into a one-person strategic apex, probably in the original owner or entrepreneur. Jonathan originally set up the pizza company and had complete control over everything in the early days. As the power lies in just one person, the success of the operation is totally dependent on him or her. The organisation is vulnerable to the capabilities and even health of its owner.

This structure's strengths are that it is fast, flexible and easy to maintain, but with increasing size this structure becomes unworkable. As you saw with Geoff Smith and Greatwear, one person could not handle the management of 20 dispersed stores, although the business had been very successful when there was just one store.

Employees are likely to enjoy working in this type of company. With a strong leader, they are likely to identify with the organisation's aims and objectives, although their relationship with the central figure is likely to be indicative of their relationship to the company as a whole.

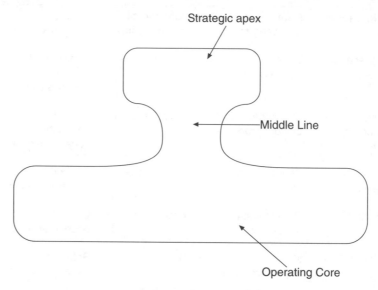

FIGURE 2.3: Simple or entrepreneurial structure.
SOURCE: Mintzberg, H., 'The structuring of organizations', The Strategy Process: Concepts, Contexts, Cases, edited by Mintzberg, H. and Quinn, J.B., 2nd edition, 1991, Prentice Hall.

SAT:
allow 10 mins

Managing tasks and solving problems ✔

ACTIVITY 1

Give three examples of a simple or entrepreneurial structure. Describe the kind of person you think would work well in this kind of organisation.

Commentary...

You might have thought of well-known examples. Apple Computers and Microsoft started out like this, though, of course, their structures are no longer entrepreneurial. Or you might have thought of a nearby store, or garage owner, or local company manufacturing a specialised product, all run by the 'boss' and all employing relatively few employees. Jonathan's Pizza Company in its early days is an example too.

The people who would probably fit well into this kind or organisation are those who like to feel part of the business and like to perform a variety of different tasks without a rigid structure, and who want to feel a part of the success of the business.

THE MACHINE BUREAUCRACY

The machine bureaucracy has highly routine operating tasks, formalised rules and regulations, a functional structure with centralised decision making and administration that separates line and staff activities. Technostructure is the dominant part of the organisation as it is required to keep everything standardised, tightly controlled and planned. There is a hierarchy of middle managers to control the specialised but probably simple operating core and ultimate control still resides in the top. You may recognises elements of this description; it describes the mechanistic structure covered in the previous session.

The organisation can perform standardised activities very efficiently. It can survive with relatively inexperienced managers as the rules and procedures cover most situations. However, this may cause problems when situations arise which require management intervention and initiative.

In this type of organisation, employees need to enjoy (or accept) routine work, the tight rules and regulations; otherwise they will become quickly discontented with the routine nature of the work and the lack of scope for personal initiative. Jonathan's Pizza Company has gone from a simple, entrepreneurial structure to a machine bureaucracy with strict rules and regulations for the mass production of his pizzas. It is unlikely that his original employees – the craft bakers – would be happy to work in this new situation.

TYPES OF ORGANISATION
STRUCTURE

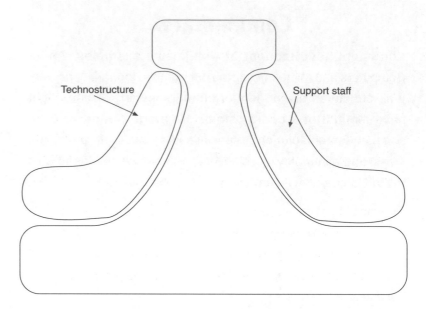

FIGURE 2.4: Machine bureaucracy.
SOURCE: Mintzberg, H., 'The structuring of organizations', The Strategy Process: Concepts, Contexts, Cases, edited by Mintzberg, H. and Quinn, J.B., 2nd edition, 1991, Prentice Hall.

There can be problems in moving to a machine bureaucracy. Staff motivation and morale can suffer. The anticipated productivity gains may not be delivered. Resource 1, at the back of the book, illustrates such a situation. Trevor Thompson went from a simple structure with teams that had responsibility for their own work to a more automated and bureaucratic structure.

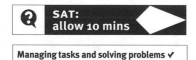

SAT:
allow 10 mins

Managing tasks and solving problems ✔

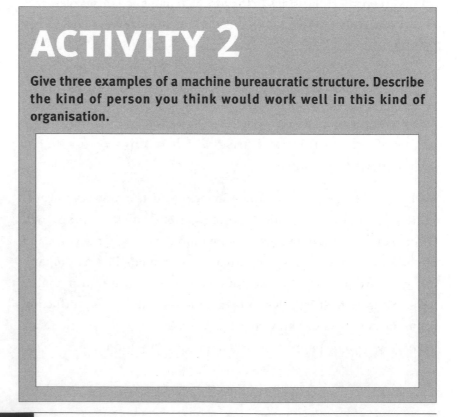

ACTIVITY 2

Give three examples of a machine bureaucratic structure. Describe the kind of person you think would work well in this kind of organisation.

Commentary...

Obviously any kind of mass production system has elements of a machine bureaucratic structure. Other examples include banks that have highly routine tasks for keeping track of money, and many government offices such as those involved in collecting taxes, administering car licences, and assessing and collecting council tax. These activities are undertaken by offices run bureaucratically with many rules and regulations, automation in some form, and centralised decision making by a few top-level managers.

The people who would probably fit well into this kind or organisation are those who are happy working in a rigid office structure where they know exactly what they are to do. They may fill a middle management position where they are content to supervise and manage other people within strict rules and procedures.

THE PROFESSIONAL BUREAUCRACY

With a professional bureaucracy, standardisation is maintained but the tasks are highly specialised. Highly trained professionals are hired in the operating core which is empowered with decision making. This means that control is decentralised from the top. As with the machine bureaucracy, rules can take over.

There is little need for a technostructure; standardisation is achieved through the training that the professionals have received outside the organisation. Professional staff operate to the codes of ethics and conduct of their professional associations. Few line managers are employed but many support staff are needed to back up the operating core of professionals.

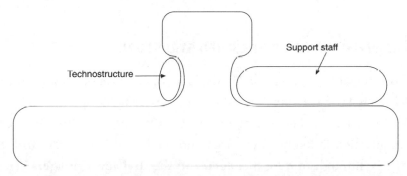

FIGURE 2.5: Professional bureaucracy.
SOURCE: Mintzberg, H., 'The structuring of organizations', The Strategy Process: Concepts, Contexts, Cases, edited by Mintzberg, H. and Quinn, J.B., 2nd edition, 1991, Prentice Hall.

TYPES OF ORGANISATION
STRUCTURE

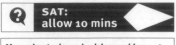

SAT:
allow 10 mins

Managing tasks and solving problems ✓

ACTIVITY 3

Give three examples of a professional bureaucratic structure. Describe the kind of person you think would work well in this kind of organisation.

Commentary...

Any hospital or university is a professional bureaucracy, with doctors, nurses, consultant, surgeons, lecturers and professors functioning in the operating core with some autonomy. Similarly, legal or accountancy practices are organised around mainly autonomous professional staff.

People who have some kind of professional training, would almost certainly want to work in this kind of environment. They would be in charge of their own particular area, governed by their own professional training and helped by support staff.

THE DIVISIONAL OR DIVERSIFIED STRUCTURE

A divisional structure is made up of a set of autonomous units which are likely to be machine bureaucracies, loosely held together and co-ordinated by a central strategic headquarters. This type of organisation is likely to be large and well established. Control is largely through middle management: the division managers. The divisions are accountable and operate as individual organisations; this does mean though that some functions, marketing for example, are duplicated within each division as this is obviously ineffective.

There may be conflict between divisions as they compete for resources. There may also be communication and co-ordination problems between the divisions. Each division is accountable but within company guidelines and policies. As an organisation's products become diversified then the structure becomes more divisionalised as market-based units replace functional departments.

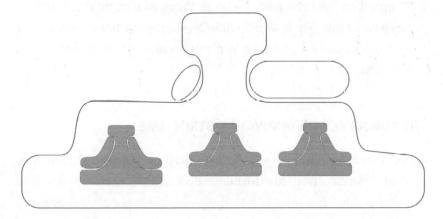

FIGURE 2.6: Divisional or diversified structure.
SOURCE. Mintzberg, H., 'The structuring of organizations', The Strategy Process: Concepts, Contexts, Cases, edited by Mintzberg, H. and Quinn, J.B., 2nd edition, 1991, Prentice Hall.

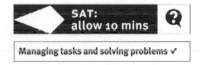

SAT:
allow 10 mins

Managing tasks and solving problems ✓

ACTIVITY 4

Give three examples of a divisional or diversified structure. Describe the kind of person you think would work well in this kind of organisation.

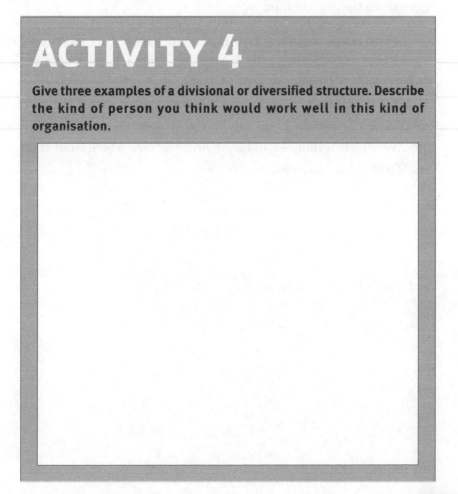

Commentary...

Examples include large corporations like IBM, Sony and General Motors, which produce, market, distribute and sell different products and services throughout the world. Another example is PFM Leisure, which we met in section one.

People who like to be part of a large successful company would work well here. They would value the better career prospects that are probably available in a large corporation compared with a smaller company.

THE ADHOCRACY OR INNOVATIVE STRUCTURE

This structure is characterised by high horizontal differentiation, low vertical differentiation, low formalisation and decentralisation. It is responsive and flexible. It has the same features as the organic structure we discussed in the previous session. There is no technostructure and a highly professional operating core. Since middle managers and support staff are professionals, the traditional lines of authority do not exist. Power is distributed unevenly throughout the organisation.

An adhocracy is really a group of teams with few rules and regulations; co-ordination is by mutual adjustment. Roles within the teams change. Conflict can arise as there are no clear guidelines or 'bosses' in control. It lacks the advantages of standardised, bureaucratic structuring and can be rather unstable, but it is very effective in certain complex, dynamic environments where innovation and flexibility are required to survive.

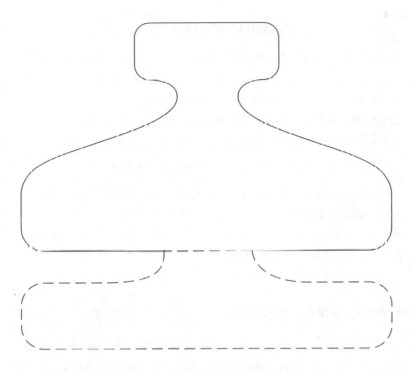

FIGURE 2.7: Adhocracy or innovative structure.
SOURCE: Mintzberg, H., 'The structuring of organizations', The Strategy
Process: Concepts, Contexts, Cases, edited by Mintzberg, H. and Quinn, J.B.,
2nd edition, 1991, Prentice Hall.

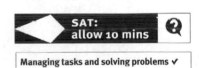

ACTIVITY 5

Give three examples of an adhocracy or innovative structure.
Describe the kind of person you think would work well in this kind of
organisation.

Commentary...

You might have found it difficult to identify examples immediately. You should be thinking here of particular environments and industries that work on a project basis. Examples include the film, music or television industries; teams of professionals come together for a limited time to put together a film, a CD, a video, a series, a documentary, etc.

The people who would probably fit well into this kind of organisation are those who enjoy an exciting if unpredictable way of working, but who are very involved and motivated in the project, and the industry itself.

THE MISSIONARY STRUCTURE

In this structure, the ideology or the culture of the organisation is dominant. The organisation is held together by the beliefs of the individuals. There is no technostructure and little specialisation of job function; there are no experts and no professionals, otherwise power would be centred in one particular area. This type of organisation could be a religious order or a small farm co-operative. You might be involved in it if you shared the beliefs of the group. It is likely to stay small as it survives by personal contact between members.

THE POLITICAL ORGANISATION

Mintzberg's seventh structure is the political organisation. No part of the organisation is dominant and there is no prime co-ordinating mechanism. Everybody in the organisation pulls against each other, leading to conflict and instability. Examples might include an organisation in a monopoly position or a government body largely protected from the external environment.

Life cycle of the organisation

We now have some ideas about an organisation's structure but we know also that it is not static. An organisation changes as it adapts to fit its environment and as that environment changes. Other changes that affect the structure are related to the 'stage' the company is at. We now analyse the company's structure in relation to its life cycle.

A series of organisational changes makes up the organisation's life cycle. The stages in this life cycle are birth, growth, decline and death. Not every organisation passes through all these stages, and each will pass through them at a different rate. But, as an organisation passes through different stages in its cycle, its structure must change to accommodate the changing organisational needs.

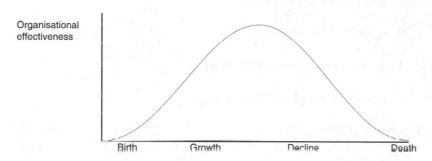

FIGURE 2.8: Stages of an organisation's life cycle.

BIRTH

This is the founding stage of the organisation and has the greatest chance of failure. A new organisation is unstable and lacks formal structure, which only gradually emerges as procedures are established and needs are met. It is flexible and responsive and it often has a simple structure as the owner or entrepreneur retains all control. In the early days of the Greatwear business, Geoff Smith had one store and retained all control. Similarly at the outset of Jonathan's Pizza Company, Jonathan Pescatore retained total control over a small number of craft bakers. He had to bring in a production manager when the company switched its production methods to increase its output.

GROWTH

As organisations grow, they increase their division of labour and specialisation in an effort to gain competitive advantage. Greatwear grew in size to 20 stores and went public, but Geoff Smith was unable to make the appropriate changes to manage this growth and was replaced by Arthur Brown. Jonathan's Pizza Company changed the means of production of the pizzas which meant changes in the management structure and the degree of specialisation of job functions in the operating core.

Several models of organisational growth have been developed. One of the best known was developed by Larry Greiner in the 1970s ('Evolution and revolution as organisations grow', Harvard Business Review, July–August, 1972). He proposed five sequential stages of growth, with each stage ending in a crisis that requires an organisation to manage and solve before moving on:

1. growth through creativity

2. growth through direction

3. growth through delegation

4. growth through co-ordination

5. growth through collaboration.

The crises at each stage are:

- leadership

- autonomy

- control

- red tape.

The organisation's structure must adjust to cope as it grows and to resolve the resulting crises. We now look in more detail at some of the factors involved and how they link with our earlier discussions on the environment and different structures.

Growth through creativity

This stage overlaps from the birth stage. The organisation is still inspired by the entrepreneur, it has found the right niche for its main products or services. At this stage, the organisation's culture and its leader are more important to survival than hierarchy and structure.

However, the organisation needs to manage its environment, using its resources to meet its goals effectively and efficiently. If the entrepreneur takes control of management, he or she may be unsuccessful and need replacing. This is what happened to Geoff Smith at Greatwear after he expanded into Europe.

Resource 2, at the back of the book, contains an article on the crisis of leadership at Apple Computers. This illustrates the kind of problems that face the original founders of companies as they try to maintain management control as their organisations grow and develop more complex structures. In Apple's case, Steve Jobs is finally forced to resign despite overseeing the remarkable growth of the company during its first ten years.

Growth through direction

The crises of leadership ends with the establishment of a strong top-management team. This team develops a strong organisational strategy that influences the developing structure and organisational culture. A functional or divisional structure will develop, and formalised procedures and rules will be put in place. Authority is centralised and decision making is formalised.

This leads to the next crisis: crisis of autonomy. This happens when the bureaucratic structure restricts professionals in certain areas from achieving results in functional areas; top management is making all the decisions and professionals further down the hierarchy have no autonomy. Employees in this situation will often leave a large company where they have been restricted and start up an entrepreneurial company on their own, using their expertise and capacity for innovation.

Growth through delegation

To solve the crisis of autonomy, many organisations delegate authority to lower-level managers in all functions and link their increased control through a reward system of bonuses and productivity. For example, Bill Gates at Microsoft has delegated authority to small teams, allowing members to act entrepreneurially and control their own activities. Success is rewarded by stock options. Perhaps Jonathan could develop a team approach to motivate his semi-skilled operators in making particular varieties of pizza, each team including a craft baker and a quality controller / scheduler and having responsibility for its own production. He may then not need the production manager to oversee total production.

This stage is characterised by more responsibility and autonomy being given to managers at all levels and functions. Decisions can be made quickly and the organisation is responsive to changes in its environment. Top managers only intervene in decision making when absolutely necessary. Each department or division can expand to meet its own needs and goals. Growth is often rapid, leading to the next crisis: a crisis of control. Functional and divisional managers begin to compete with top management for control of organisational resources. A power struggle results.

Growth through co-ordination

To solve a crisis of control, an organisation needs to find a balance between centralised control from the top and allowing lower-level managers decentralised autonomy. Top management needs to co-ordinate activities between different divisions and encourage divisional managers to support organisational aims and objectives. The management of these co-ordination activities may, however, lead to the next crisis: the crisis of red tape. Rules and procedures increase, entrepreneurship and production are restricted.

Growth through collaboration

Often, a matrix or product team approach is introduced to cope with this crisis. The aim is to reduce bureaucracy and allow more collaboration. Organisations seek to make better use of mutual adjustment and less use of standardisation. This change from a mechanistic to an organic structure is very difficult and is not usually implemented until companies are forced to by extreme circumstances. For example, both Chrysler and Xerox moved to a product team structure to streamline decision making. See Resource 3, at the back of the book, for an article on Chrysler's new team structure. There are similar moves in the British motor industry to move to a more team-based approach so it can compete with imported cars, particularly the Japanese.

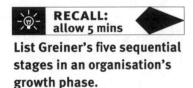

RECALL:
allow 5 mins

List Greiner's five sequential stages in an organisation's growth phase.

DECLINE

Organisational decline may come about when the company fails to respond to internal or external factors that threaten its survival. In Greiner's model, a failure to deal with any of the crises would put the organisation into a state of decline. Regardless of when decline sets in, it will affect the organisation's ability to obtain resources such as funding, staff and raw materials.

For example, Jonathan's Pizza Company could go into decline if it faces fierce competition, if it loses orders because of any unreliability or inconsistency in the product caused by bad internal structuring and controls, if the public wants a different product completely, or if health regulations have been contravened and the factory has to close.

Decline can also occur because organisations grow too large and they are simply not effective any more.

FASTEC LIMITED

Fastec Limited is a gaming machine manufacturing company. The firm has grown very rapidly since it was founded five years ago by Anne Frost, Derek Adams and Roger Stewart. The three founders, all electronic engineers in their mid-thirties, started their business as a part-time enterprise dyeing wire to sell to the computer industry. From employing one senior citizen working in Derek's garage, the firm now has a workforce of 216 employees in a factory on an industrial estate.

According to the founders, the firm survived the first two difficult years because of their considerable abilities as designers of innovative electronic devices and their willingness to work hard for long hours. They routinely worked evenings, often until very late into the night, and at the weekends, and new employees were expected to accept the same conditions. All employees worked a high amount of overtime and, as a consequence, earned nearly double the take-home pay they could expect from other local employers. These working conditions also had the effect of keeping the number of employees to the minimum, so the founders had personal contact with every employee. Employee commitment was exceptionally high and the ethos was of all fighting a common cause: the survival of the firm in a highly competitive and changing environment.

The founders enjoyed the frequent contact with the employees, and were immediately available to help them with a problem. Many employees took advantage of this accessibility; at any one time it seemed that one of the founders would be talking with an employee. Often employees would seek help with personal problems. The employees responded to this informality by producing high-quality work in poor working conditions and under the constant pressure of production deadlines.

As the firm has grown, Anne, Derek and Roger have become joint managing directors. Although the earlier pattern of operation continued, the founders have gradually begun to concentrate their efforts in different areas of the business. Anne concentrates on design and finance; she also has responsibility for the canteen. This combination of tasks arose from the need to describe and explain new product designs when visiting banks and finance houses to raise sufficient funds to continue operations. She was made responsible for the canteen because she had worked in the kitchen of a hotel during the holidays when she was a student. Derek deals mainly with the production and procurement aspects and, because he is also a skilled motor vehicle mechanic, the transport side of the business. Roger has begun to focus on winning orders and building up contacts with customers because he is the only founder with some experience of selling. Figure 2.9 shows the present organisation structure.

Under constant pressure, the founders are often short-tempered with each other; they accept this, without rancour, as a way of letting off steam to reduce individual tension. Lately, the occasions on which Roger has become angry with his co-founders has increased. Each outburst has been occasioned by the failure to meet production deadlines. A typical exchange, caused by the failure to deliver a large order to a major brewery chain on time, is given here:

Roger: I've had enough of this situation. This is the second time this month we have missed a delivery date. What's the point of me working flat out to win orders if we are not going to deliver them on time.

Derek: I know. But you don't allow enough time for all the work to be done when you quote delivery dates.

Roger: But I did ask you if this short delivery time was OK, and you said you could manage it.

Derek: I don't remember that. I just don't seem to have the time to keep tabs on everything these days.

Anne: The trouble with us is that the right hand does not know what the left hand is doing. We need to organise ourselves better.

Roger: Too right: the sooner, the better.

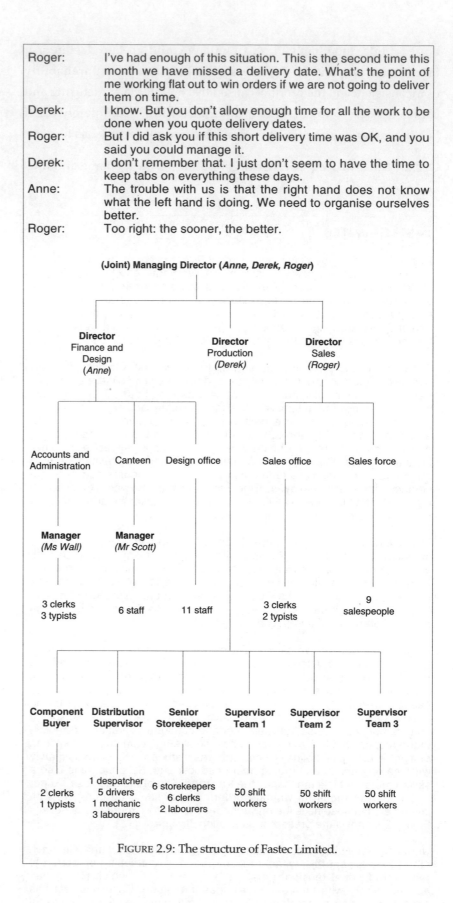

FIGURE 2.9: The structure of Fastec Limited.

ACTIVITY 6

Read the case study about Fastec Limited.

Identify the stage at which Fastec is, in the organisational life cycle. Identify the structural and co-ordinating features of the company and match them to those of the life cycle.

Consider what the founders of Fastec should do next to ensure survival of the company. Propose an organisational configuration using Mintzberg's elements and explain your proposals.

Write a 750-word report for your tutor. Summarise your key points in the box below.

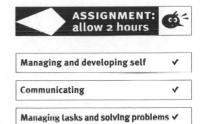

ASSIGNMENT:
allow 2 hours

Managing and developing self	✓
Communicating	✓
Managing tasks and solving problems	✓

Authority, power and control

In discussing organisation structure and the changes that are forced upon the structure from within or from the environment, we often come across structural relationships that involve changing lines of authority, control and power. We talk about organisations having centralised and decentralised decision making and different levels of hierarchy. What do we actually mean by authority, power and control? How can they be shaped and organised?

AUTHORITY

> !?! **Authority** is the power to hold individuals accountable for their actions and to influence directly what they do and how they do it.
> A **hierarchy** is a vertical ordering of organisational roles according to their relative authority.

A crucial organisational design feature is how much authority to centralise at the top of the organisational hierarchy, and how much to decentralise to lower levels. An organisation improves its control of its members by increasing the number of managers that supervise and monitor activities. This increases the number of levels making the structure taller. By increasing vertical differentiation in this way, the organisation gains better contact and control over employees by management. However, having too many levels can limit co-ordination and communication.

Horizontal differentiation can be used to control activities if there is limited direct supervision. Each functional unit – of people performing the same kinds of tasks – has its own hierarchy appropriate to its activities. For example, in a manufacturing company, the research and development department may only have one level of hierarchy, but the production department may have seven levels. Horizontal differentiation allows the organisation to stay as flat as possible.

Within the organisation, authority is given to managers at particular levels to achieve certain goals. This authority is the real source of power and individuals are subject to this power.

POWER

French and Raven proposed a classification of power ('The bases of social power', in D Cartwright (ed.), Studies in Social Power, 1959, University of Michigan, Institute for Social Research) in which they identified four bases of power. These enable you to manipulate the behaviour of others. French and Raven's four bases of power are: coercive power, reward power, persuasive power and knowledge power.

1. Coercive power depends on fear. If one individual has the authority to dismiss or reprimand or demote or assign unpleasant work activities, or generally make work difficult for another then he or she has coercive power over the other individual.

2. Reward power is the opposite of coercive. It is the power to reward with salary, bonuses and favourable conditions.

3. Persuasive power involves the manipulation of symbolic rewards, such as status and peer group approval.

4. Knowledge power (or access to information) is the ability to control the flow of information.

French and Raven make a distinction between sources of power and bases of power. Sources of power indicate how you come to hold the bases of power. They identified four sources: the position you hold, your personal characteristics, your expertise and the role you play in dissemination of information.

1. Position power is governed by the position in the structural hierarchy. This is also called legitimate power as employees believe that the manager or leader has the right to give them orders by virtue of their position in the hierarchy, and they have a duty to respond to these orders.

2. Personal power is the influence attributed to personal characteristics such as charisma or leadership skills. This kind of personal power can be demonstrated by people at any level in the hierarchy and, conversely, is not always evident in those at the top of hierarchies.

3. Expert power is attributed to skills, knowledge and training. So, for example, company lawyers and accountants would have expert power by virtue of their training and specialist skills.

4. Opportunity power is being in the right place at the right time. For example, a manager would acquire opportunity power by the chance occasion of gaining important information at a particular meeting.

CONTROL

> ⁇ **Control** is the process by which the organisation's objectives are met through its operations.

Control is achieved by setting standards, measuring performance, comparing actual performance with these standards and providing feedback and correction if necessary. It can also be achieved through the organisation structure by job descriptions that define an employee's tasks and responsibilities and standards that are required. The system of rewards and punishments operated by a company will also control an individual's actions, while control can also be effected through policies and rules, through budgets, and in mass production by machinery.

If control is lost with changes in the organisation then chaos will ensue. An organisation can operate in a situation of chaos, but only for a relatively limited time. It means that individuals, particularly managers, have a heavy work load in dealing with crises and 'fire-fighting' problems on a day to day basis. Control has to be reinstated in the long term.

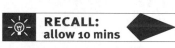

RECALL:
allow 10 mins

List where authority, power and control separately lie in Mintzberg's six main configurations:

1. entrepreneurial organisation

2. machine bureaucracy

3. professional bureaucracy

4. divisional or diversified organisation

5. innovative organisation

6. the missionary organisation.

The future

Organisations have continually to change if they are to survive. The traditional ways of doing things, managing companies, producing goods and providing services are always being challenged. As we have seen, the environment affects the organisation and its structure. There are several broad trends that affect today's organisation. We identify them here, but deal with them in more detail in the next session.

Current trends include:

- fast changing technology in automation and information processing

- increasing availability of knowledge and data about the world

- shorter product life cycles and faster turnover of fashions in services

- a more flexible workforce, with fewer permanent jobs.

Certainly, there have been major changes in the labour market with improvements in education and training, increases in part-time working, equal opportunities, and changes in family life styles. Organisations are rethinking how their employees function by re-assessing the working environment, job designs, styles of management, levels of performance and productivity. Because of environmental instability, there is now no such thing as 'a job for life' and individuals have to be prepared to adjust and retrain as necessary and work under completely different contracts than previous generations.

However, all the factors listed above are responsible for many of the changes that are now being imposed upon organisations. The difficulty that they experience is how to 'predict the changes', and how to 'adapt the business'. The strategies that companies are increasingly adopting are:

- reducing middle management

- greater use of new technology

- introducing self-managed teams

- networking

- out-sourcing and home working

- franchising

- greater use of agencies and distributors.

REDUCING MIDDLE MANAGEMENT

In the past, it was assumed that 'biggest is best'. But as you have seen, with size comes increasing complexity within the organisation, problems with too many hierarchies, communication and bureaucracy, and inflexibility to change. These days it is often the smaller companies that do well, and many of the larger companies are having to restructure to cope with the innovation and change required to stay ahead in their field.

The trend is to reduce excessive bureaucratic structure by reducing levels of middle management. Support staff can be assigned to line operations, and the span of control increased. Perhaps with the increase in size of Jonathan's Pizza Company, it would be more efficient if Jonathan were to design the structure around a team approach with a craft baker, a quality controller and scheduler and a number of operatives, avoiding the next hierarchical level of a production manager.

In 1995, AT&T the world's second largest telephone company based in the US announced plans to split into three separate companies each taking with it a specific area of its major businesses. By this restructuring, over 9000 jobs will be lost.

NEW TECHNOLOGY

Technology helps with control as one manager can now be linked directly with the shop floor through the terminal on his desk. Managers have easy access to a range of information and many activities can be co-ordinated throughout an organisation by computers.

Federal Express has 42,000 employees in more than 300 cities, but only five organisational layers. Operating spans of control are much greater than the industry average with co-ordination by computers, with up to 50 couriers operating from one dispatch centre.

Technology can obviously also contribute to the efficiency of mass production, design, scheduling, accumulating, storing and retrieving data, accounting and finance functions, sales and marketing functions, stock and warehouse control, communication and distribution. Fastec could certainly use technology to schedule and track orders through production.

SELF-MANAGED TEAMS

Employees are being encouraged to take more responsibility for themselves. Many organisations have developed a teamwork approach, with self-managed teams being set up within the organisation to produce a particular product or run a particular project. Within the team there is technical or functional expertise, problem-solving and decision-making skills, and interpersonal skills and team members take complete responsibility for their product or process.

The argument for greater team working is that with enriched jobs and direct involvement in the organisation's goals, individuals become more efficient, more interested and motivated workers. The Chrysler case study (see Resource 3) illustrates these trends. Iacocca organised the functionally organised product development operations into four product-oriented platform teams. Jonathan could do this with his pizza production and cut out the need for a middle management hierarchy at the same time.

NETWORKING

Another trend is the formation of networks: a group of people with specialised skills that come together for a particular project. An example of successful networking is the informally assembled team that built IBM's first personal computer. Resource 4, at the back of this book, is an article from The Economist which examines the ways the corporations are reorganising themselves into networks.

Many new products can be developed in this way. The making of movies, television and radio programmes, for example, is undertaken in this manner. Many film studios and television companies have reduced their permanent staff of technicians and artists. Instead, a team of people with the necessary technical and artistic skills is brought together for the duration of a specific project.

A network organisation might also be a collection of organisations that have come together to work closely together and co-ordinate activities. Nike, the sports manufacturer, has a central core organisation that carries out design, research and development. It then works with a network of partners that undertake the assembly of the component parts, product manufacturing, distributing and selling. In this way, bureaucratic structure in the core organisation is kept to a minimum, costs are kept low, but supply is guaranteed.

OUT-SOURCING AND HOME WORKING

Organisations can also trim their bureaucratic structure by out-sourcing. The organisation buys in a service from a specialist organisation rather than having permanent staff to provide an in-house service. The types of functions bought in might include advertising and promotion, public relations, marketing, computer facilities, accounting or information processing – anything that might be done cheaper and more effectively by an outside specialist party. As you can see by looking in the Yellow Pages, there are many companies running these kind of services. In the UK, local councils are no longer running refuse collection and road cleaning services, but are using outside contractors. On a slightly different scale, Scotia, a manufacturer of pharmaceuticals, is planning to market and sell new drugs directly to hospitals but use an established partner to sell to GPs.

More individuals are now working from home, either from choice or because their job has disappeared with management, budgetary or technology cuts. Many different functions can now be met by individuals having a close contractual relationship with a host organisation. For example, this book has been put together with a variety of personnel working both full-time and freelance. Indeed, with the associated reductions in overheads, space constraints and better telecommunications, many organisations are encouraging individuals to work from home as an employee, or as a 'full-time' freelancer or consultant. Part-time working is also becoming the norm, as jobs are reduced and individuals are forced or choose to work in this way.

FRANCHISING

An organisation can sell its franchise, the right to use its resources, name or operating system, for which it receives a flat fee or a share of the profits. The franchiser may provide the inputs that the franchisee supplies to the customer. This system reduces the bureaucratic costs of managing many different outlets.

McDonald's operates on a franchise basis. Although it does retain ownership of some outlets in large cities where it can rationalise its management costs more effectively, most McDonald's restaurants are run by independent franchisees. Under the terms of the franchise agreement, McDonald's ensures that all outlets are of the same standard, although it does now allow franchisees some flexibility on decor and food products. This is a new approach that it has been forced to adopt to stay ahead in certain locations. In contrast, Burger King chooses to own and manage all of its outlets.

AGENCIES AND DISTRIBUTORS

In marketing particular types of products, an organisation needs to decide on its distribution system. Does it sell directly to the customer, through a general distribution system, or through franchised dealers? Many cars or computers, for example, are sold through franchised dealers which means that the manufacturer has some control over the dealers especially on customer service. This is particularly important with a technical product. But many products just need to reach the consumer, they do not need pre-sales instruction or after-sales service, so a publisher will distribute books through a wholesale distributor or into bookshop chains to put their product on the shelves. A company might choose to run a sales force or use another company to do it for them; this is especially true for overseas sales where the company will have little control and no expertise in the local market so will use a local company to sell for them.

EXERCISE:
allow 1 hour

Working with and relating to others ✔

Managing tasks and solving problems ✔

ACTIVITY 7

Major new developments in technology are regularly reported on television and in the business and industry pages of the press. In October 1995, for example, Jaguar announced that it planned to start production of 'smart' cars. These cars will be fitted with electronic gadgets to enable the driver to detect and avoid other vehicles and to maintain a safe distance from other road users.

Review the media over a period of a few days to find other examples of technological advances. In small groups, discuss your examples with fellow students. In each case, consider how organisations in the relevant industry might be affected by the technological changes, and discuss the impact on jobs and individual workers and employees.

Summarise the main points from your discussion in the following box.

summary

▶ Mintzberg identified six key parts of the organisation: the strategic apex, the technostructure, the operating core, the middle line, the support staff and the organisation's ideology or culture.

▶ Different structures are likely to develop depending upon which part of the organisation is dominant.

▶ Using Mintzberg's analysis, seven basic structures can be characterised: a simple or entrepreneurial structure, a machine bureaucracy, a professional bureaucracy, a divisional or diversified structure, an adhocracy or innovative structure, a missionary structure and a political structure.

▶ The stages in an organisation's life cycle are birth, growth, decline and death. As an organisation passes through different stages in its cycle, its structure must change to accommodate the changing organisational needs.

▶ As an organisation grows, it adapt its structure. It is likely to face crises of leadership, autonomy, control and red tape.

▶ Organisations face clear choices about how to exercise authority, power and control. These are linked to issues of vertical and horizontal differentiation.

▶ Companies are increasingly adopting some of the following organisational strategies to meet contemporary pressures: reducing middle management, greater use of new technology, introducing self-managed teams, networking, out-sourcing and home working, franchising, and greater use of agencies and distributors.

Organisational change and its management

Objectives

After participating in this session, you should be able to:

▶ identify internal and external sources of change and how they act as forces to destabilise the organisation's equilibrium

▶ analyse the management and control of change through structures

▶ identify the effects of technology on change.

In working through this session, you will practise the following BTEC common skills:

Managing and developing self	✔
Working with and relating to others	✔
Communicating	✔
Managing tasks and solving problems	✔
Applying numeracy	
Applying technology	
Applying design and creativity	

Sources of innovation and change

For many decades, the rules of business and success have been clearly established, with the largest and most established organisations controlling industries. Then major change occurred. In most developed countries around the world, the average size of businesses has fallen. The 'biggest is best' approach which once guaranteed success, no longer applies. Newer and smaller businesses are increasingly successful and are beginning to provide direction in their industries.

With the world and external environment being so subject to change, organisations need to be adaptable to succeed. Smaller organisations can respond to change in the environment quickly and effectively. Larger organisations tend to have more complex structures, and a greater need for formal co-ordination and communication systems. They become more inflexible.

The established organisations must make changes to remain competitive, or die. They need to rethink the way that they do everything. They must first identify what they do and why they do it. They must ask a range of questions:

- Are we providing the right goods and services?

- Are we trading in the right markets?

- Are we meeting organisational objectives?

- Are we achieving competitive advantage?

- Are we maximising the use of our workforce?

- Do we have the right organisation structure?

- Are we efficient?

- Are we effective?

- Should we look at our procedures and ways of working?

We considered the example of AT&T in the last session. AT&T are restructuring into three separate smaller companies to carry out different parts of its business. This will force its major international competitors – British Telecom, Cable and Wireless, Japan's Nippon Telegraph and Telephone, and Germany's Deutsche Telecom – to rethink their strategies. They might explore the advantages of rationalising their businesses into smaller companies carrying out mature domestic business and others focused on international and more fast growing business.

There are many forces that act upon an organisation, however successful it is, which make change inevitable. They fall broadly into five main areas:

1. Changing technology
   The current rate of technological change is greater now than at any time in the past. If organisations do not respond to the developments that are taking place they will inevitably fall behind the competition and lose their competitive advantage.

2. Information explosion
   The amount of knowledge and information currently available is also far greater than at any time in the past. Organisations must ensure that they are not left behind and are fully committed to benefiting from this information explosion.

3. Product obsolescence
   The changes that are taking place in consumer preferences, together with the rapidly changing technology, have resulted in a shortening of the life cycles of many products and services. People no longer want vinyl records, record players, telex machines, and typewriters; instead they want CDs, CD-ROMs, Internet access, faxes, mobile telephones and word processors.

4. Changing nature of the workforce
   With changes in demographics and improvements in education and training, there are significant changes in the labour market. Companies are employing more women and part-time workers. More people are working from home, either as full-time or part-time employees or self-employed.

5. Quality of the working life
   People are increasingly concerned about the quality of their working life. Organisations need to address this by ensuring greater job satisfaction, more appropriate job design, more desirable management styles, and designing better organisation structures that increase individual motivation and productivity.

We can break down these main forces for change into more detailed factors that are specifically external or internal to the organisation.

EXTERNAL FACTORS

These factors arise from the organisation's external specific and general environments and will differ from one company to another:

- Information technology has affected work patterns and locations of business.

- Education and training trends
  More young people now enter higher education. New vocational qualifications have been introduced. There is a growing recognition of the need for – and value of – updating skills and knowledge through life.

- More flexible working patterns
  There has been a shift from full-time to part-time employment, and away from communal working into home working. Out-sourcing and franchising are being used to cut costs.

- Legislation
  Despite periodic calls to cut red tape, complex legislation from national governments and the EU affects all kinds of issues including health regulations on the preparation of foodstuffs, agreements on air routes between countries, policy on competition in industries, safety regulations and import / export restrictions.

- International spread of business
  Many companies now have trading partners, alliances and facilities world-wide. For example, many joint ventures have been set up with Eastern European partners. Equally, because of trade restrictions, overseas companies have set up factories in Britain to manufacture here. Japanese car manufacturers have recently opened plants in Britain. Many companies are now truly international.

- National economic trends
  It is increasingly difficult to predict the effects upon the organisation. Changes in interest rates, for example, affect funding, property prices, consumer spending, employment, inflation and a whole range of interlinking variables that affect the organisation in some manner.

- Global competition
  The increasing strength of the 'Pacific Rim' economies is well documented. Japan, South Korea and the other 'Asian tigers' have been very successful in winning new business.

Competition in the emerging markets in Eastern Europe and China is likely to be intense.

Companies can respond to these changes in two ways. One is simply to react to a crisis as and when it occurs. Although this often takes place, it is a weak and inefficient response; it means there is no initiative and control. A more competitive approach is to forecast changes and plan an appropriate response.

INTERNAL FACTORS

The factors that generate change internally can either be as a result of a conscious decision taken by the organisation to establish or maintain its competitive advantage, or, it can be as a response to external environmental changes. These factors include:

- changes that occur as part of the organisation's life cycle, e.g. the growth of Jonathan's Pizza Company means that the style of production will need to change

- innovation, involving the introduction of a new product, a new service or a new way of doing things, e.g. in 1995, Tesco, the supermarket chain, introduced their loyalty Clubcard scheme as an incentive for customers

- an entrepreneurial direction from the top, e.g. Tesco's Clubcard scheme was initiated by Tesco's chairman Sir Ian MacLaurin

- changes in key personnel, e.g. replacing Geoff Smith at Greatwear plc with Arthur Brown changed the overall style of management, decentralisation and success of the company

- actions of key competitors, e.g. the establishment of the National Lottery by Camelot in the UK has affected the football pools companies like Littlewoods and the Zetter Group, as consumers see the weekly lottery and scratch cards as a replacement for a 'flutter' on the football pools

- shortage of raw materials, whether physical or in the availability of skilled and trained personnel, through world-wide scarcity or competition, e.g. in 1995, regional water companies faced a severe water shortage caused by their inability to cope with the demands of the exceptionally dry summer. Although they maintain a monopoly, their imposition of hose pipe bans to restrict water usage will reduce their revenue from metered consumers.

PLANNED ORGANISATIONAL
CHANGE

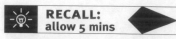
RECALL:
allow 5 mins

List the five main forces
which bring about change in
companies.

Planned organisational change

Organisations need to have strategies to introduce new developments
and to overcome resistance to change. Planned organisational change
is a set of activities and process designed to change individuals,
groups and organisation structures and processes (Beckard, R. and
Harris, R. T., Organizational Transitions: Managing Complex Change,
1987, Addison-Wesley). Organisational change involves the
restructuring of its resources and capabilities so as to contribute to the
organisation's success and improve its fit with the environment. It is
required at all stages in an organisation's life cycle. Even in decline, an
organisation needs to derive maximum benefit from its resources and
a maximum fit with its environment.

Organisational change typically involves the restructuring of human
resources, functional resources, technological capabilities and
organisational abilities. All these four resources are interdependent,
and it is often not possible to change one without changing the others.

Human resources

Changing and restructuring human resources is the key to
organisational effectiveness. It may involve training and development
of new skills and abilities, socialising employees into a new culture,
changing the culture to motivate individuals, adjusting the reward
system and physically changing top-management. It includes all the
people in the organisation, their personalities, values, beliefs,
motivation, skills and competencies.

For example, in 1995, Volkswagen agreed a new pay deal with its workers. This deal allows management to adjust production working hours to meet the market demand within certain limits, but also guarantees that no workers will be laid off over the next two years. Part of the deal also includes a pay increase but a reduction in overtime bonus payments and in work breaks. The overall deal is good for management because it allows an increase or decrease in production without any problems; it is also good for the workers as it guarantees their jobs and gives them an above-inflation pay increase. These kinds of changes will affect other companies in the German motor industry and will probably have a knock-on effect elsewhere in Europe.

Functional resources

Each function needs to develop procedures to deal with its own environment. An organisation can improve the value of functional or task-based capabilities by changes in its structure, culture and technology. Changing the functional structure, for example, to a team-based approach can motivate employees and increase product quality. It can also work in reverse; as Resource 1 illustrates, by removing the team-based approach at Trevor Thompson when mass production was introduced, staff became demotivated and many left.

Technological capabilities

An organisation's ability to develop new products and upgrade existing products or services is crucial to its continued survival. Technology concerns the manufacturing processes, tools and equipment, computers and the application of scientific knowledge. To derive the maximum benefit from technology, changes in organisational structure will probably be required. For example, IBM has made its structure more flexible, establishing divisions with the ability to compete independently.

Companies need to be innovative which can involve risks. Scotia, a British pharmaceutical manufacturer in the biotechnology sector, uses an entirely different technology from any other company in the industry, basing its drugs on lipids. In 1995, it had six drugs in late production phase, and it will be marketing these products soon. Only then will Scotia see whether its new technological approach has worked.

Organisational capabilities

Changes within the organisation structure might need to take place at all levels, and may involve changing an individual's routine, changing work-group relationships, improving integration between divisions, or changing top management. It concerns the formal framework of relationships, lines of communication and systems of authority. The new structure at Jonathan's Pizza Company involving mass production of pizzas will involve new job functions, new responsibilities and lines of control.

The systems model

There are several approaches to introducing planned organisational change. In this session, we look at three approaches, particularly in terms of the impact on organisation structure, starting with the systems model.

The systems model views the organisation as four interacting systems: people, technology, tasks and structure. A change in one system usually involves a change in another. For example, a decision to change a tall structure to a flatter structure will involve redesigning tasks, redeploying people, and probably require the introduction of updated technology to improve communication and control in the flatter structure.

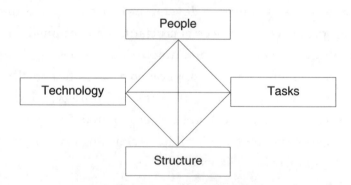

FIGURE 3.1: The systems model of change.

This model forces managers to consider these interrelationships and to decide whether to change systems individually or in combination. AT&T's restructuring could involve this kind of approach. The overall strategic approach to split into three separate companies will involve changes throughout all the existing divisions as individuals' jobs and responsibilities, chains of command and hierarchical levels are changed within the new companies.

FORCE FIELD ANALYSIS

Force field analysis was developed by Kurt Lewin ('Frontiers in group dynamics: Concept, method, and reality in social science', Human Relations, 1, 5–41, 1947). It views change from the perspective of modifying the forces keeping an organisation's behaviour stable. The level of behaviour at any time results from two sets of forces: those maintaining the status quo, the restraining forces, and those pushing for change, the driving forces. An increase in the driving forces might increase performance, but it might also increase the restraining forces. The natural reaction is to push back – driving forces activate their own restraining forces.

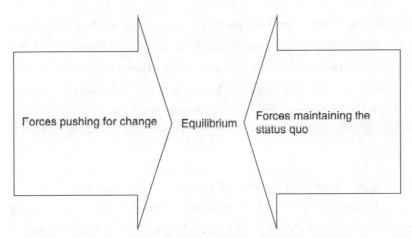

FIGURE 3.2: Lewin's force field analysis model of change.

The current level of behaviour is maintained when both of these forces are equal. To change one, the other force needs reducing or increasing as appropriate. The preferred strategy for change is to reduce the forces maintaining the status quo, the driving forces, rather than increase the forces for change.

Programmes of planned change are directed toward removing or weakening the restraining forces and toward strengthening the driving forces that exist in organisations. Lewin's model indicates that we should look for multiple causes of behaviour. Forces may be of many types and behaviour or performance can affect individuals or the complete organisation. The equilibrium concept suggests that organisations have forces that keep performance from falling too low, as well as forces that keep it from rising too high.

FIGURE 3.3: Lewin's model for change in three stages.

Lewin views the process of change as consisting of three steps:

1. unfreezing

2. moving

3. refreezing.

Unfreezing involves making the need for change so obvious that the individual or group can see and accept it. It reduces those forces that maintain the organisation's behaviour at its current level. In the Fastec case study (in the previous session), the three founders agree that they need to 'get ourselves better organised' but by refusing to give up day-to-day control of the business they cannot become better organised.

Moving involves shifting the behaviour of the group to a new level through changes in the organisation's structure. It requires a change agent to foster new values, attitudes and behaviour through processes of identification and internalisation. In Fastec's case, creating new managerial jobs to control the day-to-day activities and recruiting new managers to fill these would require the founders to change their attitudes to effective managerial behaviour.

Refreezing stabilises the organisation at a new state of equilibrium. This is frequently done by supporting or reinforcing mechanisms. In Fastec, a supporting mechanism could be a weekly meeting to enable the new managers to brief the founders on the status of production and sales.

THE ACTION RESEARCH MODEL

The action research model focuses on planned change as a cyclical process in which initial research about the organisation provides information to guide subsequent action. The results of this action are evaluated to provide further information to guide further action. The process consists of the following six steps.

1. Identify the problems or issues. This usually begins when a manager in the organisation senses that the organisation has a

problem. In the Fastec case, the founders have identified the need to get better organised.

2. Gather information about the problem or issue from other members of the organisation. Fastec's founders could appoint someone to collect information from various members of the organisation, including themselves, about the effectiveness of the current organisational structure.

3. Feedback the information to those involved in or affected by the proposed change. Once the information has been collected and organised in a coherent way, it is shared with members of the organisation involved in the change effort.

4. Diagnosis and action planning – those involved in the change effort decide on what action to take. Those involved in the change are also involved in planning specific actions. In Fastec's case, the founders need to consider the information about the current effectiveness of the structure and decide what improvements are needed.

5. Action – this is the actual change from one organisational state to another. It may require a transitional period while the new procedures and methods are introduced, new technology is installed or people are retrained. In Fastec's case, it would include designing jobs for the new managers and recruiting individuals to fill these jobs.

6. Gather data after the action – as action research is a cyclical process, data must be gathered after the change to evaluate its effectiveness. If this step leads to further diagnosis and new action, then the organisation goes through the same cycle again.

ACTIVITY 1

SAT:
allow 15 mins

Managing tasks and solving problems ✓

Consider these statements:

1. Applying the systems model of change means that the change effort must involve structure, people, task and technology.

2. Force field analysis views change as modifying the forces keeping an organisation's behaviour stable.

3. Action research focuses on planned change as a single process.

PLANNED ORGANISATIONAL
CHANGE

Are these statements correct summaries of different approaches to planned organisational change? Comment on each in turn. If needed, provide a better summary of your own.

Commentary...

The first statement is an incorrect summary of the system model. The change effort may be focused on only one of the four aspects. However, the person implementing the change should consider the possibility that the change will have implications for the other aspects.

The second statement is a good summary of field force analysis. The model views the level of behaviour at any point in time as the result of forces striving to maintain the status quo and forces pushing to change it.

The third statement misses the point of action research. This model views change as a cyclical process in which initial information gathering about the organisation provides information to guide subsequent action. The results of the action are evaluated to provide further information to guide further action.

Organisational change and the environment

The organisation needs to change to accommodate changes in the environment so that it continues to achieve the best fit that it can. We introduced this idea in session one. The contingency approach, based on work by Lawrence and Lorsch, views managers as reacting to the environment and changing the organisation using the processes of integration and differentiation.

The implications of the contingency approach is that an organisation's internal structure and processes should change to fit the general and specific environments. Two environmental dimensions – simple-complex and static-dynamic – can be identified. The first one concerns the number of sectors with which an organisation interacts and the second concerns the degree of stability these sectors experience. This gives rise to four different environments.

	Simple	Complex
Static	simple static	complex static
Dynamic	simple dynamic	complex dynamic

FIGURE 3.4: Environmental dimensions.

The environment can be characterised as simple-static where the organisation interacts with a small number of similar sectors which remain basically the same and are not changing. In this case, a functional structure can be appropriate with rules and procedures to achieve integration.

If the environment is complex-static then the organisation interacts with a large number of dissimilar sectors that remain basically the same. An appropriate structure might be a divisional organisation with moderately decentralised decision making. Integration could be achieved by training.

With a simple-dynamic environment, the organisation interacts with a small number of similar but constantly changing sectors. Appropriate structures tend to be simple with functional differentiation, moderately centralised and with direct supervision for integration.

ORGANISATIONAL CHANGE

AND THE ENVIRONMENT

With a complex-dynamic environment, the organisation interacts with a large number of dissimilar, constantly changing sectors. The structure is likely to be a matrix of decentralised divisions and integration is by training and socialisation.

This analysis of environments leads to another approach to planned organisational change. The strategic choice approach suggests that managers take a pro-active role in selecting the organisation's environment and then designing the structure and processes to fit the selected environment. With the strategic choice approach, more emphasis is given to the choices open to those managers with the power to direct an organisation.

② SAT:
allow 15 mins

Managing tasks and solving problems ✔

ACTIVITY 2

Consider these statements about approaches to organisational change.

1. The contingency approach implies that managers can decide whether or not to react to the environment.

2. An organisation will tend to differentiate itself into specialist departments when its task environment is complex and dynamic.

3. The simple-complex dimension refers to the rate of change taking place in an organisation's environment.

4. The strategic choice approach implies that managers are able to define the environment of their organisation by choosing to focus on some sectors and ignore others.

Which statements are true? Which are false? Give reasons for your answers.

Commentary...

The first statement is false. The contingency approach implies that an organisation should change its structure and processes to 'fit' its environment.

The second statement is true. Organisations tend to increase differentiation to cope with a complex and dynamic environment. This makes integration difficult.

The third statement is false. The simple-complex dimension refers to the degree to which an organisation deals with few (simple) or many (complex) sectors of its environment. The statement would be true of the static-dynamic dimension because this dimension refers to the degree of stability in an organisation's environment.

The fourth statement is true. Strategic choice implies that the contingency approach underrates the influence of managers to decide in which sectors of the environment they should operate.

Resistance to change

There are several general sources of resistance to change. These come both from individuals but also by virtue of the structure of the organisation.

- Uncertainty about the causes and effects of change
  People may worry that their work and lives may be affected, and feel threatened and manipulated. They may take action to prevent the change happening. Jonathan's pizza bakers may see the changes as threatening as there is no place for their craft skills in the new company.

- Unwillingness to give up existing benefits
  Although the change will benefit the organisation as a whole, some individuals may lose power, status or benefits in some way. Most of Jonathan's craft pizza bakers would have to take a semi-skilled operator job, although one might be promoted to the production manager or marketing manager.

- Awareness of weaknesses in the changes proposed
  People may resist change if they are aware of potential problems that may have been overlooked by the change initiators. The craft pizza bakers may have some understanding

about the mass production of pizzas and feel that the particular system will not produce a quality product for the market.

- **Lack of trust and understanding**
  The proposed change is wrongly interpreted. It can occur because mistrust exists or because of ineffective communication about the proposed change. Jonathan may not have told his pizza bakers about the proposed changes or thought out what happens to each individual in the new company.

- **Low tolerance for change**
  Some individuals are less able to adapt to new situations. Some are likely to resist change just because it is change, regardless of their personal situation. Individuals who are tolerant to change but are continuously subjected to it, may reach the limits of their tolerance.

- **Organisational resistance**
  Resistance to change is usually by individuals, but the nature of the organisation can also cause resistance. Organisations with a tall rigid hierarchical structure with well-defined specification of roles will find it harder to accommodate change than a more flexible structure. Culture can also be a resistance to change, as norms and values once established will be difficult to alter.

Jonathan's organisation functioned in its early days mainly on mutual trust and support as he developed the business in its first entrepreneurial phase. He knew everyone, and all the bakers had trained as apprentices with the company. They were willing to identify with the company and the product and to work hard. With the new company, this feeling of family may be lost. It will need replacing with something, perhaps an incentive scheme would keep his employees motivated.

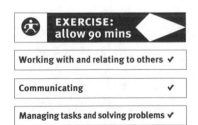

EXERCISE:
allow 90 mins

Working with and relating to others	✔
Communicating	✔
Managing tasks and solving problems	✔

ACTIVITY 3

Working in small groups, pool your knowledge and identify examples of each of the sources of resistance to change. Your examples may come from work or leisure.

Discuss the outcome of the resistance. Also describe the ways in which the groups or organisations in your examples sought to overcome the resistance.

Prepare and give a short presentation to the other groups. Use the box below to summarise your main points.

Commentary...

Clearly we cannot comment on your examples of resistance. We can however expand our identification of sources of resistance to change by indicating additional sources which you may have discussed.

- Lobbying by and negotiation between different managers can make change difficult to implement.

- An organisation's strategy may also be an obstacle to change.

- A high level of task interdependence between structures may make change difficult to achieve. If functions are interdependent, the change process becomes very complicated.

⊙ The higher up the organisational level the change is initiated, the more effect it will have throughout the organisation.

⊙ Complexity can be a problem; complex changes are more difficult to implement.

OVERCOMING RESISTANCE TO CHANGE

There are various strategies and approaches that can be used to overcome resistance to change. These are summarised in table 3.1.

Change can happen gradually – evolutionary change. This depends on a bottom-up change strategy that involves managers and employees at all levels. Or it can be revolutionary. This requires a top-down strategy that calls for direction from the top, and involves major restructuring. Many specific steps in the change process are left to individual managers to execute as the process proceeds.

Change creates uncertainty. Revolutionary change takes much less time than evolutionary, but it does not give the organisation and its individuals time to learn and respond to the new changes. As you see in section four, culture plays a key role in the recognition of the need for change and its implementation.

Jonathan felt he needed to adopt a revolutionary approach; changing the production process needed to be done in one go by the installation of the mass production line, and could not be done by gradual steps. Trevor Thompson similarly took a revolutionary approach, when he introduced the new fishing line production system; this affected all employees at once. In both these examples of revolutionary change, the way the change is handled with the individual employees, their subsequent motivation and the creation of a new and positive culture are crucial to success.

Jonathan's Pizza Company might have introduced a more evolutionary change by retaining part of the production for handmade pizzas and installing the mass production line for only part of the production. Some craft bakers could still do their original job, and they would also see that as the market for pizzas through the supermarkets grew that they would be part of a successful company. They would be more likely to accept that their future role within would have to change.

Approach	Involves	Commonly used when...	Advantages	Disadvantages
1. Education and communication.	Explaining the need for and logic of change to individuals, groups, and even entire organisations.	There is a lack of information or inaccurate information and analysis.	Once persuaded, people will often help to implement the change.	Can be very time-consuming if many people are involved.
2. Participation and involvement.	Asking members of organisation to help to design the change.	The initiators do not have all the information they need to design the change, and others have considerable power to resist.	People who participate will be committed to implementing change, and any relevant information they have will be integrated into the change plan.	Can be very time-consuring if participators design an inappropriate change.
3. Facilitation and support.	Offering retraining programs, time off, emotional support and understanding to people affected by the change.	People are resisting because of adjustment problems.	No other approach works as well with adjustment problems.	Can be time-consuming, expensive, and still fail.
4. Negotiation and agreement.	Negotiating with potential resisters; even soliciting written letters of understanding.	Some person or group with considerable power to resist will clearly lose out in a change.	Sometimes it is a relatively easy way to avoid major resistance.	Can be too expensive if it alerts others to negotiate for compliance.
5. Manipulation and co-optation.	Giving key persons a desirable role in designing or implementing the change process.	Other tactics will not work, or are too expensive.	It can be a relatively quick and inexpensive solution to resistance problems.	Can lead to future problems if people feel manipulated.
6. Explicit and implicit coercion.	Threatening job loss or transfer, lack of promotion, etc.	Speed is essential, and the change initiators possess considerable power.	It is speedy and can overcome any kind of resistance.	Can be risky if it leaves people angry with the initiators.

TABLE 3.1: Methods for dealing with resistance to change.
SOURCE: J.P. Kotter and L.A. Schlesinger, 'Choosing strategies for change', Harvard Business Review, March–April 1979. Adapted and reprinted by permission of Harvard Business Review. Copyright © 1979 by the President and Fellows of Harvard College; all rights reserved. In James A. Stoner and R. Edward Freeman, 1989, Management, Englewood Cliffs, Prentice Hall, Inc., p.370.

Technology and change

Technology concerns how people actually do their jobs, how they are motivated, controlled and supervised in their jobs, how they relate to other individuals within the organisation and external to the organisation. It can affect all transactions with the outside world.

The introduction of any new or different technology to any stage or process not only changes the immediate working environment but also has effects throughout an organisation. The effect on the primary core activities will be greater than on other departments, which themselves will not be affected equally. The effects of any change depend on the complexity, formalisation and centralisation of the organisation. These changes can affect the organisation structure itself.

Jonathan's introduction of mass production to make the pizzas affected the craft bakers' jobs. Their motivation and job satisfaction will be affected. However, it probably did not affect his accountant, except in the volume of tasks that he or she had to perform due to the increase in the company's activities. Also the structure would need to change to organise supervision of the new semi-skilled operators.

At Trevor Thompson, the introduction of technology to make fishing products affected the job functions, the team structure and the overall satisfaction and culture of his organisation. This resulted in many staff leaving. In Greatwear, Arthur Brown's use of technology probably affected his store managers more than the sales staff working in the stores.

Technology can alter people's jobs. Many people react very badly to its introduction. It is often seen as a major threat and can have a significant impact on staff morale. Its implementation has to be carefully planned. Its success is dependent on good communication and a supportive organisational culture. In section three, we look at communication issues and, in section four, at culture.

RACKET AND RUN

Racket and Run is a sports equipment shop. It sells top-of-the-range equipment and clothes for a fairly limited range of sports. By specialising and concentrating on the top end of the market, the equipment it sells tends to be expensive, although the profit margins are quite low.

The shop is run by its enthusiastic founder Peter Wilson. He employs many part-time staff, mainly young students, as well as two shop managers. The books are kept by an outside accountant. Both managers have been with him a long time; they are personal friends. Most management decisions are made in the pub after the shop closes at night.

The shop is a fun place in which both to work and to shop. However, business is a bit slow. Despite long opening hours, the shop is not making money. It is facing increased competition from local health centres that are now selling equipment, it is struggling to keep pace with changing fashions, and it is being hit by a general decline in consumer spending.

Peter calls in a consultant for advice. He wants to take a step back from the business and spend more time with his family. He's been working seven day weeks for too long. The consultant suggests that he installs a computerised stock control system to keep better track of stock and to allow a more efficient ordering system; too much money is currently tied up in stock. The new system should also mean better customer service and should simply record keeping leading to savings in accountancy bills.

Peter is also advised to take more of an executive role, by hiring a trained manager to take over the day-to-day responsibilities including supervising the two existing managers. He should review the practice of hiring so many part-time staff that need training and a high level of supervision. He should also invest in professional market analysis to find out the type of equipment he should be stocking. Previously, Peter has relied too much on his own intuition to guide both which sports the store would cover and the type of fashions it would stock.

ACTIVITY 4

Read the case study about Racket and Run. Write a 750-word report advising Peter Wilson on the changes he is being advised to make. Your report should discuss:

- how the changes can best be implemented and in what order

- whether a particular model of change can be applied

- the best way of introducing the new technology

- the likely impact of the changes on the existing staff

- the potential for resistance to the proposed changes and ways to minimise this resistance.

Finally, can you suggest any further changes that Peter Wilson might make to improve his business.

Write your report on a separate sheet of paper. Use the following box for notes and to summarise your main points.

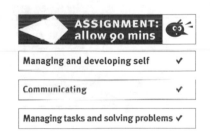

ASSIGNMENT:
allow 90 mins

Managing and developing self	✔
Communicating	✔
Managing tasks and solving problems	✔

summary

This session has considered organisational change and its management.

▶ The five main forces which make change inevitable are new technologies, information availability, product obsolescence, changes in the workforce and quality of working life.

▶ Organisational change involves the restructuring of human resources, functional resources, technological capabilities and organisational capabilities.

▶ A number of models have been developed to assist in introducing planned change: the systems model, field force analysis, and the action research model.

▶ The environment of an organisation can be classified as: simple static, complex static, simple dynamic or complex dynamic.

▶ Employees resist change for a variety of reasons and the organisation's existing structure and culture can also militate against change.

▶ Change can be evolutionary or revolutionary.

Communicating in Organisations

Communications systems

Objectives

After participating in this session, you should be able to:

> ▶ investigate various models of communication

> ▶ describe communication channels and networks

> ▶ investigate feedback and control mechanisms

> ▶ investigate the use of technology for information and communication.

In working through this session, you will practise the following BTEC common skills:

Managing and developing self	✔
Working with and relating to others	✔
Communicating	✔
Managing tasks and solving problems	✔
Applying numeracy	
Applying technology	
Applying design and creativity	

Communication

We now look at the role, functions and operation of communication within the organisation. For organisations to be effective, there needs to be communication between employees and managers, top managers and middle managers, functional departments and the environment, divisions and the corporate centre, and a whole range of other relationships that can only work and survive through communication. Good communication in an organisation is essential for achieving the organisation's objectives. Obviously, an organisation requires all sorts of communication with its environment too, and the level and type of these can also affect the internal structure.

In this session, we look at the basic process of communication, how it works within an organisation and its principal components. We investigate the role and use of technology in communication and administration and its far-reaching managerial, structural and strategic effects. In the next session, we look at communication in different organisational structures and ways of improving it.

In the first two sections of this workbook, we discussed the way in which organisation's environment and the particular stage it has reached in its life cycle shape an organisation's structure. Similarly, the organisation's structure, its size, its relationship with its environment, its culture, among other things, dictate how communication works within the organisation.

According to Scott and Mitchell (1976, Organization Theory: A Structural and Behavioral Analysis, Homewood, IL: R D Irwin), communication has four major functions within an organisation:

1. control

2. motivation

3. emotional expression

4. information.

For an organisation to perform effectively, it needs to maintain control over individuals, to motivate them to perform, to provide a means for emotional expression and to make decisions. Here we provide examples to show some facets of the major functions. To illustrate the points, we use Jonathan's Pizza Company as an example; as it grows you will see what happens to the ways that communication develops to support the new structure and way of doing things.

CONTROL

Individual workers and managers are required to follow the procedures and guidelines of their job description, and to follow company policy and instructions about conduct. Control might be through written instructions and by direct communication from a supervisor. In the early days of the company, Jonathan had loose job descriptions for his craft bakers. Control was maintained through his personal supervision. He exercised this control by feedback to the bakers on whether they had achieved the required results, and how well they performed.

MOTIVATION

Individuals require clarification on tasks, then feedback about performance and reinforcement of good behaviour. This could be through written or verbal feedback. Jonathan would congratulate particular staff on achieving high levels of quality and production in their pizza-making.

EMOTIONAL EXPRESSION

People socially interact within a work situation by expressing their frustrations and satisfactions in an informal way. This could be through written or verbal expression. Individual workers would talk among themselves and with Jonathan directly. They would discuss production problems, perhaps new ideas for new pizzas, but they would also spend a lot of time talking about their social and family lives.

INFORMATION

Individuals and groups at all levels require data to make decisions. Data are acquired and disseminated by written, electronic or verbal means. The craft bakers would need to tell Jonathan about their levels of productivity, scheduling, the stocks of raw materials, etc., to allow him to make decisions about what sales could be fulfilled and what ingredients needed ordering. This might be by a verbal or written report, daily or weekly, prepared by each individual baker to Jonathan.

Models of communication

So what is communication? Communication is a complex process or flow. Problems arise when there are blockages or distortions in that flow. We now look at the process in terms of different models of communication.

Shannon and Weaver (1949, A Mathematical Theory of Communications, University of Illinois Press) devised one model to identify the key processes of communication. It explained their work in telecommunications at the Bell Telephone Company in the late 1930s and was devised to help engineers to transmit electrical signals from one place to another.

It is a one-way system; see figure 1.1. Their concept of noise concerned the distortion and interference of static on the line; our current-day view of 'noise' includes anything that interferes between transmission and receipt of the message – a memo being lost in a pile of papers on somebody's desk, or a noisy office disturbing an important telephone call.

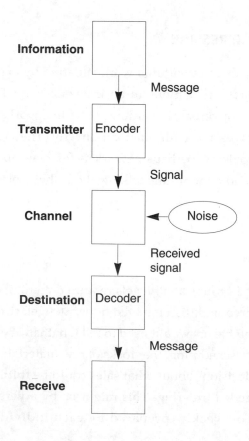

FIGURE 1.1: Shannon and Weaver's model of communication.

This simple model sees the receiver as a passive information processor. However, because the message must be decoded, or put back into an understandable form, by the receiver, so the receiver is actively participating in the process. The model also sees words as carriers relaying true meaning; however, they are subject to interpretation by the receiver, and this is therefore a subjective process. This model assumes that effective expression alone results in effective communication.

The next model includes feedback. By introducing feedback, we develop a circular model with the receiver feeding back a response to the transmitter who can then re-send a clearer modified message. The Schramm model is shown in figure 1.2 (Schramm, W. L., 1954, 'How communication works', in The Process and Effects of Mass Communication, University of Illinois Press).

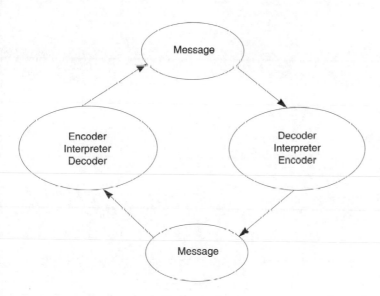

FIGURE 1.2: The Schramm model.

This model assumes that understanding means effective communication. However, we should remember that understanding does not necessarily mean agreement, or that understanding is the only goal of communication. The craft bakers may receive and understand Jonathan's message about pizzas, but that does not mean that they will necessarily act upon it.

MODELS OF COMMUNICATION

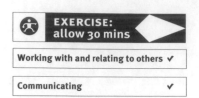

Working with and relating to others ✔

Communicating ✔

Managing tasks and solving problems ✔

ACTIVITY 1

Working in a small group, discuss factors which affect the transfer of information when communicating verbally, drawing examples from social and work activities. As you do so, identify the differences between the Shannon and Weaver and Schramm models of communication. Make a short presentation to other groups. Summarise the key points of your discussion in the box below.

Commentary...

If you think about just talking to a friend, you can see that there are many factors that affect the transfer of the message. You are affected by the location that you are in, and whether you can even hear each other – you might be distracted by loud music or some other activity taking place close by. Is your friend listening to you? Or, is he or she thinking about something else? What are you trying to say? Is it good news or bad news? Are you verbally communicating one message and non-verbally communicating another? Perhaps you are arranging to do something that you do not really want to do. Is there a good relationship between you, or do you disagree a lot?

In a work situation, there may be other factors too. A conversation between a boss and a subordinate is different from an exchange between colleagues. Both, however, are affected by whether the two people like each other, whether they respect each other, whether they understand the same jargon, whether they share the same objectives, and whether the message is an instruction or a reprimand or a commendation.

Look back at the descriptions of the two models and identify the main differences. Schramm includes feedback and develops into a circular model with the sender re-sending the message again. If you fail to 'get your message across' to your friend about, say, where you are going to meet, you repeat the message, this time maybe adding more information, like 'the coffee shop in the High Street, the one we went to last Friday', and not just the 'coffee shop in the High Street'.

If we look at the different parts of the process, we can see the problems that can arise at each stage.

Conceiving the message

You make the decision to send a message in response to a thought process or external stimulus. You want to arrange a social meeting with a friend. You consider the best means of getting the message across. You clarify exactly what the message is. You want to meet for a drink at 8 p.m. on Friday, 14th, at your local sports club.

Encoding the message

You need to choose the medium, or mix of media, that you will use to encode your message. By what means do you wish to send the message? Do you want to write it down? Do you want to show it graphically? Will you prefer to say it? You need to think through the effects and effectiveness of various media and what you want to achieve. When arranging to see your friend, you will think of ways to send the message that differ from those used to arrange a business meeting; however, in both cases, you have to decide how you want to relay the message: by a spoken or written request.

Selecting the communication channel

Technology offers us a vast range of telecommunication channels to use. If you are arranging a business meeting, do you want to send the message by a circulated memo? By letter? By fax? By e-mail? Are you looking to transmit a verbal message? By telephone? At a meeting? Face to face? You need to think about the factors involved in terms of immediacy, cost, effectiveness, documentation, confidentiality and legality. Your job responsibility might restrict your use of particular channels, without going to a superior for authorisation. In arranging to meet your friend, perhaps you decide to phone, but he is out, so you leave a message on his answer machine.

Decoding the message

In this information age, individuals can have an overload of communication and information. The receiver needs to prioritise messages and be able to understand the context and jargon of them. Also he or she needs to receive the message without prejudice against the sender, even if they do not like them or their function, or they have had some past disagreements. Your friend is very busy and picks up many messages on his answer machine; he scribbles a note to himself to call you back. He does not write down the details of your message, but thinks vaguely: 'OK for Friday.'

Interpreting the message

Because of human relationships and hidden meanings in messages, the receiver needs to ensure that he or she has received the right message. Your friend cannot quite remember what you said. Was it this Friday or next Friday that you wanted to meet? Or, maybe your message was not clear in the first place, and you had given some options.

Feedback

The receiver probably needs to give the sender prompt and clear feedback. This is obviously easier with direct personal oral communication. Feedback is likely to need more thought, time and action with written messages. In our example, your friend calls you back to say: 'Yes I can meet for a drink next Friday.' You say: 'No, I meant this Friday, the 14th.' Finally, your message is clear, and your friend's response is clear and you arrange to meet at a mutually convenient time!

All the factors discussed above may cause some distortion leading to the outcome: the message the sender intended to send is not the same as that received by the receiver. You intended to say 'a drink, this Friday' but your friend received the message of 'next Friday', because of distortion at two separate places.

ACTIVITY 2

Managing tasks and solving problems ✔

A salesperson in the sales department of a manufacturing company puts through a telephone call requesting information from a controller in the production department about the scheduling of a particular delivery.

Identify the potential for distortion in this communication. List the problems that might cause misunderstanding or an ineffective communication.

Commentary...

The salesperson is the sender of the original message, and the controller is the receiver of the message. Potential problems include the following:

- There may be **physical distortion;** the message may not be heard properly by the controller because of noise in the sales office or noise in the production office, or just a poor telephone system.

- The salesperson may not make the message clear; the controller may not be able to identify the particular job.

- The salesperson may not use the same **jargon** as the production person.

- The salesperson may be aggressive and demanding, criticising the production schedule. This tone is unlikely to encourage the controller to be co-operative.

- The controller may think that the request wastes his time, if the information is already available on the daily production report, say, through the computer system. Perhaps the salesperson could have expected a better response by sending a more impersonal e-mail.

- The controller may not be willing to tell the salesperson the true position if the production department is way behind schedule.

- The controller may not have the correct information to hand. He or she may simply invent an answer.

- The controller may be busy with something else at the time of the call and unable (or unwilling) to give the request proper consideration.

- The controller may have to refer to the request to a more senior manager before releasing the information.

You can probably think of many other problems, especially as the two employees are not in a direct line of authority. One cannot tell the other what to do; they have to rely on co-operation.

Channels and networks

The means of communication within an organisation is affected by its structure and, equally, is determined by the structure. Messages need to be dispersed throughout an organisation, but clearly the approaches you can adopt if the organisation has five employees in a single office are different to those useful for an organisation with 5,000 employees at branches throughout the country. We look now at some of the channels and networks, formal and informal, that make an organisation work.

Within the organisation communication can flow vertically, either up or down, laterally or diagonally.

VERTICAL COMMUNICATION

This is the principal route from the top to the bottom of the organisation. Downwards, it conveys directives, instructions and policies from the top decision makers to managers and employees. This top-down communication is frequently channelled through the lines of authority. Upwards, it conveys results of productivity, details about workers' and managers' performance, suggestions, grievances and problems. Reports are passed up through middle management to top management, so that senior managers have all the necessary information for decision making.

In bureaucratic mechanistic organisations with high differentiation, many hierarchical levels, high formalisation and centralised decision making, the vertical communication is very formalised. It is crucial to the smooth running of the company because so much information has to be passed upwards and downwards. The communication channels will retain the hierarchical structure imposed on them by the organisation, so the information they carry will be structured in the same way. Filtering and distortion may occur at each stage, in any message exchange between people up and down the channel.

In an entrepreneurial or simple structure, the boss is likely to know all employees individually. The boss can communicate with all employees by calling general or individual meetings or through individual telephone calls or memos. In contrast, the chief executive of a large divisionalised company needs to go through formal management channels to reach all employees. Middle managers will have to interpret and pass the message on to the operating core.

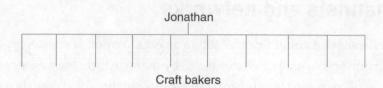

FIGURE 1.3: Communication in a simple entrepreneurial structure.

As the pizza company expands, Jonathan will need to change his way of giving instructions or information. He may need a more formal approach of instructing the many semi-skilled operators that he will need to hire. The method of communicating with these staff will depend on the organisation structure that he has designed. If he hires a production manager to oversee production then he will communicate via this person; if he goes for the team approach then he will need to communicate through the team structure.

As the organisation becomes more complex, so the communication channels will become more formal and complex. The organisation will develop its own procedures and way of doing things. For example, Jonathan's production manager may develop his own way of delivering management information to the operators using, say, a daily production meeting, or a daily production report, or a bulletin board near their clocking-in station for informal messages. And if the production line is eventually run on a shift basis, so not all staff are together in the factory at the same time, then another new way of communicating with those on different shifts will be required.

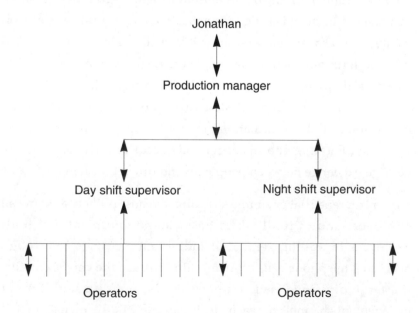

FIGURE 1.4: Communication in a more complex structure.

LATERAL COMMUNICATION

Lateral communication describes exchanges between members of the same work group, or members of work groups at the same level, or personnel of the same status. Generally speaking, individuals are likely to talk more frankly with these peer groups as there are no problems with lines of authority. Lateral communication can save time and facilitate co-ordination. It is part of Mintzberg's mutual adjustment co-ordinating mechanism discussed in earlier sections.

Jonathan's operators making pizzas may help each other with a particular production problem rather than taking it to the production manager. Or one shift worker makes sure that the next shift knows about a problem with the equipment or if the stores have run out of anchovies to make a specific order.

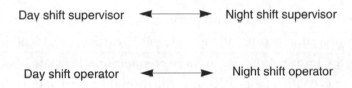

FIGURE 1.5: Lateral communication flows.

In the scenario presented in the last activity, the salesperson and the controller could co-operate and exchange the information and, if necessary, production could agree to help speed up delivery. Similarly, sales could agree to resolve the problem with the customer. This might happen if the two personnel regard themselves as being on the same hierarchical level and helping each other out. In this case, we do not know if this is a usual route for information requests, or whether it is an informal arrangement between two people who know each other well, or a desperate last resort action from the salesperson to obtain information to placate a customer.

In very functionalised or divisionalised structures, communication problems can develop when departments or divisions see themselves as rivals. The production and sales departments may be in conflict. Lateral communications need to be set up with more guidelines and procedures for middle managers to follow so that less is left to the co-operation between individuals. For example, with our sales and production people, if this was a sensible route for information to be made available on a regular basis, then management should facilitate a special daily production report for the sales team.

DIAGONAL COMMUNICATION

Diagonal communication arises in departmentalised organisations when a member of one department needs to have direct communication with a member in another department at a higher or lower hierarchical level. In this case, there is no direct line authority. Communication relies on co-operation and goodwill.

In the example in the last activity, the personnel in sales and production would be in diagonal communication if the salesperson is speaking to the production director. The success of the exchange depends on the production director being helpful, especially if this is an unusual request. If the production director is status conscious, the request for information might have been refused; instead, the salesperson's request might be passed to someone in the production department with equal standing within the organisational hierarchy.

If the organisation has a flatter structure, then there will be diagonal communication because there are fewer vertical lines of authority to carry the information. Much more co-operation is needed between personnel. With a taller structure, the formal vertical and horizontal lines of communication are more important.

These communication channels form networks up and down and around the organisation. These networks may be formal or informal.

FORMAL NETWORKS

Formal networks tend to be through the normal lines of authority: the 'official' channels that are concerned with producing the organisation's products and services and achieving the organisation's objectives. These channels are used to disseminate the organisation's directives and policies. All organisations have formal communications channels.

With a complex structure, top management relies on middle managers to pass the message on to the next level of supervisor and eventually the individuals in the operating core. A manager holding a meeting to pass on the message to the next level of supervisors may distort the message that eventually reaches the worker on the production line. In larger organisations, more people are needed to convey messages, so the communication system needs to be more structured and formal, and depends more on standard written procedures and guidelines for routine instructions.

Within these main networks, there may be smaller networks that work at a different level in disseminating information; these are formal small-group networks. These vary from the chain formation that follows the normal line of authority, the wheel formation that has a leader that relays the information to others in a team, and the all-channel formation which allows all members to actively communicate with each other. These different networks are illustrated in figure 1.6.

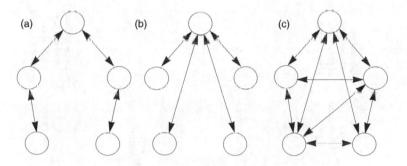

FIGURE 1.6: Three common small group networks: (a) chain; (b) wheel; and (c) all channel.

The effectiveness of small group networks is summarised in table 1.1. If the organisation has a team approach then communication within the groups is very important; there is also likely to be more informal mutual co-operation. If Jonathan takes a team approach to his pizza production, he will communicate instructions and procedures to team leaders leaving it to the teams themselves to inform all the individual members. If he takes a more bureaucratic approach, he might pass information through the production manager. The production manager continues the next level of dissemination, and may have his or her own way of communicating with employees.

Criteria	Networks		
	Chain	**Wheel**	**All-Channel**
Speed	Moderate	Fast	Fast
Accuracy	High	High	Moderate
Emergence of a leader	Moderate	High	None
Member satisfaction	Moderate	Low	High

TABLE 1.1: Small-group networks and effectiveness criteria.
SOURCE: Robbins, S. P., 1991, Organizational Behavior: Concepts, Controversies and Applications, 5th edn, Englewood Cliffs, NJ: Prentice Hall, p. 321.

If we compare the performance of centralised and decentralised communication networks in relation to what the organisation does, we can see that centralised networks are better when the organisation is performing simple, more routine tasks and decentralised networks are better with complex tasks (figure 1.7). This is linked to the overall organisation structure and where the control lies. The effectiveness of communication depends on what the organisation does, how it is structured and vice versa.

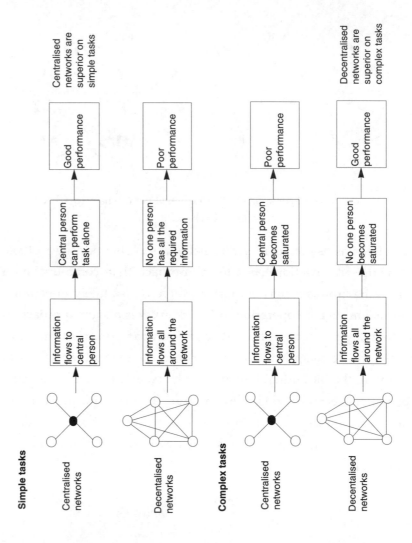

FIGURE 1.7: Communication networks and task complexity.
SOURCE: Baron, R. A. and Greenberg, J., 1990, Behaviour in Organisations, 3rd edn, Allyn and Bacon.

In the pizza company, the operating core is performing routine tasks. Jonathan, the strategic apex, may find that he still needs to centralise control in himself regardless of whether he has a team or a more bureaucratic structure under him. In contrast, in a professional bureaucracy such as a legal partnership, the people contributing to the organisation have the effective control and are performing complex tasks, therefore the communication channels will operate differently because everyone is more on a par in terms of job function.

INFORMAL NETWORKS

Informal networks describe the ways in which communication takes place outside the official channels, as information is passed on by word of mouth or at informal meetings. An underlying line of authority may still exist. Small group networks may be operating informally too, at the next level of dissemination of information.

In a more flexible organic structured organisation, with low differentiation and low decentralisation, communication is much more informal. However, the correct information still needs to reach the right people for operation and decision making, otherwise the organisation will be functioning in a state of chaos. The tea break may be a good opportunity to let employees know that there will be management changes next month, but it would not be a very effective way of telling sales staff about the features of a new product.

Some informal communication networks are free to move in any direction and operate regardless of hierarchical levels. These are usually known as grapevines. An organisation's grapevine usually fulfils a role in members' social needs but probably does not achieve any organisational tasks. It is not controlled or set up by management or anyone else so it is often seen by employees as being more reliable than official information. Anybody who participates in it probably has their own agenda, and hopes to achieve something from it.

Grapevines are based on gossip and rumour. They can cause unnecessary resentment and fear. For example, someone might start a rumour that the company is going out of business; workers will become unnecessarily anxious about losing their jobs and investors may grow jittery about their money. A disgruntled employee might start a rumour about the integrity or honesty of his or her manager or the quality of the product the organisation produces. These kinds of rumours can be very destructive. However, a grapevine does provide a means for employees to voice their grievances and it can indicate to managers the issues about which they are most concerned. Managers might manipulate the grapevine to disseminate information; this is likely to be rather negative and not good practice, but it may be seen as a 'soft' way of giving bad news to employees.

Often rumours start as a response to situations that are important to the employees. There might be some specific uncertainty, for example where people are anxious about their jobs. Perhaps the company has a major new competitor. Employees at Littlewoods Pools would not find it difficult to see that the company might experience problems because of the National Lottery; they are probably buying lottery tickets themselves. A rumour might start that there would be big reductions in staffing.

The issues that cause most problems for staff – restructuring, loss of jobs, change in job tasks, relocation, appointment of top personnel – are also likely to be the ones that management is most concerned about and trying to keep secret. This encourages and sustains the rumour. Management can minimise some of the grapevine's damaging effects by:

- giving notification of important decisions and changes

- explaining action that may appear underhand or inconsistent

- emphasising the benefits (and potential drawbacks) of future actions

- discussing the worst-case scenario.

SAT:
allow 30 mins

Managing tasks and solving problems ✓

ACTIVITY 3

Consider the different lines of communication in Jonathan's Pizza Company before and after the introduction of mass production for pizza making. Characterise and describe the two communication channels in terms of:

- vertical communication

- lateral communication

- diagonal communication

- grapevine.

Emphasise which channels are formal networks and which are informal networks.

Commentary...

	before	**after**
Vertical/formal	By direct contact with Jonathan and all individuals in the company	By contact through the production manager, or shift managers, if this is the structure that has been set up, or through the teams to individual members; increased documentation for procedures of making and results
Lateral/informal	By direct contact between all individuals all working together in the factory at the same time	By operators talking among themselves, or maybe leaving notes for the next shift worker
Diagonal/informal	All individuals could freely communicate with all others	This might only be relevant after the company expands even more and differentiates into sales and production departments
Grapevine/informal	Individuals are likely to approach Jonathan directly with grievances and worries	Individuals are more likely to discuss problems with with each other, maybe within their team structure, or maybe with their production manager, but they are unlikely to go directly to Jonathan.

A grapevine is likely to develop and if it carries any destructive rumours, such as a worsening cash flow, then Jonathan will need to defuse it directly. For instance, he will need to clarify that suppliers are being paid, before outside suppliers themselves start to hear the rumours and become anxious about payment.

Principal communication media

There are many channels that individuals, managers and top management can use for communication; they vary from face-to-face exchanges (i.e. talking to someone in the same room) to the printed word and sophisticated electronic media. Here are some of the options.

FACE-TO-FACE

This is the richest but most restrictive way of communicating between people. It is the richest because of the many factors that come into play: language, tone of voice, body movements, facial expressions, eye contact and a whole range of subtle ways that we have of relaying a message to someone else. There is also the potential for immediate feedback and clarification, if there is any misunderstanding or misinterpretation.

When Jonathan instructed his craft bakers to make a batch of 400 of a particular variety of pizza, they could respond in a face-to-face situation by saying that there were only enough anchovies for 200 pizzas. He could then make a judgement about whether to make another variety, order some anchovies urgently from a supplier that could deliver quickly, or renegotiate the order with the customer.

However, talking face-to-face is a restrictive form of communication. We do need to be in the same place at the same time as the person; this may often not be possible in a busy modern diversified organisation. When the pizzas are mass produced on a shift basis, operators may not be able to tell Jonathan or maybe even their production manager that they have run out of anchovies for the order. As companies grow, there are new and increased communication needs. Perhaps, Jonathan has to issue written guidelines to the operators about what to do if they run out of an ingredient when on a night or a day shift. Also, he needs a better system to control his supplies of raw materials, so constant feedback from the factory about stocks is required.

Individual or group meetings are essential for achieving some types of communication and problem solving within an organisation. All employees need some face-to-face contact even if it is only with their immediate supervisor. It is a major part of lateral and informal communication and so is important in mutual adjustment and team building. Also, it is often important for top management to be seen to be around; it plays a part in building up corporate culture.

TELEPHONE

We often use the telephone if we cannot meet the other party for face to face communication. However, a conventional telephone cannot transmit visual information; we cannot use it to transmit graphics and pictures or any other visual cues, and hence we lose all non-verbal communication.

As the sender determines the timing of the call, it is not an ideal communication medium if the receiver does not have the time or inclination to take the call. Look back at activity 2; the production controller may be involved in doing an important job for his or her manager, and although relevant information might be available, the controller may say that he or she is too busy to answer (or be too distracted to concentrate on the problem).

Many phone calls are unproductive because the people we want to talk to are unavailable. Time is wasted in either calling the person back or receiving a return call when we are not available. Answer machines cope with some of these problems, but messages can be poorly left and badly interpreted.

Phone calls are also unsuitable if personnel do not have easy access to a telephone; often workers on the shop floor are not able to leave their work station to make a telephone call to a superior to ask what to do in a particular situation, but they could easily consult a manual on procedures and guidelines that they keep by the machine.

GROUP MEETINGS

Departmental meetings, training sessions, and group conferences require organisational time and resources. They do provide means of co-ordinating activities, stimulating motivation and commitment, communicating corporate culture and solving problems. They should not be used to disseminate information – like office procedures and regulations – that could be delivered with less cost and people involvement. Unnecessary meetings waste valuable organisational time. They should be run to a fixed agenda so that time is not wasted. However, they benefit from the richness of face-to-face encounters. Jonathan could hold weekly meetings with his production manager, marketing manager and purchasing manager to schedule the week's production and sales, and look at any problem areas on supplies, for example, that might arise.

FORMAL PRESENTATIONS

These are used to present a new product, or safety procedures or a training programme. They are an extremely efficient and effective means of disseminating information if the presenter is skilled, well prepared and a good speaker. Feedback is restricted as individuals are less likely to ask questions or offer criticism in a large group. At the next stage of Jonathan's company's growth, he may make a formal presentation about the opening of a new factory and what it means to the existing factory. By doing this, he would inform all personnel about the company's plans, and also defuse the rumours that have come to him about personnel being transferred from one factory to the other.

MEMOS

Writing a memo demands that the sender of the message makes the message clear and precise. This is a skill that can be learnt. Memos cannot receive any instant feedback, but they do provide a permanent – and formal – record of communication. The receiver can spend time taking in the information and deciding on a response. They are useful as a means of informing routine organisational changes, notification of meetings and similar information. Jonathan might use them to tell his production manager, accounts, and purchasing manager about a new customer or supplier, but would be unlikely to use them to tell individual workers about a new customer order. However, he would use it to tell all employees about a change in working hours or an individual's annual salary review.

MAIL

This is now an expensive and relatively slow means of communication given the electronic alternatives. It can be used to reach a large number of people in different geographical locations, and is suitable for important but not time sensitive information. Jonathan might use the post to communicate with all his suppliers and his bank manager to tell them about the changes in the company. The government might use it to notify small businesses about changes in legislation. Jonathan would probably use it to send payment to his suppliers, rather than transfer funds electronically, and he would use it to send invoices to his customers.

Think about your own mail: it might contain information about your account from your bank or building society, your gas or telephone bill, a letter from a friend overseas, a circular from your sports club about a forthcoming event, a renewal form for your house or car insurance, a book that you have ordered from a book club, a DIY item ordered from a specialist mail-order company, or even flowers a relative has sent for your birthday. Many types of communication are still sent by mail.

FAX (FACSIMILE)

Faxes have replaced some types of traditional mail because facsimile transmission provides immediate delivery. It is an easy channel to use, and very reliable. Senders control the timing. Confidentiality may be a problem if the fax is received in an open office situation. Jonathan might use it to confirm his order for a new batch of anchovies from his supplier.

STAFF AND CUSTOMER NEWSLETTERS

A company newsletter can help to promote corporate culture. It can help employees to keep in touch with the activities of other parts of the company and with what other company employees are doing both inside and outside the company. Features might be written on new products or services, or employee or customer benefits; it can be just used as a vehicle for employee recognition or product promotion. A newsletter takes time to produce so the information may not be up to date.

Newsletters are often used by large bureaucratic organisations to project themselves as more 'human' and 'user friendly' to their staff and customers. For example, the Automobile Association produces a publication on a regular basis. In addition to motoring features, it carries information about other AA services like insurance. CompuServe uses its magazine to advise users of its new products and services, and offers advice about problems that customers might encounter in using its product.

BULLETIN BOARDS

This is a traditional way of communicating with employees in a single location. They are useful for posting work schedules, job vacancies, for-sale announcements, notices of local events and employee functions. They are usually located in 'high-traffic' areas, like close to the coffee machines or the clocking-in area so employees cannot miss them. Messages need to be simple and the information easily remembered. The boards need to be maintained, kept up to date and uncluttered.

PUBLICATIONS

There is still a place for printed materials within organisations. Booklets and manuals are a useful way of drawing together information that employees would need to retain as reference material. They might contain instructions about how to operate machines, or what to do in cases of malfunction, or guidelines of what to do in certain situations. A company may produce a manual for their salesmen to carry, which lists answers to typical customer enquiries and gives instructions about how to take the order and what information is required for each order.

This type of publication is suitable for conveying information that does not require frequent updating. Although it might take a lot of time and collaborative effort to prepare it in the first place, it can be a very efficient way of relaying a large volume of routine information to a large number of people who may be in different locations. In a large bureaucratic organisation, this type of publication is essential for providing information about company rules and regulations. It might also draw together all procedures and ways that different job functions and departments are expected to communicate with each other, and what information is to be transferred between them and how it is to be transferred.

Annual reports are designed for a wide audience of customers, potential and actual investors, suppliers, particularly those in the organisation's specific environment. (See the companion workbook Managing Finance and Information.) They contain detailed financial, strategic and management information about the organisation. As such they need to be very carefully prepared documents.

A school, college or university needs to publish student regulations that govern the award of qualifications and annual prospectuses that notify new and existing students about courses and programmes that are being offered in the forthcoming academic year.

AUDIOTAPES AND VIDEOTAPES

These are now just as easy to produce as printed materials. They have many of the same advantages, and can reach a lot of people in different locations. However, videos and cassettes cannot be as easily scanned for pertinent information as printed documents. But, in their favour, they do have an aural and visual image that can help in relaying the message. They might be used to help to sell a new product or idea; a research department might produce a video to explain a new product to the sales team.

HOTLINES

During a crisis – such as a takeover or merger – a company may set up hotlines to answer employees' queries. This can help to alleviate fears and control rumours. They may contain a taped message that is updated on a daily basis detailing corporate changes, stock prices etc. Hotlines may also be used as a confidential system for employees to ask questions about the company.

ELECTRONIC MAIL (E-MAIL)

This is a method of transmitting a message electronically from one computer terminal to another. It can be used purely as internal communication system or, if the particular system has the required telecommunications facility, it can be used for external communications. The message is instantaneously sent from the sender's computer to the receiver's mail box from where it can be picked up and read at any time. The same message can be sent to many different addresses at the same time. It is quick, easy to use and cheap as connection between the computers is through the normal internal or external telephone system. It is best for brief, simple, time-sensitive information.

Dialogues are easy to set up, although they may become rather informal, but generally the feedback is quick and effective. Individuals need to check their e-mail box regularly, just as they would a normal mail box. Clearly its use is limited if not all individuals and organisations have the technology for electronic mail.

Within an organisation, electronic mail can substitute for memos and faxes or telephone calls, particularly for organising meetings, providing information about orders or supplies, etc. It can obviously only be used between personnel that have a computer on their desk. It is usually regarded as a very confidential means of communication as only the receiver is likely to pick up the message.

It can also be used to send graphics and complete document files. The software is generally speaking not difficult to use, and the hardware required is a networked computer system for a single site operation and a modem and telephone line for wider communication.

Computer conferencing

Computer conferencing can be used to link small groups of employees. It is useful for sharing new ideas and brainstorming. Messages all look alike regardless of the status of the sender, so it is a great 'leveller' as more attention is paid to the message rather than the sender. It can achieve the same results as a normal meeting in much less time, but obviously misses some of the richness of face-to-face contact, and top level people may find it a problem as they 'lose' their status. Corporate culture cannot be effectively communicated through technology. It can help in organisations that are trying to develop creativity at all levels.

Voice mail

A computer digitises the caller's voice and leaves it in the receiver's voice mail box. The receiver can pick it up via a special code number thus retaining privacy and the confidentiality of the message. The same message can be sent to many different addresses. Most voice mail replaces short memos and telephone messages that do not require an immediate reply. It is not possible to scan messages, so you have to listen to all of them before you reach the important ones. Voice mail like e-mail is only effective if sufficient people have the facility.

Tele-conferencing

Tele-conferencing is the telephone equivalent of the group meeting. Small and large groups can simultaneously communicate in a single conversation via a phone line. It means that travelling is reduced for personnel in different locations. It is often used for the first stages in new personnel recruitment especially if the prospective employee is in a different country. It is best for information rather than negotiation. It could be used for sales meeting where sales reports need to be made with little comment or interaction.

VIDEO-CONFERENCING

Video-conferencing is tele-conferencing with a visual image. It provides a telecommunications alternative to face-to-face and group communication. It transmits audio and video images via a satellite connection. Some systems are one-way; others are interactive allowing parties at different locations to communicate with each other. It is more effective than tele-conferencing because it includes visual cues. It will probably replace many face-to-face meetings in the future. 'Meetings' tend to be quicker and more focused than actual 'real' meetings. This is an invaluable means of bringing together busy and expensive managers in a large organisation from, say, overseas divisions for regional or head office meetings. It is particularly effective for sales and marketing meetings but less effective for, say, research and product development where more interaction is required from participants and a face-to-face meeting may be essential.

SAT:
allow 20 mins

Managing tasks and solving problems ✔

ACTIVITY 4

Review the different types of communications media. What would be the best ways of achieving the following communications:

1. Jonathan informing all staff about changes in the company

2. Jonathan ordering tomato sauce from his supplier in Italy

3. your bank informing you that you are overdrawn

4. checking the balance at your bank account

5. ordering a pizza from your local take-away.

Commentary...

Clearly, in each case, there are a number of alternatives that could be used. The choice of best method is, to some extent, subjective. Here are our suggestions.

1. Jonathan should hold a face-to-face meeting with his staff.

2. If Jonathan wants the supplies as soon as possible, and to make the order clear, especially if he is dealing in another language, he should send a fax.

3. Some banks may inform you by phone, most will send a letter so that there is a formal record of the notification.

4. Here there are many possible methods: you could check your account directly if you happen to be in the right branch; you could find out electronically from a cash dispenser; or with banks that provide a telephone service, you could ring.

5. You would order your pizza by telephone or by calling round personally. You want the pizzas delivered tonight, not tomorrow or some time next week.

In choosing a channel for communicating, there are several questions that you need to ask. Go back to the key factors of communicating to see where they all fit in to the process.

- What kind of response do I need and how quickly do I need it? For example, you want your pizza at 8 p.m. tonight.

- How many different parties can I send my message to through this channel? For example, you want to reach all suppliers and customers.

- Is the message confidential? For example, you are dismissing an employee for consistently bad performance.

- Can I easily and quickly use the channel to send my message? For example, do you have a telephone in the house to call the pizza take-away?

- Can the receiver of the message easily and quickly use the channel? Does he or she have the facility available? For example, the pizza take-away will always need someone to answer the phone, not have to rely on the pizza maker who may not be able to reach the telephone every time if he is in the middle of making an order.

- Do I need to be in the same time zone and place as my receiver? For example, if you want to reprimand someone then you should do it face-to-face if possible, but it might be a divisional manager in Australia that you cannot possibly meet, so you might have to use the telephone or preferably video-conferencing if you have the facility.

- How much does it cost to use this channel? Are other channels cheaper? For example, a fax to Italy is cheaper than making a lengthy peak-rate international telephone call.

- Can I project my personality through this channel? Jonathan might want to use the occasion for telling the staff about changes to inspire them about the expanded company.

- Is this channel too formal? Not formal enough? For example, Jonathan might hold his meeting with his staff in a formal meeting room that he rarely uses, or informally at a 'day-out' for the staff, depending on his relationship with them and how he would normally do things.

- Who exercises control about when the message is received? Is this important? Messages sent by electronic mail or left on answer machines are only read when the receiver checks his or her electronic mail or listens to the telephone messages.

- Do I have the authority to use this particular channel? For example, you may want to phone for a late night pizza delivery but your landlord may prohibit you from using the telephone after 10 p.m. in the evening.

- Does the receiver have the authority to use the chosen channel? For example, the pizza company may have a policy of only receiving orders in person and not by phone.

PRINCIPAL COMMUNICATION
MEDIA

Finally, in choosing the channel, you must align your needs as the sender, with those of your receiver, the characteristics of the message and the logistics of the channels.

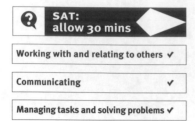

Working with and relating to others ✔

Communicating ✔

Managing tasks and solving problems ✔

ACTIVITY 5

Working in a small group, look at the following three situations. What is the best communication channel in each case? Justify your answers.

1. A medium-sized construction firm wants to announce a new employee benefit scheme.

2. A manager wishes to confirm a meeting with 10 employees.

3. You work in a medium-sized insurance company. You want to foster support for a programme that encourages employees from different departments to work effectively together on the same project team.

Commentary...

In the first situation, the best choice would be through small group meetings, so that the details may be verbally explained and employees allowed to ask questions. Alternatives are by memo (but this would not allow any feedback and may not be simple enough to convey the message), or a large staff meeting, possibly after a memo has been circulated, (but this would not allow proper opportunities for employees to ask questions – clearly only a limited number could speak and some might be intimidated about speaking at such a large meeting).

In the second situation, if the employees have access to the facility then voicemail or e-mail would be suitable because there is no requirement to respond. Equally a memo would do. The telephone could be used but this is a more time-consuming option; if people are not available to take the call, then the call has to be remade, unless they have an answer machine.

In the final scenario, the best way would be either on the telephone or, preferably, through face-to-face contact. You would want to alter and add to your message in response to how the receiver reacts. You are trying to win people over to the idea of team working and that requires a communication medium which allows you to be persuasive and permits instant feedback so that you can hear people's concerns.

As you can see, there are various options for sending different types of messages. It is easy to see what works best in certain situations, like phoning for a pizza, but there are constraints on the sender and receiver in all cases. The advantages and disadvantages of principal communications media are summarised in table 1.2.

PRINCIPAL COMMUNICATION
MEDIA

	Advantages	Disadvantages
Written communication Letter Memorandum Report Abstract Minutes Article Press release etc.	**Provides written record** and evidence of despatch and receipt; capable of relaying complex ideas; provides analysis, evaluation and summary; disseminates information to dispersed receivers; can confirm, interpret and clarify oral communications; forms basis of contract or agreement.	**Can take time to produce, can be expensive;** communication tends to be more formal and distant; can cause problems of interpretation; instant feedback is not possible; once dispatched, difficult to modify message; does not allow for exchange of opinion, views or attitudes except over period of time.
Oral communication Face-to-face conversation Interview Meeting Oral briefing Public address Oral presentation Telephone call Conference Training session etc.	**Direct medium of communication;** advantages of physical proximity and, usually, both sight and sound of sender and receiver; allows for instant interchange of opinion, views, attitudes – instantaneous feedback; easier to convince or persuade; allows for contribution and participation from all present.	More difficult to hold ground in face of opposition; **more difficult to control when a number of people take part;** lack of time to think things out – quality of decision making may be inferior; often no written record of what has been said; sometimes disputes arise over what was agreed.
Visual communication Non-verbal communication – expression, gesture, posture Diagram Chart Table Graph Photograph Film slide Film Video tape Model Mock-up etc.	**Reinforces oral communication;** provides additional visual stimulus; simplifies written or spoken word; quantifies – provides ideas in number form; provides simulations of situations; illustrates techniques and procedures; provides visual record.	**May be difficult to interpret** without reinforcing written or spoken word; requires additional skills of comprehension and interpretation; can be costly and expensive in time to produce; may be costly to disseminate or distribute; storage may be more expensive; does not always allow time for evaluation.
Computerised telecommunications Local/wide area networks Fax Telex Packet switching Tele-conferencing Computer conferencing /networking	**Speed of transmission**: WAN messages, London to Sydney, Australia in 11 seconds. **Versatility**: Fax can transmit text, number, graphics, artwork and photographs all on one side of A4 if need be. Tele- and computer conferencing provide interpersonal exchanges visually and via VDU screens. **Accuracy**: Instantaneous message-reading and checking of electronic circuits operating between sending and receiving equipment during the transmission of high-speed 'bits' of the message in packet switching of computer data to ensure the message is accurately received in remote locations. **Feedback/instantaneous exchange**: Computerised telecommunications allow for a virtually simultaneous exchange of information and responses.	**Volume of transmitted data:** The volume of telecommunicated information is increasing at such a rate that business personnel are unable to absorb it within relevant time limits. **Costs:** Telecommunicated messages have billing premiums placed upon them to pay for the enormous development and hardware investments made nationally and internationally. However, the cost of fax, telex and communications modems etc. is falling rapidly in an expanding market. **Legal implications**: Words printed on paper at source still have a legal currency that a faxed message does not (but which telex does!). **Instant delivery**: The almost instantaneous delivery of LAN/WAN e-mail messages etc. can cause upsets if messages are composed in anger or are 'half-baked' and then despatched irretrievably.

TABLE 1.2: Advantages and disadvantages of written, oral, visual and electronic communication.

SOURCE: Evans, D. W., 1990, People, Communication and Organisations, 2nd edn, Pitman, pp. 32–3.

Feedback and control

In investigating the merits of different communication media, we have stated that one consideration is the need for feedback. For example, in telling employees about a new employment package, there ought to be opportunities for dealing with questions so that employees' fears can be quickly addressed.

Positive feedback is likely to be given to any communication quickly and without hesitation. Negative feedback is likely to be delayed or avoided. When you phone for a pizza, you want to hear that they will be round directly with a 'four seasons with extra cheese topping', or whatever. But if the pizza company is extremely busy, it will probably fail to mention that it might not be able to make your order for 40 minutes, and it will certainly 'forget' to mention that the driver is having problems with deliveries. Similarly, management will not mention the full implications of the new employment package if it is linked to a level of productivity that has yet to be achieved.

Positive feedback is more readily and accurately perceived by the receiver than negative feedback. You want to hear that your pizza will be 'straight round'. The employees want to hear about the benefits of the employment package and how much more money it means to them.

To make negative feedback more acceptable, it should be backed up by facts and figures. The pizza company might say that delivery will be no later than 45 minutes, or you could have a 'pepperoni, now'. The feedback is more likely to be accepted if it comes from someone in a position of power, authority or knowledge. If you have a problem with the '45-minute' delivery, you might ask to speak to the manager.

It obviously also helps if the person who is giving bad news is liked or respected by the receiver. If a well-respected manager is delivering the message about changes in the company, the bad news is likely to be more acceptable or, at least, more palatable. As always, an individual's personal view is critical to the effectiveness of the transfer of information. An employee, who is not happy working for the company, may receive the news badly whatever the chief executive has to say.

FEEDBACK AND CONTROL

SAT:
allow 20 mins

Communicating   ✓

ACTIVITY 6

Imagine you are a manager telling employees about changes in the company that will affect their job functions. List the tactics you could adopt to ensure that the news is properly heard and, where possible, well received. Consider ways in which you can make feedback more effective.

Commentary...

The manager can adopt several tactics to improve effective feedback and improve communication. These include:

- focusing on specific points – emphasise positive aspects such as the new prospects for the company and the value in staying ahead of competitors

- keeping feedback impersonal – the changes will affect all employees including yourself, and you are just doing your job by telling them about the changes

- making feedback timely – answer specific questions as they are asked, do not try to avoid the issue

- keeping feedback goal-oriented – the changes need to be made for the benefit of the company, otherwise it will not be successful

- ensuring understanding – make sure that everyone understands what is happening and why and what will be done to help them in the future, and what the changes means to them personally

- making criticism constructive, and able or possible to be acted upon – the manager may be able to suggest to the staff ways that they can help management and themselves to achieve the aims of the changes.

For some individuals, feedback about their performance at work is a reward or recognition and motivation. For others, it is a source of information and a means of correcting behaviour, and building motivation and self-esteem. In both cases, it acts as a control mechanism, and so, becomes part of the co-ordinating mechanisms of the whole organisation.

For feedback to work as an effective control mechanism, it depends on:

- each individual's own view about what they do in the company and how well they do it

- employees and management agreeing on levels of performance and productivity, through job descriptions, company regulations, and productivity and incentive schemes

- allowing employees to contribute to the overall success of the company by their own personal contribution

- ensuring that everyone receives useful positive and negative feedback about achievement

- criteria that are used for measuring achievement are regularly re-evaluated.

We can summarise this by saying that the success of any organisational control system depends on employees knowing what their job responsibilities are and the standards to which they are expected to perform. It also requires effective informal systems – managers praising and complementing individuals – and formal feedback systems such as performance appraisals.

Communication plays a key role in ensuring that the employee knows exactly what he or she is supposed to do. It is vital in ensuring that all employees are aware of the performance standards they must meet. As we have seen, it is also important in motivating and controlling the individual, particularly through feedback mechanisms.

The ways of providing this feedback will change as companies grow. In Jonathan's Pizza Company, in the early days Jonathan was in a position to supervise his craft bakers directly, to make sure that they knew what they were doing and to give them immediate feedback on their performance. Their job responsibilities and performance criteria were loosely set out in their job descriptions; control and feedback were very personal issues between Jonathan and his individual bakers. As the company has grown, he cannot maintain that very personal touch – there are simply too many staff. He needs to introduce more precise job descriptions for all workers, more detailed company regulations about general performance and behaviour, and detailed procedures for manufacturing, attaining consistency, quality control, scheduling, etc. Employees will be measured against these performance criteria in a systematic way, and an impersonal feedback system will control and motivate staff.

As a company grows, therefore, different demands are placed on the communications system. We now look at how technology can help. But first, do the following exercise to appreciate just how far reaching technology is.

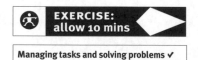

EXERCISE:
allow 10 mins

Managing tasks and solving problems ✔

ACTIVITY 7

List below the times that you have used technology in your own personal transactions in the last two days.

Commentary...

Here we list some of the huge range of possibilities. You might have:

- used a cash dispenser to withdraw funds from your bank account

- phoned up to make a credit card booking for some cinema tickets

- called to make enquiries about flight and seat availability for your next summer holiday

- made a purchase using your Switch card

- made a purchase and added to your Shell air miles, or Tesco's bonus points

- phoned a broker for a new insurance quote on your car and been given instantly several quotations from different companies.

Maybe, you have access to Internet through a service like CompuServe and have used it to call up information or to contact any friends who have the facility. This is just in your personal life; think about the enormity of technology's involvement in your business and student lives.

Communication, information and technology

The information technology explosion of the past decade has changed the way in which organisations communicate. Computerised telecommunications mean that people throughout the world can communicate electronically. And the process of decision making has changed as individuals now have access to much information about the organisation through centralised computer facilities. In Greatwear, Arthur Brown's European managers could access central data for information about sales and stock from their stores, and he could have central control of information and decision making.

It is likely that the nature of many people's jobs, and the locations where they work, will change as they become more accustomed to using new technology. For example, linking of computers in people's homes to a central office system via a modem and a telephone line means that individuals can work at home to save office accommodation and overheads or as an out-sourcing operation.

The use of computers means that some office tasks are more likely to be carried out by managers themselves rather than delegated to clerical and other support staff. Users will be able to communicate directly with each other 'anywhere, any time' through the use of laptop and notebook computers and the cellular phone system.

Let us now consider information technology and its applications in more detail.

USE OF NETWORKS

Networks connect computer terminals to each other and, possibly, to a central database. A local area network (LAN) is a private network that operates over a small geographic area. Wide area networks (WAN) use a private or public telecommunications system and operate over wide geographic areas by using satellite and other links. Increased use of LANs and WANs – along with fax, e-mail and other telecommunications – means that a manager has access to world-wide communications facilities from his or her desktop terminal. Through this a wealth of information about the organisation's specific and general environment is available by drawing on national and international databases and the Internet.

Communication with world-wide personnel is much easier. Video-conferencing facilities, and telephone and computer conferencing, mean that global meetings can happen without personnel moving from their own offices, providing savings of time and money on travel. Arthur Brown can communicate with his European managers at Greatwear, without leaving the UK if he has access to these facilities. What he can do, and they are all able to do from their respective locations, is to access and input data into the central computer system, so information about sales and stock figures, for example, are available to everyone from the computer terminal on their desk.

Managers are more likely to take control over their own communication; reading and sending their own e-mails, faxes, etc. from their own terminal, cutting out the need for another level of support staff. Scheduling of group meetings and diary management can be done by an individual manager through his computer.

Networking means better communication within the organisation and with its specific environment of suppliers, customers, etc. Data can be entered and received directly into the main computer by end-users. Details of a customer can be keyed into the database by the salesperson and then used by the accounts department for issuing the invoice and chasing up payment. Or details of a raw material and the supplier can be entered by the purchasing department and used by accounts department to pay. A manager can directly access sales and production information entered by each department.

Resources such as software, printers and storage facilities can be shared. Expertise in other locations can be shared throughout the organisation regardless of location. An expert in design, for example, can be shared between divisions in different locations with tele-conferencing or video-conferencing used for meetings, and draft designs with graphics sent by computer or fax.

MANAGEMENT INFORMATION SYSTEMS (MIS)

Within the organisation, technology can aid communication in several ways. Through a centralised management information system, it makes information readily available at middle and top management levels to aid decision making. It also means that better control can be exercised by middle managers over employees as information on productivity, performance, etc. is readily available.

This means that flatter and more flexible organisational structures can be implemented as co-ordination of staff and tasks is much easier. Information is readily available through the management information systems and does not require formal transmission through a communication channel network.

In an organisation dealing with life assurance, for example, the sales team can feed information from customers directly into the company's main computer at headquarters. This information can be accessed throughout the organisation through the office information systems; it can be used by the internal administrator for drawing up the policy, by an accounts person for issuing the invoice, and by management to analyse sales and trends that will affect policy and strategy decisions. This reduces the need for paperwork, probably reduces errors, and may reduce the need for a middle management level. A flatter structure can be introduced as information is readily available; control can be exercised with fewer managers and with an increase in their span of control.

A computerised system also makes financial reporting, charging of clients for services, invoicing, issuing of statements, chasing up late payments more effective. These transactions become an ongoing part of the system from receipt of order, to despatch, to invoicing, and follow-up of payment. Internal financial and accounting packages also ease the laborious tasks of accounting personnel.

DESKTOP PUBLISHING (DTP)

Information can be professionally produced in-house by desktop publishing facilities. This means the organisation can control costs, confidentiality and schedules of some or all of the official documents that it produces. It will mean effectively less out-sourcing. It also means that a manager (or his secretary) can produce more professional internal memos and reports. Better design should help to convey messages and instil confidence in employees. This can enhance corporate culture.

As you saw earlier, as Jonathan increases the number of staff at his pizza company, the need for printed materials increases. Employees will need more detailed job descriptions, and the company will need more detailed regulations and procedures. Desktop publishing allows the information to be presented more clearly and efficiently. Jonathan may produce a monthly staff newsletter to spread positive messages about the company: the expansion is proceeding smoothly; the company has the money to produce this kind of publication; senior managers and Jonathan still need and value individual contributions from the employees; and even though the company is bigger, it still cares about them. He could produce a manual for the operators to help to direct their work, and give him more control. Again, this would enhance a professional image.

Graphic software programs allow clearer presentation of numerical data. This can help the reader who may not be an expert in the field and who could be located in a different department or division. For example, a salesperson may need a manual with a non-technical description and diagrams of a new engineering product to show to customers. Research and development could produce this in-house, for the company's salesforce. Materials for training or safety presentations can also be given a more professional look.

STORAGE OF INFORMATION

Computer files can replace paper files. They can be indexed so records can be retrieved in a similar fashion. Customer files storing records of transaction, etc. can be electronically filed, retrieved and even annotated. Paper documents can be scanned into the system. This paper document processing reduces the need for clerical support and cuts down on errors. CD-ROM will become the technology of the future for storage and retrieval of information that started out as a paper document with words and graphics. Sound can also be included.

DATABASE MANAGEMENT SYSTEMS

Database management systems allow end-user access to an organisation's database. For example, sales orders received by the salesforce in the field could be entered into the central database, with a single inventory keeping track of stock in the warehouse and a single price file updating prices. The information can be used by the salesforce themselves, the marketing department to analyse trends and figures and the finance department to keep track of billing and customer accounts. Inventory and production personnel (who need to provide the flow of goods into the warehouse) and top-management (making decisions about product line viability, stocking, financing, etc.) would also have the necessary access.

There are some problems associated with many people using the same information. Ownership needs to be protected by a security system because when many individuals have access to the same information it can mean that its use as a source of power and control by management is undermined. Similarly, it may be necessary to restrict access to financially sensitive information, such as individual product profit levels or employees' personnel files.

Often, end-users use the basic information in different ways and from different perspectives, so they are more likely to take what they need from the central database and hold it in their own files. This may then defeat the object of having communal files. This problem can, however, be managed by a corporate information management policy.

ELECTRONIC DATA INTERCHANGE (EDI)

EDI has been used for many years in the banking industry for electronic transfer of funds. This is a quick, reliable and safe means of transferring money both nationally and internationally. EDI initially developed in the airline and transportation industries. Airlines have central reservation systems, tickets are issued and invoiced electronically. You can book a ticket via the telephone using your credit card and the seat can be confirmed and the ticket issued. With cargo shipments, all parts of the process – the reservation systems, airlines, forwarders, carriers, customs authorities and port operators – are interlinked electronically. Bookings can be made by the customer directly and shipments can be traced and tracked. Airway bills, import/export documents, bills of lading, invoices and associated payment through letters of credit can all be transmitted electronically.

In the US transportation industry, automobile manufacturers and trucking and railroad companies have also developed an EDI system to save time in processing paper documents, increasing the speed of delivery and allowing better stock control and just-in-time purchasing by the customer. It allows matching of invoices, delivery notes and statements electronically, cutting out the need for laborious clerical work and consequently affects personnel involved in purchasing, logistics, scheduling and accounts payable. This electronic transfer of documents means that contracts, and conditions and procedures of trading need to be set up at the start of a business relationship as there is no negotiation on the individual operations by any personnel. It is likely that once these arrangements are set up between suppliers and customers, that they remain so for some time and these trading partners obviously develop a very close relationship.

EDI can facilitate the setting up of networks between organisations, where a central corporate body utilises a 'network' of other companies that are interrelated, and interdependent but not owned. For example, Nike, the sports manufacturer might use this system to communicate with its partners that are manufacturing their products; its main core function is to do research and development.

As you can see, the implications of information technology exist throughout our world now. Information technology concerns each and every organisation and not just in the production and design departments of a high-tech industry. In fact the availability of data and information and the effect of information technology on communication throughout the organisation are critical to its success.

The control and dissemination of information in new ways allows different structures to exist and function efficiently. Flatter, less formal, decentralised organisations with less hierarchy can succeed because the technology allows more flexible information and communication channels replacing the need for formal rigid channels. This enables organisations to be more flexible and responsive in today's changing world.

ACTIVITY 8

Look back at the case study on Racket and Run (see section two, session three).

In implementing the changes suggested by the consultant, Peter Wilson has made several innovations. The store is now called Racket and Sail. The business has grown; it now has a computerised stock control system, a full-time manager and several full-time staff. The range of goods has changed and Peter has found several new cheaper overseas suppliers for several product lines. He is even manufacturing some of his own lines which he is distributing through other specialist shops.

Peter is setting up new branches in neighbouring towns to sell the same range of stock. He intends to hire two new shop managers, who will report to his existing manager and some more full-time sales staff.

Write a 500-word report on how technology can now help Peter improve communication within his expanding business. Comment particularly on how Peter should set up communications between the branches. Consider also:

- **what lateral and horizontal communications should be set up**

- **how ordering and stock control needs to be managed across the three stores**

- **whether other technologies such as EDI may be useful for, say, overseas orders**

- **whether Peter needs a customer database.**

Write your report on a separate sheet of paper. Use the box below for notes and to summarise your main points.

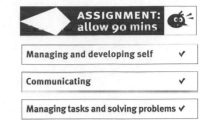

ASSIGNMENT:
allow 90 mins

Managing and developing self ✓

Communicating ✓

Managing tasks and solving problems ✓

summary

▶ Communication has four major functions within an organisation: control, motivation, emotional expression and information.

▶ In analysing communications, six processes must be considered: conceiving the message, encoding, selecting the communication channel, decoding, interpreting the message and giving feedback.

▶ In choosing an appropriate communications channel, you need to align your needs as the sender, with the needs of your receiver, the characteristics of the message and the logistics of the channels.

▶ The main communications media include face-to-face, telephone, meetings and printed material. Electronic communication media such as e-mail are increasingly used.

▶ The means of communication within an organisation is affected by its structure and, equally, is determined by the structure. As the organisation becomes more complex, so the communication channels will become more formal and complex.

▶ An organisation is likely to utilise a variety of communication networks. These networks may be formal or informal.

▶ It is important for employees to have feedback about their performance. It requires effective informal systems – managers praising and complimenting individuals – and formal feedback systems such as performance appraisals.

▶ Information technology is supporting the trend towards flatter, less formal, decentralised organisations with less hierarchy.

Communication and the organisation

Objectives

After participating in this session, you should be able to:

▶ **investigate the role of communication in relaying information in an organisation and its relationship with different types of organisational structure**

▶ **investigate the part played by communication in organisational change and culture**

▶ **describe ways of improving communication and information transfer.**

In working through this session, you will practise the following BTEC common skills:

Managing and developing self	✔
Working with and relating to others	✔
Communicating	✔
Managing tasks and solving problems	✔
Applying numeracy	
Applying technology	
Applying design and creativity	

Organisational concerns with information

The main role of communication is to convey information: from one part of the organisation to another; and from the organisation to its specific and general environment. Information is required for decision making by senior management at the top of an organisation, but it is also needed by the workforce for doing their job tasks in the operating core lower down the organisation. It concerns not only what jobs people do, but how they do them, how well they do them and what controls the organisation has over them. Managing this information is one of the functions of middle management. It is also a key part of the co-ordinating mechanism of the organisation.

In this information age, there is a massive amount of readily available data. With the increasingly widespread use of information technology within organisations, individuals have direct access to information previously unavailable. The manager needs to know what information is available, how it has been processed and what it means to the organisation.

This gives rise to four different perspectives (quadrants) on information:

- processed information

- unprocessed information

- knowledgeable ignorance

- absolute ignorance.

PROCESSED INFORMATION

Processed information is data, letters, reports, etc., that have been assimilated and noted by the relevant parties. It does not mean that the information has been understood and acted upon. Jonathan knows that he needs new stocks of tomato sauce and has faxed an order to his supplier in Italy. He knows that the order has been received, because it has been acknowledged, but he will not know if it has been acted upon until he receives some delivery details. With this type of information the message has to be very clear and unambiguous. Jonathan will probably have requested supply within three weeks, or immediate notification if this is not possible.

UNPROCESSED INFORMATION

Unprocessed information and data are communications that have not been assimilated, such as unread reports and unreturned telephone calls. Some information may be unprocessed because of critical filtering that occurs at each level of an organisation. This occurs, for example, when managers control some channels of communication, only allowing through specific and necessary information.

This filtering process, although in one sense a barrier to information flows, is important. Organisations need effective filtering mechanisms to modify the information from top management via middle management to the shop floor. Top management may not be sufficiently aware of the implications of a organisational change, for example, on a shop floor worker's job function, so the change will need explaining by the middle management in the context of what is actually happening on the shop floor.

For example, Jonathan may not understand the precise operation of the production line; the manual is available but he has not had time to read it. So, if there is a malfunction and the automated production line is not producing as many pizzas as it should, it is the production manager's job to relay this information and the exact nature of the problem to Jonathan. And, if Jonathan wants increased production, then the more knowledgeable production manager can modify the demand into something that the operators can actually respond to.

KNOWLEDGEABLE IGNORANCE

Knowledgeable ignorance concerns the 'known unknowns'. The manager needs to be able to ask the right questions and accept that there are gaps in his or her understanding or knowledge. However, if one manager does not know something, there may be another manager elsewhere in the organisation who has received the information and processed it. Then it is a question of putting the two managers together to exchange information. Jonathan's production manager may not understand precisely why the production line is not working efficiently, but he or she knows a technician who can explain the problem.

ORGANISATIONAL CONCERNS
WITH INFORMATION

ABSOLUTE IGNORANCE

Absolute ignorance is complete unawareness of information; it challenges managers to deal effectively with uncertainty. The production manager may have no idea what to do when supplies of anchovies run out for a particular batch of pizzas. Should the pizzas be made without anchovies, possibly wasting the batch if these are unacceptable to the customer? Should production be switched to fulfil another order? Should production be shut down completely? The production manager either needs guidelines from Jonathan to cover situations like this, or enough knowledge of the business to make a decision. Otherwise, he should ask Jonathan what to do whenever this might happen, or a stock control mechanism should be implemented so that production is not started unless there are sufficient ingredients.

Category	Appropriate questions
Processed information	Does the information arrive on time?
	Does the information arrive at the right place?
	Is the information understandable?
	Is the information specific enough?
Unprocessed information	Has the proper information been transmitted?
	Has too much or too little information been transmitted?
	Has the information been screened effectively?
	Has nonuseful information been discarded?
	Do employees have access to needed information?
Knowledgeable ignorance	Have the proper questions been asked?
	Have the 'holes' in the information fabric been detected?
	Do we know where to find the answers?
	Can we prioritise our information needs?
Absolute ignorance	Is there some mechanism built into the system so that certain information is randomly encountered?
	Are new perspectives being sought?
	Are new sources of information being tapped?
	Should consultants be hired to expose the organisation to new trends?
Second-order concerns	In which quadrant do the major organisational concerns lie?
	What is the proper mix of organisational strategies used to cope with the issues above? (i.e. should the organisation be more concerned with absolute ignorance or unprocessed information?)

TABLE 2.1: Organisational concerns with information.
SOURCE: Clampitt, P. G., 1991, Communicating for Managerial Effectiveness, Sage, p. 83.

Table 2.1 summarises these different concerns with information. Clampitt (1991) goes on to list the factors that affect the efficiency of communication. These include:

- the number of links in the communication chain

- the way the message is presented and/or sent

- the way the information is organised

- the relationship of the receiver to the sender of the message or communication

- the extent to which information is grounded within experience

As the number of links in the communication chain increases, there is likely to be more distortion of the information or message. At each level of the organisation, some factors may be highlighted and others reduced. For example, managers may choose to manipulate information as it passes them to give the appearance of them having more control. Inferences become facts, so the final message delivered to each employee bears little relation to the first message from top management. Even with a written memo, interpretations can be different at different levels. Managers may choose to modify selectively the overall message so that it fits their particular department's requirements.

Presentation is important. The way that the message or information is presented or sent can mean as much as its content. A badly worded memo containing spelling mistakes is likely to be ignored while a professional-looking document is likely to carry more weight. A scribbled note from Jonathan to his Italian supplier is not likely to be as effective as a typed letter on headed stationery.

Images are powerful ways of communicating. We all know the saying: a picture is worth a thousand words. With easy-to-use software packages, graphics can be used in any report or internal document to convey messages about performance. Improved technology has enabled desktop publishing to be used by anyone, not only graphics experts. User-friendly, cheap and versatile packages are available for general office use. New technology also allows the cheaper production of audio and videotapes and the use of video-conferencing as an alternative means of communication.

The way in which the information is organised affects the meaning. You can show different results by 'stretching' the data in different ways, or failing to mention some significant point. It is especially

ORGANISATIONAL CONCERNS
WITH INFORMATION

easy to do this with graphics; bar charts or graphs can convey quite different messages with 'adjusted' axes. For example, when newspapers (or television) display changes in interest rates, mortgage rates and foreign currency rates they rarely start with both axes at zero; any changes are thus amplified.

The sender of the message or information may be as important as its content. You may respond to your boss if he or she tells you some information, but fail to respond to your colleague. The pizza operators will respond to an instruction from the production manager, but might choose to ignore a comment from a colleague on the production line. You may listen to a known expert or your teacher on a subject but not to the security man at the college campus where you study. If someone you like or respect tells you something then you will probably respond much more positively than if you dislike them.

The quality of the information decreases as it goes beyond our experience. Information about next year's budget is more accurate than the forecast about the year after that; information about a new market is less accurate than an established market. Jonathan will know the company's operational requirements – for cash flow, supplies, income, staffing – for his existing small market, but he will not be able to estimate easily for next year with the large increase in production and staff. He will understand his small market for hand-crafted pizzas, but will be less clear about sales of mass produced pizzas through the supermarket.

In, addition, several factors affect an individual's information load:

- The way messages are channelled through an organisation's network is important. The network sub-grouping plays a big part in this. For example, Jonathan's production manager may have leaders of shift groups or teams who work on a particular line who deliver the final message to the operators in their own way.

- The physical setting provides a variety of distractions, e.g. information will be more difficult to convey on a noisy factory floor.

- The person's own characteristics – intelligence, skills, personality, mood, stress level – combine with the characteristics of the message. An employee may be having a bad day, perhaps feeling under par, and cannot take in any new information.

RECALL:
allow 5 mins

Explain what is meant by:

- **processed information**

- **unprocessed information**

- **knowledgeable ignorance**

- **absolute ignorance.**

Communication and organisation structure

The level of integration and differentiation in the organisation structure makes different demands on its communication systems and information management systems. A number of different organisational factors have implications for communications:

- the number of levels in the hierarchy

- the number of managers supervising subordinates and their span of control

- the use of computerisation to supervise and control employees and their job tasks

- the use of rules and regulations to standardise activities and control employees

- the access to information for decision making by middle and top management

- the requirement for interdepartmental, interdivisional and environmental interaction

- the size of the organisation – with increasing size comes increasing complexity, more differentiation, more integration and more requirement for rigid communication channels

- the stage in the organisation's life cycle – as the structure adjusts to fit with its environment then the ways of communicating change, but communication is also the means for implementing the required changes

- the organisation's culture – this affects whether employees are generally happy and motivated. With a motivated workforce, informal channels of communication are much more effective, a flatter more flexible structure might be possible, with a less rigid communication system being required. A favourable culture also enables change to be implemented more effectively.

All these organisational factors affect and interrelate with a company's communication and information systems. Let us now explore them further.

COMMUNICATION PROBLEMS ARISING FROM STRUCTURAL FACTORS

Tall hierarchies with many management levels can hinder effective communication. Messages may be distorted at each level in the hierarchy, and it takes more time to pass information between the top and the bottom as the chain of command lengthens; it also slows down decision making. This means that the organisation may not be able to respond quickly to the actions of competitors or other changes in the organisation's environment. In a multi-divisional structure, it may take too long for decisions to come from the corporate centre to the individual divisions for them to respond to local conditions.

In tall hierarchies, middle managers may have the chance to manipulate information and control may be lost by the top. Top management may have no idea of what is really happening under them and, by losing sight of the real picture, they may make poor or ineffective decisions. With multi-divisional organisations, divisional managers working at a distance from the corporate centre may disguise and selectively inform top management about the division's performance. For example, at Greatwear, Arthur Brown's store manager in Paris may be presenting the sales figures in a way that covers up the fact that sales are down. The pressures to be successful mean that there can be an incentive for managers to disguise or fail to report, poor results.

With increased specialisation and differentiation into a functional structure, the need for effective communication and integration between functional departments increases. Departments are not only functionally distinct; they may also be geographically separate. They may have different accounting procedures, different priorities, different operating procedures, different professional codes of practice and ethics, different jargon in their specialisation, different expertise and skills, and different lines of authority. With technology, more information is readily available throughout the organisation, not just retained within departments, and this may mean that departments feel they have lost their power base.

As an organisation adds a new department, the number of communication linkages are necessarily increased as all existing departments must now liaise with the new one. What appears as a simple structural change increases dramatically the linkages that are required to co-ordinate activities. This may then force the introduction of rigid policies to control communication.

Poor communication of relevant information – new products, new services, new pricing structures – between departments may lead to poor customer service. There may be unnecessary conflict over a product, for example, between sales and production, on scheduling or product enhancements. There may be conflict between managers on competition for resources, or accountability and performance. Departments may not have clearly identified responsibilities, say in relation to a customer problem, and may simply pass it on to another department. One department may feel that another is not doing its job properly and making their own function more difficult. This produces tension and conflict. Jonathan's marketing manager may feel that the production manager is being deliberately unhelpful by saying that the operators cannot make a particular type or quantity of pizza. The marketing manager is worried about the sales figures, but is powerless to achieve results without production's effective co-operation.

There may be communication problems between general staff and technical experts, arising from a failure to understand the area or the jargon. For example, perhaps Arthur Brown hires an IT specialist to help with his warehousing, stock control and bar coding system. The sales assistant will not want to know about the technical details, just about how he or she is expected to use it, explained in simple language; accounts will not want to know the details of the system, just how much it costs to buy and to maintain.

This type of communication problem can also occur in professional bureaucracies where departments are staffed by highly trained specialists with their own codes of practice and ethics. Accountants, doctors, lawyers, architects all belong to professional bodies; codes of ethics and conduct cover their professional behaviour.

OVERCOMING COMMUNICATION PROBLEMS

The problems we have identified here are not insoluble, and a company can do many things to reduce or eliminate the problems.

A corporate communications policy can be the basis of easing interdepartmental communications problems. This needs to be based on corporate culture and values, individuals need encouragement to develop a commitment to corporate goals not just their own departmental goals. Training and initiation of new employees should stress this. Rivalry between departments and their managers must be discouraged.

Linked to a communications policy, a company may need different accounting procedures to reward individuals equitably for performance if they are dependent on other departments outside their immediate sphere of control.

In our case studies, Jonathan will need to see that production's capabilities are taken into account when setting sales targets for marketing team. Fastec had problems with production not being able to meet orders; these need to be resolved and the sales people need to be discouraged from thinking that there is no point in winning orders if they cannot be delivered on time.

Other factors that can help communication are office design and the physical location of individual departments. Open plan offices can be designed so that managers are more approachable and accessible, and there is no 'us and them' mentality. If top management is 'on the top floor' then they will be seen as being very separate from the rest of the workforce.

Departments that deal with each other on a regular basis – for example, purchasing and accounts – could be located next to each other. Managers at the same hierarchical level should have the same type of office accommodation and equipment.

Organisations can introduce a pro-active communications strategy. A company may have an 'open-door' policy, whereby managers allow any staff to walk in without an appointment. Other managers may set aside a particular time in the week when they can be approached about issues that are worrying employees. Company-wide seminars and new product presentations can help to inform all employees about what is going on in the company. A newsletter provides a further communications channel, and might be used to preview new developments and products before employees see them in the newspapers. Social gatherings can help to inform individuals informally about the company.

The introduction of teams and groups into the organisation structure can cut across functionalisation. Permanent executive committees meeting on a regular basis – consisting of all the functional heads from one level in the hierarchy – can be beneficial. At other levels, multi-functional teams and task forces could be set up to deal with particular problems, projects or development of new products. This brings together wider knowledge and information. It also helps to win acceptance of the final decision as it will be seen throughout the organisation as being a more legitimate process than had an autocratic decision been taken by one department. However, the use of groups and group decision making is more time-consuming.

ACTIVITY 1

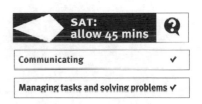

Remembering that communication controls, motivates, allows emotional expression and provides information for decision making, outline the different ways that communication will work in each of the following types of organisations:

- ● **simple entrepreneurial**

- ● **professional bureaucracy**

- ● **divisional organisation**

- ● **adhocracy or innovative structure.**

Commentary...

In a **simple entrepreneurial structure** the boss is in charge! So, that is the control. It is likely to be a small company and the owner is likely to be able to communicate formally and informally with all employees. The culture that fosters commitment and motivation among employees makes lateral, diagonal and informal communications very easy because staff are co-operative. Job descriptions, procedures and company regulations are unlikely to be formal or well documented. Administrative paperwork is likely to be kept to a minimum, although information technology may be used by the entrepreneur to keep track of all activities and acquire information for decision making. Individuals are likely to approach the boss directly if they have any grievances.

The **professional bureaucracy** has standardisation and formalisation, but it is a decentralised organisation with specialists in the operating core being mainly autonomous. Communication is crucial in passing information both between interdependent units and vertically to the top, particularly as senior management has relinquished some of its control to experts in the functional units. Employees will have detailed job descriptions, and there will be formal procedures and company rules and regulations. Conflicts may arise as departments (particularly when filled with specialists) may see themselves as rivals within the organisation. These conflicts can be reduced by a strong communications policy which promotes a single organisational culture.

With a **divisional structure,** communication is likely to rely more on formal rigid channels, as the organisation is diversified and, possibly, in separate geographic locations. Middle or divisional managers will have a lot of control and be a main avenue of information dissemination. They will channel instructions and directions from the top to the operating core. Vertical communication is obviously very important because of the size of the organisation and the need for top management to retain some control and to direct operations. Horizontal communication is essential if the different divisions and departments are to be integrated to achieve the organisation's aims and objectives. To some extent, a rigid formal system will be required, especially given the size of operation, although informal co-operation will still be needed. The organisation is likely to rely heavily on information technology for global communication and to gather the necessary information for decision making. Again, employees are likely to have detailed job descriptions, formal written procedures and formal company rules and regulations.

With an **adhocracy,** a team approach means that communication can be much more informal. An adhocracy is dependent on mutual co-operation between individuals who are at the same hierarchical level. There is little differentiation, integration and formalisation. Within the groups or teams, power and control will change as the project develops and it has different needs from the participants. There will be loose job descriptions and procedures as functions will change as the team changes. There will be overall company regulation though.

Communicating change and culture

CHANGE

One essential function of communication within the organisation is the part that it plays in the implementation and management of change. Change is an inevitable and essential part of a successful organisation's development. To ensure its successful and effective implementation, the support of the whole organisation is required. Each change process is unique, but it is useful to have an understanding of some of the common patterns and stages in each implementation process.

Change can be instigated by the top management and then carried out by middle management in a top-down strategy. Alternatively, employees may be involved at early stages, even in suggesting, initiating and implementing change. An integrative approach combining management's vision and control and employees' participation and acceptance is the most effective change process.

Change can be either routine or non-routine. Routine changes occur on a regular basis and might include small changes in procedures, policy, government legislation, pricing and packaging of the products or services. For example, in Jonathan's company, a routine change might be adapting the printing of labels on his packaging to include information of all food additives used in manufacture, because of a European regulation requiring this to be done.

Non-routine changes include major changes to culture, structure, management or operations and are often linked to the organisation's stage of development. For example, Jonathan's Pizza Company's move to mass production would count as a major change. It needs handling with care. Fastec grew from an entrepreneurial company with three founding members to a departmentalised structure that still needs more co-ordination and control to work effectively.

The possible problem areas that are associated with stages of the organisation's life cycle are identified in table 2.2.

Routine and non-routine changes present different communication challenges. Routine changes are relatively easily communicated. Staff can be informed of these changes by memo, bulletin boards or by a weekly updating facility via e-mail. Jonathan could have some printed labels produced, send a memo to each craft baker informing them of the requirement, and leave it to them to organise sticking the labels onto the packaging.

Non-routine changes can generate much more significant problems. Many employees react badly to non-routine changes regardless of what it actually means for them, but simply because it is change and they have no control over it. They go through stages of denial, anger, bargaining, depression and acceptance. At each stage, managers need to be responsive to the individual to ensure that there is a smooth transition. Jonathan will need to think carefully about how best to inform his craft bakers about what will happen to their jobs in the new automated production environment.

Organisational stage	Identifying characteristics	Possible Resistance Points
Birth and early growth	Emphasis on entrepreneurship Heavy influence of 'founding fathers'	Speculation over CEO's reaction Diminish CEO's control Impact on corporate vision
Maturity	Creation of standard operating procedures Institutionalising vision Solidifying departmental responsibilities	Interdepartmental differences Protection of 'turf' Control of resources Budgetary allocations
Decline or redevelopment	Dramatic change in competitive environment More bureaucratic structure Quest to reshape corporate vision	Indifference and lethargy Impact on established careers Power relationships Waiting for 'crisis' to institute change

TABLE 2.2: Change and the stages in an organisation's life cycle.
SOURCE: Clampitt, P. G., 1991, Communicating for Managerial Effectiveness, Sage, p. 199.

In general terms, for non-routine change to be implemented, employees need first to be informed of the changes – structural, management, details of job tasks, responsibilities, remuneration, relocation, etc. To effect this process of information, it is worthwhile for management to look at historical patterns of behaviour to see how employees have responded in the past to change. This may give some indication for the future as it will reflect the organisation's culture. It might also show whether employees were prepared to follow a leader's vision in the past.

In Jonathan's case, if he had previously moved the location of his factory and all his employees had then been willing to make an inconvenient move, he might take this as evidence that the bakers wanted to work for him regardless of any other factors. He might now judge that they are prepared to stay and make the new company work, regardless of whether their job functions change. This willingness of employees to follow their leader 'no matter what' can be a crucial factor in successful implementation.

Changes need to be well thought out. All aspects should be considered and covered where possible. Do job descriptions need changing with an organisational restructuring? Have the implications for staff performance and remuneration been worked out? Will jobs disappear with the introduction of new technology? What new positions or functions arise because of the changes? Is retraining required? Jonathan's craft bakers will have new job specifications, and these will need to be linked to new criteria of performance and remuneration. He must think these details out carefully in planning the change.

Managers need to be aware of how employees perceive change. What does it mean to them personally and financially? How important are their work relationships? Is the physical location of the company an important factor? If incremental change is possible, it may help to ease some of this kind of resistance. Retaining part of the market for handmade pizzas, and not producing all the pizzas on the production line, may help to smooth the implementation of the changes in Jonathan's Pizza Company.

Before managers communicate information about change, they should ask the following questions:

- Will change improve the current situation? What happens when we've done this? Is there a next stage?

- Is it obvious why we have to do it? Are our competitors doing it this way?

- What happens if the new way is no better than the old way?

- Does the change fit our organisational culture and organisational mission? Or are these going to have to change too?

- Can we actually implement this change or is it virtually impossible to carry out?

If managers are satisfied with the answers then employees should be provided with sufficient, consistent, reliable and frequent information on the planned changes. By supplying information willingly, managers will help to overcome staff resistance to change and defuse the effects of the grapevine. An organisation should seek to provide employees with answers to the following questions:

- Will it affect our jobs, salaries or bonuses?

- Will our job tasks change? Will they be boring? Will we not want to come to work any more?

- Will we still work with, and for, the same personnel?

- Will we have to move location or have some other major social or physical disruption?

- Do we need training for new skills?

- What is it going to cost? Can the company afford it? Would the money better be spent on something else?

- Will the company survive by doing this? Is the company in serious trouble?

In informing personnel of change, management needs to select carefully both the communication channel and the timing of the messages. Employees do not want to hear about major changes from third parties, they do not want to receive the information in a situation where they cannot ask questions and receive some feedback. So, the best way is in a face-to-face meeting with their line manager or, in a small company, with the boss.

Line managers can feel uncomfortable conveying what might be perceived as 'bad news'; they may want the personnel officer to explain the changes. However, this shows weak leadership. It would be better to let the personnel department organise a follow-up meeting, perhaps to iron out remuneration details. A memo, an e-mail or a large formal meeting is not the best means of communicating. However, a follow-up memo could be useful in explaining the changes in more detail, and would give staff the opportunity to take time over digesting the information.

Timing is also important. The manager should not hold any meeting at 4 p.m. on a Friday, so the employees take their problems and unanswered questions home for the weekend. He should try earlier in the week and earlier in the day. First thing on a Monday morning is also a poor choice; staff have not had time to settle into their work routines and complete their exchange of weekend news with colleagues.

COMMUNICATING CHANGE
AND CULTURE

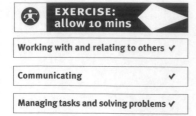

Working with and relating to others ✔

Communicating ✔

Managing tasks and solving problems ✔

ACTIVITY 2

Review the Trevor Thompson case study in Resource 1 in the back of the book.

In small groups, discuss how the implementation of the major changes in production could have been made more successful. Note the main points of your discussion in the box below.

Commentary...

The changes introduced at Trevor Thompson necessarily led to a complete change of the employees' work tasks, their remuneration and their relationships with others. These changes should have been thought through carefully, with particular attention paid to the possible demotivation resulting from the routine nature of working in the new production system.

The new system should have been carefully discussed and negotiated with staff in what is a small company that had been previously working very effectively as a team. The culture appeared to be very supportive and co-operative and very much based on the employees' relationship with Trevor. Staff should have been given the opportunity of voicing their comments and concerns and, with a team work arrangement already in place, they could have been given the responsibility of making the new system work for themselves.

In a small situation like this, formal and informal meetings could have been held for all staff. Training should also have been more carefully scheduled. Simply to inform employees about the production system after their return from holidays displays a very heavy-handed approach. Staff would undoubtedly be disappointed with the boss and demotivated in their work; it is not surprising that some employees 'voted with their feet' and left the company.

CULTURE

Culture influences how the company will respond to change. In high-tech industries, for example, the corporate culture may recognise a continual need for innovation and change. Companies will foster this innovative approach in its employees, and in their reaction to change itself. Individuals welcome change as it means that management is looking ahead and responding to the environment. They know that this will give their companies a better chance of survival.

In a simple entrepreneurial structure, the implementation of change will depend largely on the employees' view of the boss, their motivation to 'stay with him', and on the enormity of the changes. In the pizza company, whether the craft bakers stay with Jonathan, or not, depends largely on how much regard they have for him as a boss, and how severely the changes affect their jobs and remuneration.

The culture of the organisation needs transmitting to all employees. This is easy in a simple structure where the culture is largely determined by the entrepreneur, but more difficult in larger organisations, where the culture has to be generated and retained. Managers use a gradual socialisation to convey the corporate culture to new employees. It starts with the selection procedures, the training procedures, the office design and environment, the company's logo and other printed materials, and the image that is presented to the outside world. The manager can have lengthy discussions with employees about the company, what it has achieved, how it operates, and its philosophy and values. Managers may also be able to symbolise critical corporate values in some way.

If organisations are successful in establishing a positive culture, employees will be proud to be part of something. They should be motivated to contribute their best, not regard working as 'just a job'.

Increasing efficiency of information and communication

Communication and information are inextricably linked, but how do we improve one or the other? We can start by looking at the possibility of physical improvements.

Staff that are required to use particular hardware and software for communication or to obtain information need to have easy access to appropriate equipment. This might include telephones, fax machines, computers, word processors, e-mail, graphics software and video-conferencing. If managers need a computer system for information receipt, processing and sending, then they should each have a terminal on their desk, and not share the use with another manager, or with a secretary. If there are many users wanting to use expensive equipment like a laser colour printer, then these facilities should be networked, and an equitable means of usage agreed. Those personnel that need telephones should have them on their desks, but perhaps they can share a fax machine in a general office, provided there is a fast system for distribution to other offices, and the fax is not likely to be used for confidential material.

Other physical measures include the following:

- Meeting rooms should be available for use, with easy booking and attractive design, particularly if managers are in very small or open plan offices, so they are reliant on a general room in which to meet staff.

- The general office design can be changed to, say, an open-plan office to increase communication and enhance team building.

- Use should be made of ergonomically designed work stations and office equipment, which minimises noise and distractions as much as possible.

- Departments can be geographically located near to each other where possible.

- Departmental in-trays and bulletin boards, and increased efficiency and scheduling of internal mail service between departments can help in easing the flow of materials, memos, etc. around the office building.

- Internal printed materials can be made to look more professional by the use of desktop publishing and the use of colour or graphics.

- A social and informal environment can be created by the provision of a staff canteen used by all employees, or smaller tea or coffee areas. These could become regular meeting places for informal transfer of information.

- Library facilities could be provided (or upgraded) for access to company or industry information.

Information loads can be reduced by introducing filtering devices into office procedures:

- Bulletin boards should be organised and kept up to date by a designated person.

- Written and electronic messages should be flagged as routine or urgent, so the receiver can prioritise and deal with them accordingly.

- Junk mail should be screened as it comes into the mail room, or by a departmental or manager's secretary.

- Junior personnel and receptionists should be trained to cope with the first level of filtering of calls and customer queries.

Technical devices can also help to make communication and information handling more efficient:

- New technology can allow direct electronic contact for meetings, transfer of information, funds, orders, etc.

- EDI and networks can directly link suppliers and customers, reducing paperwork and transmission delays.

- User-friendly networking facilities can make it easier to transfer information from the field to management. Modern telephone and telecommunications resources in a location should be used to the full.

- The latest software can speed up information flow, storage and processing.

- An 'expert' database of typical customer questions and answers can be put together about a product or service to replace (or reduce) the involvement of specialists.

Finally, employees and management can themselves help in the communication and information process by:

- rationalising their own information needs

- finding out their own required information from company sources

- undertaking training to cope with information processing.

Management can rationalise routeing of information through the communication channels; for example, some written reports may no longer be necessary if the information is directly available through the manager's desktop terminal.

Organisations can also rationalise procedures so that budgets are kept, purchases made, contracts signed, production schedules adhered to, product design monitored without involving lengthy paperwork and signing off procedures by many different levels of personnel. The aim should be to limit the reporting and documentation required internally. Technology allows management at all levels to monitor progress directly.

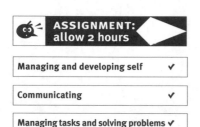

ASSIGNMENT:
allow 2 hours

Managing and developing self	✔
Communicating	✔
Managing tasks and solving problems	✔

ACTIVITY 3

Organisational change can cause uncertainty both among employees and customers. In recent years, British Rail has been restructured into different businesses. Senior managers are trying to encourage a more commercial culture in the run up to possible privatisation. Perhaps, inevitably, some employees are worried about whether they have a future on the railway; passengers are concerned about future prices and levels of service.

Review the newspapers and television for stories about British Rail. You might wish to use a library to look through back issues of newspapers. Choose a paper like the Financial Times which has a good coverage of industrial stories. In this media review, also look out for any advertising.

Visit your local railway station to see the ways in which British Rail is trying to communicate with its customers. Look at the literature it produces, the displays of posters and other customer information.

On the basis of your research, produce a 500-word report on the way in which British Rail is communicating with its customers. Your report should:

- discuss some of the problems that British Rail faces in trying to reassure its customers about the impact of the changes that it is undertaking

- look at different messages that British Rail is trying to convey and the communications media used

- suggest ways that British Rail could improve its communications strategy.

Prepare your report on a separate sheet of paper to submit to your tutor. Use the box below to summarise your findings.

summary

This session has considered communication as a means of relaying information within the organisation.

▶ There are four different types of information which give rise to organisational concerns: processed information, unprocessed information, knowledgeable ignorance and absolute ignorance.

▶ The factors that affect the efficiency of communication flows within an organisation include: the number of links in the communication chain, the way the message is presented and/or sent, the way the information is organised, the relationship of the receiver to the sender of the message or communication, and the extent to which information is grounded within experience.

▶ Different organisational structures have different communication requirements.

▶ Strategies for improving communications include introducing corporate-wide communications policy, improved office design and physical location of departments, an 'open-door' policy for managers and greater use of networking through teams and groups.

▶ Communication is vital in the implementation of change and in developing an organisational culture.

▶ There are a number of ways of increasing the efficiency of communication for relaying information.

Identifying and Changing Organisational Culture

Organisational culture

Objectives

After participating in this session, you should be able to:

> ▶ understand the meaning of organisational culture

> ▶ identify the characteristics that make up an organisation's culture

> ▶ identify different types of organisational culture and how they operate in particular organisations.

In working through this session, you will practise the following BTEC common skills:

Managing and developing self	✔
Working with and relating to others	✔
Communicating	✔
Managing tasks and solving problems	✔
Applying numeracy	
Applying technology	
Applying design and creativity	

Organisational culture

We have discussed the importance that organisation structures play in ensuring the smooth running of organisations. We have also emphasised that in these times of change and development organisations need to be more responsive and more flexible than in the past. However, as Watson (1994, In Search of Management: Culture, Chaos and Control in Managerial Work, Routledge) put it: 'Since the early 1980s, there has been a move away from emphasising structures as the most important organising device of organisations and a shift towards managing through values.' This involves managing through the establishment of a shared culture with key values about, among other things, how employees should behave.

Both concepts – structure and culture – are important. Certainly, organisation structure does facilitate productive co-operation and the process of integration helps to link the activities of the various organisational groups. The organisational culture, however, provides an additional binding force and helps to deliver overall organisational harmony. Rules and procedures cannot cover every eventuality and the basic assumptions of the culture help to prevent individuals 'doing their own thing' in the face of uncertainty. The organisation culture makes sense of situations and sets out what would be deemed the 'correct response' in ambiguous circumstances.

The concept of culture originates in social anthropology but, as you will see, it is often used selectively in ways that suit the interests of management. Nonetheless, the image that it conjures up of an organisational tribe with its own language and ritual and way of seeing the world is a potent one. It is not difficult to imagine how a strong culture would aid integration. But what about the notion, which we have referred to, of the organisational culture assisting in situations of uncertainty or ambiguity? We start with an exercise before going on to define organisational culture.

ACTIVITY 1

In small groups, think of three 'uncertainty situations' at your college or at work which the organisational culture clarifies, or could potentially clarify. Write down the key points in the box below.

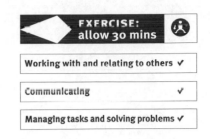

EXERCISE:
allow 30 mins

Working with and relating to others ✔

Communicating ✔

Managing tasks and solving problems ✔

Commentary...

Here we give two illustrations against which you can compare your ideas.

A supermarket employee has been instructed to fill an empty shelf as quickly as possible. The task has hardly been started when a customer asks the employee where the cereals are displayed and requests to be taken to them. What should the employee do? If the culture stresses that customers always come first then the assistant's response is clear.

A student arrives 15 minutes late for a lecture, and hesitates at the door, wondering what to do for the best. In the absence of formal rules governing such situations, the college culture will ideally 'solve' the problem by socialising students into an understanding that late-comers disturb both fellow students and staff and that it is not acceptable behaviour to enter when the lecture has begun.

What are your three 'uncertainty situations'?

Now that you have been introduced to the concept of organisational culture, we can formally define it.

> **!?!** Culture is the basic assumptions and values which are shared by, guide and shape individual and business behaviour in an organisation.

These values are manifested in tangible factors – artefacts – like stories, rituals, ceremonies, language, office and factory buildings and layout, decoration and the way that organisational members dress. There are many different definitions of culture. Table 1.1 gives some examples. Take a look at these different, but fairly similar, ideas about culture to broaden your perspective.

The culture of an organisation refers to the unique configuration of norms, values, beliefs, ways of behaving and so on that characterise the manner in which groups and individuals combine to get things done. The distinctiveness of a particular organisation is intimately bound up with its history and the character-building effects of past decisions and past leaders. It is manifested in the folkways, mores and the ideology to which members defer, as well as in the strategic choices made by the organisation as a whole. (*Eldridge & Crombie 1974: 89*)

Culture....is a pattern of beliefs and expectations shared by the organisation's members. These beliefs and expectations produce norms that powerfully shape the behaviour of individuals and groups in the organisation. (*Schwartz and Davis 1981: 33*)

I will mean by 'culture' a pattern of basic assumptions – invented, discovered, or developed by a given group as it learns to cope with its problems of external adaptation and internal integration – that has worked well enough to be considered valid and, therefore, to be taught to new members as the correct way to perceive, think, and feel in relation to those problems. (*Schein 1985: 9*)

The culture metaphor points towards another means of creating organised activity: by influencing the language, norms, folklore, ceremonies and other social practices that communicate the key ideologies, values and beliefs guiding action. (*Morgan 1986: 135*)

Corporate culture is the implicit, invisible, intrinsic and informal consciousness of the organisation which guides the behaviour of the individuals and which shapes itself out of their behaviour. (*Scholz 1987: 80*)

TABLE 1.1: Definitions of culture.
SOURCE: Adapted from Brown, A., 1995, Organisational Culture, London: Pitman, p. 6.

LEVELS OF CULTURE

We can think of the elements in our definition as being in a hierarchy with three levels:

1. tangible elements of culture

2. values

3. basic assumptions.

The tangible elements of culture are at the surface: the most visible level of an organisational culture. These elements are sometimes referred to as artefacts and include behaviour patterns or norms of behaviour, rites or rituals, modes of dress, language, physical office or factory layout, logos, publications, annual reports and corporate image. They also include rules, systems and procedures. What is important about these tangibles is the meaning that organisational members attach to each of them. And their meaning is only grasped in terms of the values that underlie them.

Values concern what is important and they are culturally learnt by organisational members. They are connected to moral and ethical codes. They shape, predict and explain what happens at the surface level. So, for example, it is organisational values that guide people when dealing with uncertain situations. They deal with what people think they ought to do or how they think they ought to behave and include honesty, integrity and being fair with people. This category also includes beliefs – what people believe is or is not true. In practice, values and beliefs are difficult to distinguish. You may value honesty in your organisation and believe it to be an essential part of its effectiveness.

Attitudes connect values and beliefs to feelings. You might have been in situations where staff honesty has helped to solve organisational problems, say conflicts between departmental heads, so you have developed a positive attitude to honesty in your workplace. For example, a manager may develop a negative attitude to the effectiveness of teams because of some past experience, so he or she will be negative about implementing a top management change to a team approach in the organisation.

However, just as our daily living habits become automatic, so organisational values may become taken for granted and drop out of consciousness. They gradually become basic assumptions. So, to be able to grasp the overall pattern of values and acquire a deeper level of comprehension, we need to understand the third level of the cultural hierarchy – the basic assumptions.

Basic assumptions deal with the fundamental aspects of culture. They tell members how to think, feel and perceive and yet they too may be taken for granted. It is only when they surface that the whole cultural pattern is illuminated and clarified. Basic assumptions may relate to, for example, human nature, organisational goals and the organisation's relationship to its environment.

As an example, consider a hospital; we can assume that saving lives is part of the objectives of the organisation. We can also take for granted that this is not mentioned any more. However, if a rumour starts to circulate that top management has made a policy decision that the hospital can no longer afford to try to save the lives of all premature babies in the future, then the underlying basic assumption will resurface and fierce debate will ensue.

A basic assumption in a manufacturing company might derive from the fact that its founders had felt that most organisational problems could best be solved by close supervision and an emphasis on downward communication. They might have taken this approach because they believe that people are naturally lazy, have little to contribute and need to be policed and told exactly what to do. This basic assumption is likely to result in a very centralised organisation which allows very little discretion. Jobs then will be highly specialised and controlled by procedures.

This example brings out an important point. The basic assumptions of the culture are likely to influence the organisational structure and indeed the processes, particularly the communication process, that take place within that structure. Also, the resultant structure, the design of jobs and the nature of communications, may well in turn affect the culture. The employees in the manufacturing company may come to perceive the organisation in a negative light and become resentful, even though the way they were being treated is officially seen to be the correct way to do things.

Schein (1985, 'How culture forms, develops and changes', in R.H. Kilmann, M.J. Saxton, R. Serpa and associates (eds), Gaining Control of the Corporate Culture, Jossey Bass, pp. 17–43) has suggested a typology of basic assumptions with five dimensions:

1. humanity's relationship to nature

2. the nature of reality and truth

3. the nature of human nature

4. the nature of human activity

5. the nature of human relationships.

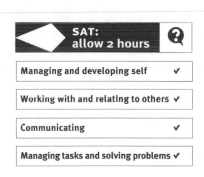

RECALL:
allow 15 mins

Describe the three levels of
organisational culture.

Having defined organisational culture and explored the idea of the
three levels of culture, we can now examine its characteristics in more
detail. Before proceeding, however, it would be helpful for you to find
out more about the culture of an organisation with which you are
familiar. Then you can examine a number of theoretical characteristics
of culture in a real life situation and thus develop your understanding
of them.

ACTIVITY 2

This activity requires you to carry out a further interview in your
chosen organisation; see activity 6 in section one, session one.
Again, the aim is to obtain two sets of responses from different
people connected to the organisation.

However, if your chosen organisation is the one in which you work,
you will need to select only one person to interview, as you can be
the other source of the data required. Your single interviewee should
be in a management position, and quite senior if possible. If you used
your own college, then you can also be one of the sources of data this
time. Certainly it will be helpful if you are already familiar with the
organisation.

An interview schedule is given here, but you should feel free to
rephrase or add further questions if you feel that this would be of
benefit. Also, if you are using the same organisation as you have

SAT:
allow 2 hours

Managing and developing self ✓

Working with and relating to others ✓

Communicating ✓

Managing tasks and solving problems ✓

used before, you may find your previous data useful.

Before the interview, prepare separate sheets (listing your questions along with any relevant comments gleaned from your earlier data) on which to record your interviewees' responses. Allow plenty of space to make notes during the interview. After the interview flesh out your notes and read your answers carefully both to refresh your memory about what you have learnt and to make sure that what you have written, accurately and completely reflects what you were told.

You may find it useful to read the following pages on the characteristics of organisational culture before conducting the interview.

INTERVIEW SCHEDULE

1. What is the name of your chosen organisation?
2. How many staff does your organisation employ?
3. How many sites or branches does your organisation operate from?
4. What does the idea of an organisation having a culture mean to you?

(You may need to prompt a little here. Perhaps, you could mention the image of the organisational tribe. Remember however, if you prompt too much there is a danger that you will only be given back the information you gave.)

5. To what degree are you aware of your organisation's culture?
6. Tell me about the culture.
7. Is there anyone in the organisation who for you symbolises the culture? Describe him or her.
8. How did you learn about the culture?
9. (a) Tell me about the *visible* aspects of your culture.
   (b) Tell me about the values or basic assumptions that underpin them.

(You may need to give a few examples – uniform, fostering sense of family/team, separate catering facilities indicating them/us ethos, etc.)

10. Cultures often have their roots in the history of the organisation. Can you think of any cultural elements from the past still affecting the existing culture?
11. Are there any subcultures? On what basis are they differentiated? Do you think they add or detract from efficiency?

(The process of differentiation is the process of allocating tasks within the organisation which have important elements, like shared knowledge and shared skills, to different teams, sections and departments within the organisation. This process of differentiation leads to subcultures developing around different 'groupings'. You will already have information about your teams and departments from the section one questionnaire.)

Characteristics of organisational culture

Using some of the information that you have acquired from your questionnaire, we will now examine the characteristics of organisational culture.

Commonly, six characteristics have been isolated:

1. Culture is learned from the organisation's internal and external environments.

2. The organisation's internal environment from which the organisational culture is partly learned has itself been influenced by that culture.

3. Culture is partly unconscious.

4. Culture is influenced by the past.

5. Culture is commonly held.

6. Culture is unlikely to be wholly uniform throughout the organisation.

Let us look more closely at each of these characteristics.

CULTURE IS LEARNED FROM THE ORGANISATION'S ENVIRONMENT

Organisational members learn about the culture from such internal factors as:

- selection, induction and training

- decision and communication processes

- planning and control procedures

- styles of management

- behaviour of colleagues

- favourite topics of conversation

- technology

- the physical impression of the organisation

- rituals and ceremonies

- the main dos and don'ts.

CHARACTERISTICS OF
ORGANISATIONAL CULTURE

SAT:
allow 20 mins

Managing tasks and solving problems ✓

ACTIVITY 3

Consider the various aspects of an organisation's internal environment from which members learn about their culture. You asked your interviewees how they learned about their organisational culture. However, their answers to questions 4–7 may in part have also indicated how they were socialised into their organisational culture. For example, question 4 asked what the idea of an organisation having a culture meant to them, and the notion of tribe may well have been mentioned and how this sense of tribe was brought about. In their answer to question 6, they may have mentioned characteristic management styles or, in answer to question 7, they may have mentioned symbolic or influential people from whom they learnt about the culture.

Look at your interview answers in terms of the internal factors listed above. Make a note of any factors mentioned by your interviewees which are in the list. Make a note of any additional factors which may have been mentioned.

Culture also is a product of the external environment of the organisation. Organisations operating in different sectors will have different markets, for example, and the needs of these separate markets demand different technologies and different skill. Williams, Dobson and Walters (1989, Changing Culture: New Organisational Approaches, IPM) give the example of 'Differences in skill requirements between a manufacturing organisation and a Civil Service department resulting in the recruitment of individuals from differing social and educational backgrounds'. These variations, they point out, 'are likely to be reflected in differences in management behaviour, in work methods, in reward and training procedures, etc.'.

External environmental influences can impact on the internal environment and so influence the culture into which the organisational members are socialised. Hence, particular characters and behaviours are reinforced. For example, if the organisation is operating in a risky business in a world-wide recession, or is dealing with suppliers in a foreign unstable country, then this will affect the internal culture by acting as a destabilising influence.

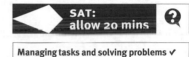

SAT:
allow 20 mins

Managing tasks and solving problems ✔

ACTIVITY 4

Refer to your questionnaire answers and list any mentions of external environmental influences. On the basis of your knowledge of the organisation, suggest possible external influences which were not mentioned.

List some of the ways in which the overall political and economic environment in the UK has changed in recent years. Suggest possible organisational culture changes that particular political and economic factors may have brought about.

Commentary...

The political and economic environment has been changed in the UK in several ways. Recent trends include:

- increased involvement in Europe, and the effect of EU regulations on a variety of issues

- world-wide recession

- greater promotion of market forces and enterprise

- privatisation programmes

- the state becoming more a purchaser than a provider of services

- introduction of increased competition into services traditionally provided by public bodies

- accountability of public services managers to customers and not simply politicians through customer charters.

The general effect of these changes tends to be a more customer-oriented and entrepreneurial culture. It is best to say 'tends' since we are talking about an issue that still needs investigation. Also, although there is evidence that such changes have happened to some degree, the traditional cultures have not been fully replaced.

CULTURE INFLUENCES THE INTERNAL ENVIRONMENT

The organisation's internal environment from which the organisational culture is partly learned has itself been influenced by that culture. One way in which organisational members absorb culture is through the various facets of the internal environment – the structures, procedures, styles, ceremonies and so on. This internal environment, however, is itself (partly) a product of the culture, created and recreated by those immersed in it.

ACTIVITY 5

SAT:
allow 15 mins

Managing tasks and solving problems✓

Refer to your questionnaire data and see if you have any information on the way that the internal environment is both shaped by the organisational culture and influences that culture.

Ask yourself, for example, whether or not some of the visible aspects of the environment from which culture is learned are at the same time products of that culture. In other words, are they at the same time shapers of culture and manifestations of culture?

Commentary...

To illustrate the point, consider an example from Jonathan's Pizza Company. In the early days of his pizza company, Jonathan's craft bakers all wore white uniforms with a distinctive red logo on the sleeve that they acquired after they finished their apprenticeship. They saw themselves as part of a team with a professional approach to their work. We could see the uniforms with the logos as a product of the culture but also as part of how the culture has developed. With the change to the mass production line, the bakers may fear that not only will their job functions change but that they will lose the 'special' nature of their uniform; they might be required to wear the same uniform as the newly recruited semi-skilled workers.

CHARACTERISTICS OF
ORGANISATIONAL CULTURE

CULTURE IS PARTLY UNCONSCIOUS

Basic assumptions can become so taken for granted that they are rarely stated; in fact, we can cease to be consciously aware of these assumptions. Strongly held values may lead to certain behaviour or procedures. Over time, these values can be transformed into underlying assumptions which drop from awareness.

Take, as a simple example, the case of a medium sized, manufacturing company. In the 1960s, the company introduced common dining facilities for all employees in an attempt to break down 'them and us' attitudes. The value this imbued was that all employees in the company were important. Thirty years later this arrangement continues but goes unremarked. The value that originally underpinned the change has been long dropped from conscious discussion or action.

At a more mundane level, while organisational members may well be formally introduced to many aspects of culture, they will also learn about it unconsciously. They will pick up culture intuitively, just by being there. For example, employees may know how best to approach colleagues from other departments without ever being expressly instructed to do so.

SAT:
allow 15 mins

Managing tasks and solving problems ✔

ACTIVITY 6

Refer again to the answers to your questions for any data relevant to the way that culture is partly unconscious. For example, you asked about awareness of culture. You also asked your interviewees about how they gained knowledge of the organisational culture. Did anything that was said reveal or imply unconscious learning? Finally, you directly asked about the non-visible aspects of culture, both values and basic assumptions. Did you receive any helpful answers to this question?

Commentary...

Again, we take an example from Jonathan's Pizza Company. In the early days, Jonathan may have spent some time with each new baker when they first joined the company as an apprentice, explaining what the company expected from them in terms of behaviour and performance. But other aspects of the company's culture may have been learnt either directly from the other bakers or indirectly, just by watching their behaviour. The new baker may have learnt that everyone helps each other, and that you are expected to work late if there is an urgent delivery to be made.

CULTURE IS INFLUENCED BY THE PAST

The original culture of an organisation, reflecting, for example, the values of the founders and the environment which faced them, may still influence the contemporary culture. In answer to question 7, your interviewees may have named the founders as people who symbolised the organisational culture. Indeed, photographs of founders are often displayed in prominent positions in organisations. Also, of course, as we have already suggested, the culture of the past still exerts influence because decisions affecting an organisation's future are inevitably conditioned by the culture within which they were taken.

ACTIVITY 7

Refer to answers to question 10, in which you asked whether or not the interviewees could think of any cultural elements from the past still affecting the existing culture. Working in small groups, share and discuss this data with others in your class.

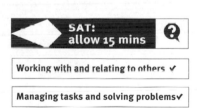

SAT:
allow 15 mins

Working with and relating to others ✔

Managing tasks and solving problems✔

CHARACTERISTICS OF
ORGANISATIONAL CULTURE

CULTURE IS COMMONLY HELD

Culture is a collective phenomena. It is about organisational members adopting similar behaviours and ways of perceiving events and activities, even if they do not work at the same branch or on the same site. The organisational culture is expressed in the characteristics of the particular organisational tribe and this differentiates it from other 'tribes'.

The imagery is of the culture being external to the organisation's members, shaping their thoughts and actions, but it only does so because they have been collectively socialised. What they do both expresses and reproduces the organisation's culture which they have gained from common experiences and learning, and from the common environment. It is due to this characteristic that we can say, for example, that a certain individual is very much in Marks and Spencer's or IBM's mould.

CULTURE IS UNLIKELY TO BE WHOLLY UNIFORM

Within most organisations, the culture will almost certainly never be completely homogeneous. Let us consider the reasons why culture is unlikely to be uniform.

Consider an organisation in which the predominant culture is one in which managers feel that employees needed to be 'policed' and told exactly what to do. While this treatment of employees is sanctioned at the deepest cultural level, naturally some employees are likely to feel resentful; it is likely then that some or all, often or occasionally, would seek to resist this 'official' culture. This official culture is the organisational leader's preferred way of doing things – this is sometimes referred to as the corporate culture. The resistance then would stem from the 'unofficial' culture.

When managers seek to manage through values or culture, they must try to ensure that their corporate culture actually does pervade the whole organisation. If successful, then the culture is referred to as a strong culture. However, even when strong cultures exist, there will almost always be a degree of heterogeneity (i.e. variety) between organisations. This is because most organisations are characterised by subcultures. These arise, for example, around different roles and functions. You might be aware of this phenomenon from your questionnaire data.

Groups in the same functional area face common problems. They will develop a shared view of how to respond to them. From their set of common experiences, groups will hold common values. But these values will not always be shared by groups in other parts of an organisation. So, there will always be degrees of cultural variance whether at functional or hierarchical levels. For example, a department that relies on innovation and creativity (like research and development) is likely to be less hierarchy-focused than a task oriented department (like production). Production personnel will be more controlled by roles, rules and procedures, while the research scientists will have more autonomy and place much more emphasis on common goals. We look at these cultural variations when the types of organisational culture are examined later.

Cultural heterogeneity, then, is to some degree inevitable; it is also desirable and necessary. It is these subcultural differences which give, for example, functional specialists their particular professional perspectives and make each grouping so valuable to the organisation in their own distinctive way.

SAT:
allow 40 mins

Managing tasks and solving problems ✔

ACTIVITY 8

Remembering that organisational cultures are unlikely to be uniform throughout an organisation, review the answers to question 11 on the questionnaire. Look back at the responses to the questions about teams and departments in the interviews you conducted in your chosen organisation in section one.

Now answer these five questions about your chosen organisations.

1. We have emphasised that functional differentiation can generate different subcultures. Are any functional areas mentioned in the data? If so, which?

2. Are subcultures differentiated on any other basis? If yes, explain.

3. Does your research provide no evidence of subcultures? If so, given your knowledge of the organisation, do you think this is really likely?

4. Do your interviewees feel that, where they exist, subcultural differences contribute or detract from organisational effectiveness? On what basis do they make their judgements?

5. Are there any discrepancies in view between your two respondents? If so, on what issues do they disagree? Suggest why they may disagree.

CHARACTERISTICS OF
ORGANISATIONAL CULTURE

Commentary...

Remember that individual's perspectives are likely to be influenced by their position in the organisation. Senior personnel, for example, may be more likely to stress cultural harmony. Perhaps, also, they may have a sense of the organisational culture fundamentally being their culture. They might place more stress and importance on culture than the average employee, and see the contribution it can make to organisational effectiveness.

Subcultures might arise as a result of organisational changes. With the new structure at Jonathan's Pizza Company, it is likely that a subculture develops within the semi-skilled operators. They may see themselves as separate from the craft bakers, and certainly different from the marketing manager and the other marketing staff.

Types of organisational culture

We now examine the types of organisational culture in more detail. Handy (1993, Understanding Organizations, 4th edn, Penguin) has developed a useful, four-fold classification of cultural types, each with their own respective structures and systems:

1. power culture

2. role culture

3. task culture

4. person culture.

POWER CULTURES

These are typically found in small entrepreneurial organisations dependent upon a single power source which may be either one individual, or, more usually, a core group. Its structure is best pictured as a web (see figure 1.1), with rays of influence spread out from the centre. There is little bureaucracy, and unencumbered by formal structures and systems, reactions to opportunities and threats can be quick. Success, however, hinges on the quality of the power source and whether or not the power holders make the right decisions. Again, given the absence of bureaucracy, control is exercised by the small core group. Most of the organisation can then be left largely alone to continue with their jobs with occasional policing.

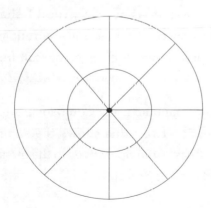

FIGURE 1.1: Web format of a power culture.

Power cultures place much faith in individuals; but they judge by results, so life within them can be tough for the individual. If those outside the 'power' source fall out of line with 'official' thinking and make a 'wrong' decision, they will be pushed out of the organisation. Organisations are likely to grow, of course, and it is very difficult to retain this kind of culture in large firms.

Jonathan was running a power culture in the early days of his company. His craft bakers would respond to him directly, and if one of them did not 'fit in' he would not be likely to stay very long. It will be impossible for Jonathan to behave in the same way in the new expanded company. He will need more written policies and procedures, and he will have to maintain his control through indirect supervision.

ROLE CULTURES

These are typically found in large bureaucracies and work by logic and rationality. They are called role cultures because the positions in the organisation are more important than the individuals who fill them. In this way, a company can survive over time. It exists beyond the contributions of particular individuals and successively recruits people into pre-set roles. Given this, position power is the main power source rather than personal power and the main sources of influence are rules and procedures.

Handy has suggested that the accompanying structure to a role culture can be best pictured as a Greek temple (see figure 1.2). The pillars of the temple can be seen as the functions, for example, finance, marketing and production, and their work, and the relations between them, are controlled by roles, rules and procedures. Crowning the pillars are senior management, co-ordinating at the top. However, temples become unstable when the ground shakes and role organisations are only successful in stable environments. When the market changes and product needs change, role cultures are no longer appropriate.

Look back at the Acme Manufacturing Company's organisation chart (see section one, session two); this shows the significance of the positions in the hierarchy, from operatives to the managing director, and is an example of a role culture.

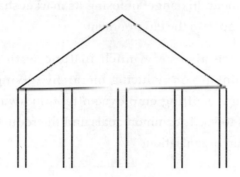

FIGURE 1.2: Greek temple format of a role culture.

TASK CULTURES

Task cultures are likely to be project oriented. They are characterised by a culture of team work rather than individual effort. The accompanying structure is best seen as a net (see figure 1.3). Another structural form of a task culture is the matrix organisation (see section one, session two).

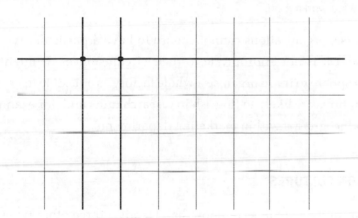

FIGURE 1.3: Net format of a task culture.

Task cultures depend on bringing together the appropriate resources and the right people, then leaving them to run the project within certain guidelines and using specific organisational procedures. Influence depends more on expert power than on position or personal power. The unifying power of team work means that task cultures lead to a focusing of the individual member's attention on the overall task rather than their specific contribution.

Task cultures are appropriate where flexibility and sensitivity to the market and the environment are very important. In Oticon's case (see case study below), a task culture was appropriate because the company was seeking growth through product innovation and market development. In danger of losing its market share, it needed to become more open to the environment.

Task cultures are also very much in tune with fashionable management thinking on reducing hierarchy, giving employees greater autonomy, shifting employee attention away from their individual roles towards common goals and the reduction of status differences within organisations.

OTICON HOLDING

The board of Oticon Holding, a Danish hearing-aid company set up in 1904, had by the mid 1980s recognised that it was in great danger of being ousted by one of the big players in its field. The board was also aware that to a large degree the company was prisoner of its traditional culture. A major change was necessary and the board head-hunted a new chief executive.

A new approach was initiated at head office. The chief executive dismantled the traditional management structure and put everybody to work in ever-changing, project-based teams. The staff helped to develop the details. All of the office people had to become multi-skilled, and take on three to five jobs each. They were free to decide what to do and worked in shifting teams gathered around projects that interested them. The new office set-up was open plan with just 140 work benches with terminals. Staff moved about within the office according to the projects that they were working on.

Of course, organisations cannot choose to have a particular type of culture if it is not appropriate to their circumstances. It might be inappropriate to try to organise a whole factory as a flexible team, but task cultures are likely to flourish in research units and, for example, in product groups within marketing departments.

PERSON CULTURES

Person cultures are less common than Handy's three other types. In person cultures, the individual is the central point. For example, a group of solicitors may form a partnership to share the benefits of organisation. They do so purely because they feel that this is the best way to forward their personal ambitions. Each has an office, they share administrative assistance and office equipment and they keep the structure as minimal as possible. The resulting 'organisation' would have a person culture. It can be seen as a cluster of individuals (see figure 1.4).

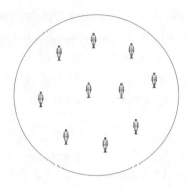

FIGURE 1.4: Cluster format of person culture.

Obviously, the majority of organisations have objectives over and above those of the individuals who comprise them. Control simply by mutual consent would be insufficient. However, forms of person cultures may be found in the pockets of large organisations. For example, computer specialists or hospital consultants may feel little loyalty to their organisations. Instead, they see themselves as very much doing their own thing with certain benefits going to the overall organisation. These individuals are likely to be bonded by professional training, codes of practice and professional associations.

RECALL:
allow 10 mins

Summarise the central sources of power in each of Handy's typical cultures:

○ power

○ role

○ task

○ person.

TYPES OF ORGANISATIONAL
CULTURE

Other researchers have also generated typologies of organisational cultures, and we investigate these now. This helps us to see not just how the different cultures relate to different structures but also how they are likely to respond to change. As with Handy's ideas, there is a direct link to the organisational structure, the type of organisation and its environment.

DEAL AND KENNEDY TYPOLOGY

We start with Deal and Kennedy's typology (1982, Cultures: The Rites and Rituals of Corporate Life, Addison-Wesley). Deal and Kennedy identify four generic cultures:

1. tough-guy macho culture

2. work-hard/play-hard culture

3. bet-your-company culture

4. process culture.

These cultures are determined by the degree of risk that the organisation's activities have and the speed with which feedback on decisions and strategies is received.

The tough-guy macho culture concerns organisations in high-risk situations with rapid feedback. These organisations focus on speed and change and short-term gain. Conflict and tension are fostered internally, staff turnover is high and a strong culture fails to develop. Examples might be management consulting firms or companies in the entertainment industry.

The work-hard/play-hard culture is a low-risk high-feedback culture. Examples are computer firms and other manufacturing companies and highly visible consumer product companies like McDonald's. They tend to be very dynamic customer-oriented companies, with rules and procedures to minimise risks. A reasonably strong culture is helped by staff functions, office outings, etc.

The bet-your-company culture is developed in organisations in a high-risk long-feedback environment. Examples include large aircraft manufacturers like Boeing, and multinationals in the oil industry like Shell. These companies make substantial investments in long-term projects; they tend to centralise decision making and have a fairly tall hierarchy.

The process culture is a low-risk slow-feedback culture. Typical examples include banks, the Civil Service and insurance companies that operate in a fairly stable environment. The organisations are likely to be bureaucratic, formal and hierarchical and not able to react quickly or effectively to any kind of change.

QUINN AND MCGRATH'S TYPOLOGY

Quinn and McGrath (1985, 'The transformation of organisational cultures: A competing values perspective', in P.J. Frost, L.F. Moore, M.F. Louis, C.C. Lundberg and J. Martin (eds) Organizational Culture, Sage, pp. 315–34) identified four generic cultures:

1. the rational culture (market)

2. the ideological culture (adhocracy)

3. the consensual culture (clan)

4. the hierarchical culture (hierarchy).

Their classification is based on the transactions or exchanges within the organisation. Details are given in table 1.2. As you can see, Quinn and McGrath's ideas of culture is very much linked to the organisational structure that fosters it and vice versa. You can see the types of organisational structure emerging – the simple entrepreneurial structure, the professional organisation, the machine bureaucracy, the adhocracy and large divisionalised companies.

TYPES OF ORGANISATIONAL
CULTURE

The market

This is a rational culture designed to pursue objectives using productivity and efficiency as the prime criteria of performance. The 'boss' is firmly in charge of this culture, and competence is the basis of his or her authority. The style of leadership is directive and goal-oriented, decision making is decisive and the compliance of employees guaranteed by contractual agreement. Individuals are judged according to their tangible output and are encouraged to be achievement-oriented. According to McDonald and Gandz (1992) the salient values of market cultures are aggressiveness, diligence and initiative.

The adhocracy

This is an ideological culture which can support broad purposes as indicated by its favoured criteria or performance, namely, external support, growth and resource acquisition. Authority is held on the basis of charisma and power is wielded by referring to values. In such organisations decisions are often taken as a result of intuition, leaders tend to be inventive and risk-oriented, and employee compliance is enforced by their commitment to organisational values. Individuals are evaluated according to the intensity of their effort and interested in growth rather than achievement. McDonald and Gandz (1992) suggest that these cultures are characterised by values such as adaptability, autonomy and creativity.

The clan

This is a consensual culture the organisational purpose of which is group maintenance, and which gauges performance in terms of whether or not it facilitates cohesion and morale. Authority is vested in those who are members of the organisation generally and the basis for the exercise of authority is informal status. Decisions tend to be arrived at through participation and consensus and the dominant leadership style is one of concern and support. Employees comply with agreed decisions because they have shared in the process by which they were reached. Individuals are evaluated in terms of the quality of the relationships they enjoy with others and are expected to show loyalty to the organisation. For McDonald and Gandz (1992) the dominant values of a clan include courtesy, fairness, moral integrity and social equality.

The hierarchy

This is a hierarchical culture that exists to execute regulations while remaining stable and controlled. In these organisations authority is vested in the rules and power is exercised by those with technical knowledge. Decisions are made on the basis of factual analysis and leaders tend to be conservative and cautious. Here the compliance of employees is maintained by surveillance and control and they are assessed against formally agreed criteria and are expected to value security. According to McDonald and Gandz (1992), some of the values associated with the hierarchy are formality, logic, obedience and orderliness.

TABLE 1.2: Typology of organisational cultures.
SOURCE: Brown, A., 1995, Organisational Culture, London: Pitman, p. 72.

SCHOLZ'S TYPOLOGY

Scholz based his classification on strategy, and considered three different dimensions of culture (Scholz, C., 1987, 'Corporate culture and strategy – thr problem of strategic fit', Long Range Planning, 20(4), 78-87):

1. evolution – how culture changes over time

2. internal – how the organisation's internal environment affects its culture

3. external – how the external environment affects its culture.

He identified five types in his evolution dimension:

1. stable

2. reacting

3. anticipating

4. exploring

5. creating

and three types in his internal dimension:

1. production

2. bureaucratic

3. professional.

Organisational structures emerge with these different classifications, as the environment, environmental uncertainty, strategy and the internal requirements to perform tasks are reflected in both the underlying structural framework and its developing culture. The influencing factors are:

- the organisation's life cycle

- the original owner or entrepreneur

- size

- technology

- the organisation's mission and strategy

- the specific and general environment

- its employees.

These typologies are useful ways of studying and trying to understand culture. Remember though that no organisation will fit directly into one category.

summary

▶ Culture is the basic assumptions and values which are shared by, guide and shape individual and business behaviour in an organisation.

▶ Values concern what is important. They are culturally learnt by organisational members and are connected to moral and ethical codes. Attitudes connect values and beliefs to feelings.

▶ Culture is shaped by the organisation's internal and external environments. The organisation's internal environment from which the organisational culture is partly learned has itself been influenced by that culture.

▶ Other characteristics of culture are that it is partly unconscious, it is influenced by the past, it is commonly held, and it is unlikely to be wholly uniform throughout the organisation.

▶ Handy identified four main types of organisational culture that affect the organisation's structure and systems: power culture, role culture, tasks culture and person culture.

▶ Other researchers – including Deal and Kennedy, Quinn and McGrath, and Scholz – have develop different ways of characterising organisational culture.

Culture in action

Objectives

After participating in this session, you should be able to:

▶ describe the major internal and external determinants that affect an organisation's culture

▶ identify the functions and importance of organisational culture

▶ evaluate social responsibility and culture.

In working through this session, you will practise the following BTEC common skills:

Managing and developing self	✔
Working with and relating to others	✔
Communicating	✔
Managing tasks and solving problems	✔
Applying numeracy	
Applying technology	
Applying design and creativity	

What determines specific organisational cultures?

The last session examined some of the main characteristics of culture. Here, we look more closely at what determines particular cultures and how they link to the organisational structure.

Although we have not directly addressed why one organisation differs from another, certain ideas we have introduced about cultures are obviously relevant. For example, when considering the idea that organisational cultures are very likely to be heterogeneous, we saw that the degree of heterogeneity varies between organisations. Also, we discussed the impact that the founders may have on an organisational culture and the fact that external environments also affect the organisation.

The culture of a specific organisation is a result of the impact of:

- the founders

- the internal environment

- the external environment

- current management

- the national culture.

We now look at each of these factors in turn. At each stage you should seek to relate the culture of your chosen organisation to these determinants.

IMPACT OF THE FOUNDERS

The entrepreneurs, or founding group, tend to make a significant and lasting impact on the organisational culture. They were (in some cases still are) the heart of the organisation. They both create the culture and bear it into the future. It is their vision, their successes, and their personalities that become the stuff of folklore. The culture affects the selection and recruitment procedures to ensure that culturally like-minded people are recruited. It is also reflected, to some degree, in the other systems and in the structure of the organisation.

Davis (1984, Managing Corporate Culture, Ballinger, p. 8) suggests that: 'if the leader is a great person, then inspiring ideas will permeate the corporation's culture. If the leader is mundane, then the guiding beliefs may well be uninspired. Strong beliefs make for strong cultures. The clearer the leader is about what he [or she] stands for, the more apparent will be the culture of that company.'

The founding family of what was to become IBM believed very strongly that people should not drink alcohol at work. This basic assumption regarding abstinence in working hours is said to be still reinforcing such other key cultural values as dedication and hard work.

IMPACT OF THE INTERNAL ENVIRONMENT

The cultures of specific organisations also result from the systems and structure of the organisation. Remember, of course, that this internal environment is at the same time a reflection of culture and is perhaps still partly shaped by the impact of the founders. We noted relevant elements of the internal environment when discussing the general characteristics of organisational structures.

Among other internal factors which may affect organisational culture are:

- organisational size
- degree of differentiation
- extent of formalisation
- the degree of freedom allowed to subordinates to show initiative
- criteria for appraisal and reward
- use of technology
- information and control systems.

Criteria for selection are also an important determinant of culture, especially where there is a major emphasis on fitting in.

Conversely, recruitment and selection can be used as a major cultural change mechanism. So, for example, the electricity boards in the UK have sought to make radical changes to their traditional culture by switching staff recruitment from (predominantly) engineers to sales professionals.

IMPACT OF THE EXTERNAL ENVIRONMENT

Organisations operate in different sectors and have different markets. The servicing of these markets will, for example, determine resource and skill needs and technological requirements. The particular environment places different demands and constraints on organisations and their cultures change in response to these market-driven environmental factors.

We looked at the different types of environment in section two. Here, we showed that how the particular environment – and the degree of environmental uncertainty in each case – affects organisational structure. You should remember that there is a specific environment (including customers, competitors, suppliers, distributors, government, and shareholders) and a general environment (including demographics, political forces, technological advances and other factors that are not specific to that organisation).

Think back to the changing environmental demands made on the public sector. For example, the new environment, with its greater emphasis on enterprise and market forces, demands that public services managers be accountable to customers and not simply to politicians. This is placing their organisations under much greater pressure, altering their skill requirements and, among other things, forcing them to introduce a number of changes to their internal environment with the aim of fostering a more entrepreneurial culture.

IMPACT OF CURRENT MANAGEMENT

Initially, the founders have the most influence on culture. This lessens as the organisation grows and develops. The habitual ways of doing things are no longer appropriate. Again, as we discussed in section two, the organisation goes through stages in its life cycle that make new demands; it will grow and change from a simple entrepreneurial structure to something more complex. Changes in the environment necessitate new responses.

As the environment changes and as new demands on the organisation grow, then current managers will have a greater potential impact on the culture. There can be limits to how far – or how quickly – current managers can change culture. The entrenched culture will have provided them with ways of making sense of the external setting of the organisation. Also, of course, there may be simply a recasting of core beliefs to suit new circumstances.

Take, as an example, Jaguar. The company went into decline between 1972 and 1980. Part of British Leyland, this decline was largely due to changes brought about by the corporate leaders of the parent company. In 1980, it was given a year's notice of closure by British Leyland's chief executive. However, it was turned around by re-emphasising the traditional Jaguar culture of engineering excellence and craft pride. These were extended and recast to include high standards of competitiveness in productivity, quality and reliability. Tangible aspects of the new culture included monthly dealer award schemes, successful employees had their names put on a plaque in reception and an annual award ceremony was established for the best performing suppliers. We look in more detail at the changes at Jaguar later.

IMPACT OF NATIONAL CULTURES

An organisation's culture is also influenced by the wider national culture in which it operates. Hofstede (1980, Culture's Consequences: International Difference in Work related Values, Sage) surveyed managers and employees who worked for IBM in 40 different countries and found five significant patterns in their national cultures. Employees of the same company replied differently to Hofstede's questions depending on the country in which they worked.

Hofstede characterised different national cultures in the following terms:

- uncertainty avoidance

- power distance

- individualism (versus collectivism)

- feminine (versus masculinity).

An 'uncertainty avoidance' culture likes to be quite clear about what is permitted and what is not, so that there can be a respect for order. The Japanese culture, where this pattern is strong, values clarity, legality and orderliness. British respondents, on the other hand, do not place a high value on them. Japanese companies are more likely to have extensive rules and procedures for staff to follow.

Power distance cultures accept the fact that power in its institutions and organisations is distributed unequally. This pattern was strong in Japan but weak in Great Britain. Japanese employees are more likely to accept that the chief executive is extremely wealthy and they never see him functioning within the organisation.

WHAT DETERMINES SPECIFIC ORGANISATIONAL CULTURES?

Power distance

High power distance countries		Low power distance countries	
Malaysia	Philippines	Austria	New Zealand
Guatemala	Mexico	Israel	Republic of Ireland
Panama	Venezuela	Denmark	Sweden

In general, Hofstede found that Latin American and Latin European countries (like France and Spain) had high power distance values, as did Asian and African countries. Low power distance was found to be a feature of the USA, the UK and its former colonies, and the non-Latin parts of Europe.

Individualism/collectivism

Individualist		Collectivist	
USA	Canada	Guatemala	Venezuela
Australia	Netherlands	Ecuador	Colombia
UK	New Zealand	Panama	Indonesia

Hofstede found that nearly all wealthy countries (Hong Kong and Singapore were two exceptions) scored highly on individualism, while nearly all poor countries were found to be more collectivist.

Masculinity/femininity

Masculine		Feminine	
Japan	Italy	Sweden	Denmark
Austria	Switzerland	Norway	Costa Rica
Venezuela	Mexico	Netherlands	Finland

The UK and West Germany were ranked equal ninth most masculine nations out of 53, with the USA in fifteenth place.

Uncertainty avoidance

High uncertainty avoidance		Low uncertainty avoidance	
Greece	Uruguay	Singapore	Sweden
Portugal	Belgium	Jamaica	Hong Kong
Guatemala	Japan	Denmark	UK

Hofstede found high uncertainty avoidance scores for Latin American, Latin European and Mediterranean countries, Japan and South Korea. The German-speaking countries (Austria, West Germany and Switzerland) were medium-high. Except for Japan and South Korea all Asian countries scored medium-low, as did African and Anglo-Nordic countries plus the Netherlands.

Confucian/dynamism

Long-termist		Short-termist	
China	Japan	Pakistan	Canada
Hong Kong	South Korea	Nigeria	Zimbabwe
Taiwan	Brazil	Philippines	UK

Hofstede found that the USA tended towards being short-termist, while the Netherlands was the most long-termist European nation, ranked tenth out of twenty-three countries surveyed.

TABLE 2.1: Hofstede's analysis of national cultural differences.

SOURCE: Brown, A., 1995, Organisational Culture, London: Pitman, p. 43.

Individualistic cultures prize taking care of oneself and one's immediate family. Hofstede found that this pattern was strong in Great Britain. A British employee is less likely to accept redundancy for the sake of the company, as it will affect his life and his means to look after his family, whereas a Japanese employee would see his (or her) lack of job in the wider context of the success of the company.

Feminine cultures prize caring for others, the quality of life and putting people before money and other things. This pattern is weak both in Great Britain and Japan. Both societies cultivate a material approach to the world which would be reflected in employees' views about remuneration and organisational objectives.

National cultures help to determine organisational cultures as they determine what values and beliefs are likely to be set up, and what basic assumptions are likely to exist in the company. Organisational cultures will reflect the national culture's approach to power and means of control, approach to the individual and approach to the overall company and society.

Table 2.1 summarises Hofstede's analysis. These national cultures then, as Pheysey (1993, Organisational Cultures: Types and Transformations, Routledge) put it, 'provide "compass points" by which key people in organisations attempt to orient themselves and to pursue other goals'. We further discuss Japanese organisational cultures later in this section.

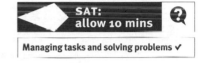

SAT:
allow 10 mins

Managing tasks and solving problems ✓

ACTIVITY 1

Before reading on, list possible functions of organisational culture. Some functions have already been mentioned; for example, culture functions as a 'binding force'. Look back through this section and list other uses you can find.

Commentary...

Culture is a social glue or an integrating mechanism. Culture shapes and guides behaviour, especially in situations of uncertainty or ambiguity. Finally, cultures give a sense of belonging and even identity.

Functions of organisational cultures

We now introduce a number of additional functions of culture. Edgar Schein (1992, 'Coming to a new awareness of organisation's culture', in G. Salaman (ed.) Human Resource Strategies, Open University), an influential writer on organisational cultures, identified other key functions that they perform:

- functions of culture that resolve problems of internal integration

- functions of culture that resolve problems of external adaptation and survival.

First of all we examine some of the key functions which help to resolve internal integration problems. Within an organisation, individuals must agree how they are going to communicate, the communication channels that they will use, and how power and authority is to be exercised. They must agree details about the co-ordination and control of functions, about appraisal and reward systems, and how to deal with unexpected situations.

Schein identifies four key functions that culture plays in this process:

1. a common language

2. criteria for inclusion and exclusion

3. criteria for success and failure

4. social guidelines.

Culture provides a common language which emphasises important concepts like quality and customer service. Listening in to the routine conversations held in organisations is an important way to learn about culture. The buzz words, the catch-phrases and the dominant legends influence the way that the organisational members make sense of their organisation and come to know what is deemed to be important. Phrases like IBM's 'IBM means service' or Interflora's 'Say it with flowers' are not only powerful slogans; they also relate back to the subsurface cultural levels of values and basic assumptions of the companies concerned.

Culture provides criteria for inclusion and exclusion and so helps to set boundaries. At a visible level, for example, the boundaries of a strong culture will be clear at the level of characteristic behaviour and perhaps mode of dress. The level of customer service at supermarket A will clearly distinguish it from supermarket B. Even prior to training, an organisation may well have a clear view of the type of person it wants to recruit. It was said of BBC appointment boards that when a candidate left the room the most common comment heard was that either the individual was, or was not, a BBC person. A BBC person was seen to have a special kind of tact, together with the ability to learn quickly by trial and error, since the Corporation did not then put its most important rules on paper. Some organisations set out their expectations in great detail, prior to recruitment, and then invite those who do not feel that they can match up, to withdraw.

Culture gives legitimacy to the organisational pecking order both by highlighting criteria for success and failure and by socialising organisational members into 'recognising' them as fair and reasonable. Jonathan's new operators in the bigger company will have written performance criteria to meet, as Jonathan will not be able to supervise them directly. As they join the company, these criteria will be discussed and any queries can be dealt with at that stage.

Cultures performs a social function in setting out the rules of the game in terms of peer relationships and relationships between the sexes. It provides guidelines in an area where it is difficult to lay down precise rules and where uncertainty may lead to misunderstandings and conflict. Culture provides then for a more secure environment where both friendship and a sense of belonging can flourish in the context of pursuing the purposes of the organisation. For example, in terms of relationships between male and female employees, the cultural guidelines may relate to avoiding body contact and the use of non-sexist language.

Now we examine the key functions identified by Schein which help to resolve problems of external adaptation and survival. These concern the organisation's mission and goals, the evaluation of meeting these goals and the strategies if the goals are not being met. In each case, culture helps to develop a common understanding. So, in regard to the organisation's goals, culture helps to develop a common understanding of the organisation's mission and the strategy which will enable the organisation's objectives to be achieved.

FUNCTIONS OF ORGANISATIONAL
CULTURES

SAT:
allow 15 mins

Managing tasks and solving problems ✔

ACTIVITY 2

In section one, session one, you identified the mission of either your place of work or college/university or chosen organisation. Check back and write it in the box below. Is there any discrepancy between the organisational culture as you know it and the mission statement? Explain your answer.

Commentary...

Any discrepancies between a mission statement and what is actually happening 'on the ground', can be seen as discrepancies between what we have called the 'official' or **corporate culture** and the **'unofficial' culture**. You may have found examples of this. We gave an example earlier – an organisation may specifically declare itself to be an equal opportunities employer but, in practice, a group of employees in a particular department may decide not to work with women or members of racial minorities.

It is important – in the interest of organisational effectiveness – that the official and unofficial cultures are matched as closely as possible.

Despite a strong corporate culture, individuals within an organisation may show different actions. Golden (1992, 'The individual and organizational culture: Strategies for action in highly-ordered contexts', Journal of Management Studies, 29(1), 1–21) identified four different approaches by an individual in a strong culture:

1. With unequivocal adherence, the individual follows and reinforces the norms of the culture. For example, in the early days of the company, Jonathan's craft bakers are happy to work late to meet a specific order, without being paid overtime.

2. With strained adherence, the individual follows the norms but has some problems with doing so. For example, one of Jonathan's craft bakers may work late to help his colleagues, but actually resents doing so.

3. With secret non-adherence, the individual openly and apparently follows the norms, but in reality does not. For example, another of his bakers may apparently be very happy to work late, but always manages to find good excuses not to do so.

4. With open non-adherence, the individual does not follow the norms, and quite openly and directly challenges the culture. For example, one baker never works late to help anyone else; instead he goes home at the usual time saying that it is not his problem and the company should hire more full-time staff if it wants to meet production schedules.

In reality, unequivocal adherence is unlikely all the time, and although it would provide control, it would be a bad thing as it would not provide a conducive environment for change. Attitudes can change in the longer term; unequivocal adherence can turn into strained adherence. For example, if the bakers might be happy to work late in the early days of the company to make it a success but, in the long run, they may start to complain about the amount of (sometimes unpaid) overtime they are expected to work on a regular basis. Jonathan would need to look at both his internal scheduling and his remuneration system to resolve the problem.

In tackling problems of external adaptation and survival, culture also helps to develop a common understanding of the organisation's operative goals as derived from the mission and on the means to be used to attain them – for example, the organisational structure and the reward system.

The reward system of an organisation is another means for management to achieve its organisational goals. When managers pay special attention to particular types of accomplishment and rewards them, it is because these accomplishments relate to areas which are crucial to the achievement of the organisational mission. For example, in certain public services in the UK prior to privatisation, seniority for its own sake, brought reward. In today's more entrepreneurial culture, performance in areas like sales, for example, which are seen as critical to competitive success, determines reward.

Finally, in terms of external adaptation and survival, Schein argues that culture helps to develop a common understanding of what will happen if organisational goals are not being met. If performance is down, then there may be staff cutbacks, or changes in the remuneration package, for example. Criteria for performance will need to be set up and monitored, and agreed procedures followed if they are not being met. Then it will be no shock to employees if changes have to be made.

CULTURE AND CHANGE

Culture pervades all aspects of organisational life. It is likely to influence the type of people who are selected for leadership positions. It constrains strategy and, indeed, it affects the organisation's orientation to the future. This is because organisational culture will affect how organisational leaders interpret their task, how they perceive the opportunities and threats in the environment, their decision-making processes, the structures and systems put in place and the behaviour, motivation and commitment of organisational members.

The danger for organisations is that cultures tend to be self-perpetuating. This makes things difficult when organisations do need to change their strategic direction. It many cases, it means that they have changed the culture in order to implement a new strategic approach.

If we remember that, to varying degrees, change is an inevitable feature of organisational life then organisations should obviously be always externally focused and prepared for change. And, of course, the openness or closed nature of an organisation is as much a determinant of their culture as it is a product.

In changing from his small craft-based operation to a large mass-production operation, Jonathan will need to change the culture and also use the existing culture to make the changes.

Social responsibility and organisational culture

Culture is also important in shaping attitudes to social responsibility. Managers are increasingly recognising that the means to attain goals must also be ethical. And when things go wrong in the area of ethical business behaviour, managers increasingly look to the organisational culture to provide a solution. There are two schools of thought on how culture can enhance ethical behaviour and they relate back to the notions of homogeneous and heterogeneous cultures.

One approach is to build a strong, unified, homogeneous culture in which resides the corporate conscience. The danger here is that the existence of a corporate conscience discourages individual members, or even professional subgroups, from taking responsibility for ethical decisions. In such circumstances, a person with integrity and voicing their misgivings, becomes labelled as a potential whistle-blower or troublemaker. The silent majority of organisational members are likely to put their faith in the corporate leaders. It is argued – or at least assumed – that they have the full picture and must therefore know what they are doing.

The second approach stresses cultural heterogeneity, valuing differences but not, of course, to the point where integration would be threatened. The idea is that in this cultural climate, individuals are more likely to feel able to take ethical stands. It is expected that professionals will also have commitments to their professional associations and subcultures will criticise other subcultures. Advocates of this approach argue that ethical business behaviour ultimately stems from the conscience of individuals and will not be assured when a culture leans towards demanding single-minded conformity to the way things are done in their organisation.

Cultural heterogeneity is almost always both desirable and inevitable. However, cultural homogeneity is both likely and appropriate in small family firms and small entrepreneurial firms dominated by a power culture, or in solicitors' offices, barristers' chambers or architects' practices where the person culture prevails. Small branches of banks or building societies are also likely to have homogeneous cultures.

The idea of social responsibility also arises from the interdependence of organisations and their social environment. Certain areas of social responsibility, like employee and consumer protection, and

SOCIAL RESPONSIBILITY AND
ORGANISATIONAL CULTURE

environmental safeguards are regulated by law. But not everything can be legislated for, nor is the law of itself sufficient to make either managers or other organisational members behave in a socially responsible manner. Managing ethical matters through culture is therefore very important.

Aspects of social responsibility covered by the law include the following areas:

- Employees are safeguarded by the Health and Safety at Work Act (1970), and by equal opportunities and labour legislation. However, a glance at any newspaper will reveal cases of abuse of the law which have been brought to court and other examples of possible infringement of the law. For example, in September 1995, there is a case of a company hiring underage schoolgirls to work in a factory for £2.50 a day. The company is being investigated by the Health and Safety Executive. The law states that no one under 16 should work in a factory. In another recent case, some lettuce growers have been found to be using illegal pesticides that carry a sterility risk for the workers. The growers may be prosecuted and would be subject to unlimited fines if found guilty.

- The environment is safeguarded by the Environmental Protection Act (1990), but again this is abused. For example, in 1995 Britain's water companies were discharging sewage into the rivers killing wildlife. The National Rivers Authority has prosecuted but the companies continue to offend. By September, the ten privatised water companies had already been convicted 22 times. Although the companies have spent money on improving water and sewage treatment, they still need to do more. In another 1995 case of water pollution, many sea birds off the Yorkshire coast were killed by an oil slick resulting from a ship illegally cleaning its oil tanks at sea. The chances of tracking the culprit are remote and the fines, if it were caught and prosecuted, are small.

- Consumers are also protected by legislation on the safety of products, pricing, content, advertising etc., but some companies flaunt the rules. In 1995, food manufacturers have been reducing the size of cans of foods like baked beans, but retaining the same price, so effectively increasing the price.

In addition to the law, groups such as Friends of the Earth, Greenpeace and animal rights campaigners exert 'political' pressure on companies to act in a socially responsible way. The media can also exert pressure; for example, in 1995, a Sunday Times disclosure about the undervaluing of property, resulted in the Halifax Property Services, one of Britain's biggest chains of estate agents, abandoning a controversial scheme of paying bonuses to salesmen for persuading owners to cut the prices of their homes.

However, as you can see from the examples of breaking of the law, there is still an important role for culture to play in the ethical behaviour of companies.

ACTIVITY 3

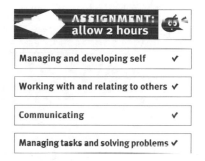

ASSIGNMENT: allow 2 hours	
Managing and developing self	✔
Working with and relating to others	✔
Communicating	✔
Managing tasks and solving problems	✔

Working in a small group, discuss to what extent you feel that there is a conflict between the pursuit of profits and ethical business behaviour.

Carry out some research by reading local and national newspapers, and watching or listening to the news and investigative programmes on television and radio. You will find many examples of companies either directly infringing the law or contravening 'the spirit' of the law. But you should also find many examples of companies creating an environment for ethical conduct and many examples of different regulatory bodies within industries that support – and, in some case, go beyond – legislation by establishing professional codes of conduct. The examples given so far should give you some ideas.

Look at all industry sectors, not just those that may appear more obviously contentious such as pharmaceuticals and the testing of drugs; or financial institutions that are dealing with people's money; or food manufacturing firms that supply what people eat. Almost all companies are in a situation where they have to exert some social responsibility because they exist in a real environment.

Summarise your discussion – with examples drawn from your research – in a 750-word report for your tutor. Summarise the key points in the box below.

Planning cultural diversity

Different cultures are appropriate in the same organisation at different stages of its life cycle. Different cultures can also be appropriate in different parts of the same organisation. Both of these points have implications for organisational design. As you saw in section one, one of the key questions that Child draws to the attention of organisational designers is: 'How should jobs and departments be grouped together?'

To further your understanding of this 'grouping', and of the different culture types, we now examine the different types of activity which tend to characterise different parts of organisations. It is only by looking to these that organisational leaders can plan for the appropriate mix of cultures.

Handy (1993, Understanding Organizations, 4th edn, Penguin) has isolated four principal activity types:

1. Some activities are routine, as opposed to non-routine and, in a large organisation are likely to account for the work of the greater proportion of personnel. Such routine activities include, for example, accounts, administration and most production and sales activities. It is suggested that a role culture is appropriate for those parts of organisations where these activities prevail.

2. Some activities are directed towards changing what the organisation does or the way that it does it. Such activities include, for example, corporate planning, organisation and method, the development side of production and certain aspects of marketing. It is suggested that a task culture is

appropriate for these parts of organisations where these activities prevail.

3. Some activities are directed towards dealing with the unexpected. Obviously those parts of the organisation that have the closest interface with the environment, like aspects of marketing and the middle levels of management are relevant here. It is suggested that power cultures are appropriate for those sectors and departments where such activities prevail.

4. Some activities are directed towards the overall guidance of all of the other activities. Such activities include, for example, priority selling, allocation of resources, initiating action and standard setting. It is argued that power cultures again, are appropriate where these activities prevail.

Organisations, then, should seek to differentiate their structures and cultures as appropriate to the dominant activities that take place in the different sectors. However, as we have already made clear, these subcultures must work together, and differentiation is only successful where there is also integration. Certainly, cultural heterogeneity is almost always both inevitable and desirable. However, underlying the unique contributions of each of the subcultures, there must be a commitment to the core values and basic assumptions of the wider organisation culture so that each is making its own distinctive contribution to the overall aims of the company.

The bottom line is that planned diversity must be managed so that the various organisational groupings, each dominated by different key activities, are effective.

summary

▶ An organisation's culture results from a number of factors: the impact of its founders, the impact of the internal environment, the impact of the external environment, the impact of current management and the impact of the national culture.

▶ Hofstede characterised different national cultures in terms of uncertainty avoidance, power distance, individualism and femininity.

▶ Culture helps to resolve problems of internal integration, by providing a common language, criteria for inclusion and exclusion, criteria for success and failure, and social guidelines.

▶ Culture can also help to resolve problems of external adaptation and survival. It helps to develop a common understanding of an organisation's mission and goals, the evaluation of meeting these goals and the strategies if the goals are not being met.

Culture and change

Objectives

After participating in this session, you should be able to:

▶ identify the influence of culture in organisational
performance

▶ understand the process of organisational culture
change.

In working through this session, you will practise the following
BTEC common skills:

Managing and developing self	✔
Working with and relating to others	✔
Communicating	✔
Managing tasks and solving problems	✔
Applying numeracy	
Applying technology	
Applying design and creativity	

Strength of an organisational culture

A culture can be regarded as strong or weak – examples of strong cultures are IBM and Japanese companies; examples of weak are a supermarket and a large production company. How can we say this? Is this an intuitive or a subjective judgement? Strength can be judged by the number of artefacts that are displayed by the organisation, or by the strength of agreement or consensus of individuals on core beliefs, values and basic assumptions.

Payne has done some work in this area (Payne R.L., (1990), 'The Concepts of culture and climate', Working Paper 202, Manchester Business School). Using a different approach, he categorised a culture as strong if it determined basic assumptions, less strong if it only determined values and beliefs, and weak if it determined attitude and behaviour (see figure 3.1). His 'strength of consensus among members' axis incorporates these factors.

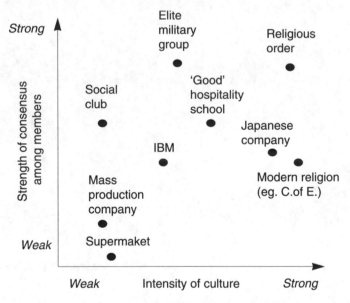

FIGURE 3.1: Examples of strong and weak cultures.
SOURCE: Brown, A., 1995, Organisational Culture, London: Pitman, p. 75.

The burst of interest shown in the idea of organisational cultures began in America. Commentators had been agonising about the economic success that Japan and other South East Asian countries enjoyed and unfavourable comparisons were being made between American and Japanese managers.

In contrast to their own traditional, rather bureaucratic organisations, Ouchi (1981, Theory Z: How American Business Can Meet the Japanese Challenge, Addison-Wesley) recommended to American managers the art of Japanese management. He argued that America's productivity problem would only be solved when managers learned to do their job in such a way that their employees could work together more effectively. Ouchi invited the managers to think of cultures, not only in terms of races or nations, but in terms of particular organisations.

Ouchi suggested that companies ought to become Theory Z organisations. In Ouchi's descriptions, Theory Z organisations display the following characteristics:

- an emphasis on long-term, even life-long, employment

- relatively slow processes of evaluation and promotion

- an emphasis on the development of company-specific skills and only a moderately specialised career path

- an emphasis on implicit, informal controls, but supported by formal explicit measures

- participative, consensus-oriented decision making but with the individual ultimately responsible

- a broad management concern for the welfare of their employees as a normal part of the working relationship

- an emphasis on informal relationships between organisational members.

In a climate ripe for new solutions, American managers began to focus on culture as a potential answer to some of their problems. Management texts started addressing the issue. In 1982, Corporate Culture by Deal and Kennedy explicitly focused on culture as an answer to organisational problems. And, in the same year, one of the most widely read management texts ever published appeared; it was written by Peters and Waterman (1982, In Search of Excellence, Harper & Row).

Peters and Waterman's message came as a boost to the confidence of American managers. It told them that the solution to their problems did not lie in the East, but in the cultural practices of the best American companies. The central message, which was echoed in a spate of American and English books which came out at that time, was that successful companies have strong cultures and these make a significant contribution to their commercial success. In Search of Excellence led managers to think about running their organisations as much through culture as through the traditional methods.

STRENGTH OF AN
ORGANISATIONAL CULTURE

Peters and Waterman examined successful American companies and concluded that it was their organisational cultures, incorporating eight characteristics of cultural excellence, that they all had in common and that had determined their success:

1. Bias for action – practical; get on with job; try it and see if it works; do not ask for permission.

2. Close to customer – get things right for the customers; learn from them.

3. Autonomy and entrepreneurship – many leaders and innovators; encourage ideas; trying is the thing, with success as a bonus.

4. Productivity through people – trust rather than control; people are the key to productivity; no 'us and them' attitudes.

5. Hands-on, value-driven – top people keep in touch with all aspects and areas of the organisation.

6. Stick to the knitting – stay close to core business.

7. Simple form, lean staff – simple structure; shallow hierarchy.

8. Simultaneous loose-tight controls – centralised values, loose formal controls, decentralised product development.

Watson (1994, In Search of Management: Culture, Chaos and Control in Managerial Work, Routledge) made the point that this eighth and final cultural characteristic underpins the others. It brings home the whole issue about placing the emphasis on managing through values rather than through structures and systems. The organisation does not tightly control through, for example, close policing, rules and closely prescribed roles; rather, the tightness comes from the organisational members themselves who choose to do what they are supposed to do because 'they wish to serve the values which they share with those in charge'. Unfortunately, the eight cultural characteristics came to be seen as a simple recipe for success. Obtain them, it was argued, and your organisation will perform well. Peters and Waterman themselves went on to advocate their ideas further into a flat, almost non-existent structure.

ACTIVITY 1

In small groups, discuss the following question: Why could managers be viewed as naive if they believed that obtaining Peters and Waterman's recommended cultural attributes would deliver success to their organisation?

Note your key points in the box below.

Commentary...

How many reasons occurred to you? The key one is that cultures, and their characteristic structures, are situationally determined. Cultures are contingent on circumstances. Peters and Waterman seemed to assume that there is one best organisational culture which is appropriate to all circumstances. So, while it is likely that a strong culture could give rise to patterns of behaviour which can help to promote success, the type of strong culture will presumably vary in different organisations in terms of their environmental context. The same strong culture cannot be appropriate in all circumstances.

Another important reason is that there is no simple causal relationship between strong cultures and organisational performance. Corporate economic success cannot depend only

STRENGTH OF AN
ORGANISATIONAL CULTURE

on the culture. What about changing environmental influences which render a once, perhaps 'excellence' culture, no longer appropriate?

In 1984, Business Week monitored the progress of the 'excellent' companies investigated by Peters and Waterman. Even then, only two years after the publication of their book, at least fourteen had gone into decline and Business Week's analysis suggested that in many cases the decline could be explained in terms of external factors.

Denison (1990, Corporate Culture and Organizational Effectiveness, Wiley) suggested that there are four different aspects of culture that affect an organisation's effectiveness and hence its performance:

1. consistency

2. involvement

3. adaptability

4. mission.

A consistent culture is what we also call a strong culture: basic assumptions, beliefs and values are shared solidly throughout the organisation. It is also likely to have a charismatic owner or leader. The culture allows alignment and achievement of organisational goals because of the sharing of basic assumptions. Employees (and managers) are likely to be 'pulling in the same direction'. Control and communication will be easy to achieve and there are few internal conflicts. Because of the sharing of a common language and way of doing things, communication is likely to be more effective as there will be less distortion in the process – everyone is communicating with a common theme.

Employees will be highly motivated as they can identify with the strong culture, its good parts and its bad parts. It is distinctive and it is 'theirs'. This type of culture also tends to foster employee participation. Employees have a set of rules and norms of behaviour that are easy to follow as they have been worked out over the years in a variety of organisational situations and through various change processes. In a strong culture, employees are contributing with maximum effort, and resources are not being dissipated on internal conflict.

The level of involvement – informal or formal – of the employees is also linked to organisational effectiveness. A project, task team or quality circles approach fosters this involvement as individuals have ownership and responsibility for a particular piece of work such as a new product. Individuals feel a greater commitment to the project and the organisation, perform better and require less control.

A culture has to fit into the organisational environment for high organisational effectiveness. This fit is affected by many internal and external factors and is subject to change, so unless the organisation successfully adapts it may mean short-term but not long-term success. The organisation's adaptability is a key factor in responding to the internal and external environment. An 'adaptable' organisation will be able to read changes and, with a positive adaptable workforce, it can restructure and respond to these changes.

Finally, a mission gives employee a shared objective for the organisation and contributes to effectiveness by giving them a sense of purpose and precise goals to meet.

Involvement and consistency are primarily concerned with the internal environment of the organisation; adaptability and mission are concerned with the external environment. Involvement and adaptability are concerned with flexibility and change; consistency and mission are concerned with stability and direction.

You should now be able to link the different aspects of culture, with the different aspects of organisational structure, and the requirements for adaptation and change in our changing environment. When we look at different models of organisational culture change, we will again see these links between culture and structure. We also know from earlier sessions that the structure changes with the organisation's growth and changes through its life cycle.

As different structures give rise to different cultures, the organisational structure needs to be designed to create the culture. With mechanistic structures, with a tall hierarchy, formal procedures and centralised decision making, the culture is likely to be predictable and stable, individuals have little autonomy and accept mainly authoritarian rules and procedures. With organic structures, the flatter, more informal, decentralised structure lends itself to innovation and flexibility with individuals having responsibility and control over their own actions and being involved in actively taking risks.

The structure and the culture need to match each other. Given the varied and diverse functional units within an organisation, and the varied types of tasks they perform with different types of personnel and with different types of environment, then you can see that different cultures will evolve in the functional sub-units. Those parts of the organisation that deal with a rapidly changing environment will be flexible task cultures, using Handy's classification. The operating core may follow more of a role culture.

To address some of the imbalance that these subcultures create, organisations may adopt a team approach, and create project or new product teams that can operate more flexibly in a bureaucratic organisation. Remember the Oticon case study (in the section four, session one); here the management adopted a team approach as a way of improving organisational effectiveness. Conversely, the study of Trevor Thompson (see Resource 1 at the back of the book) illustrates the problems that can arise in going from a team approach to a rule-based automated production process.

Autonomous work groups may also be involved within the operating core. Tasks can be arranged differently so that an individual team has responsibility for, say, production of a particular product. This is the approach taken in the Japanese automotive industry and now adopted in Britain. In the previous session, we saw this approach adopted at Jaguar. Again the group has responsibility for its own actions, but it may generate its own norms and behaviours outside of the corporate culture.

Quality circles are voluntary groups of workers with shared responsibility. They occur extensively in Japan. Management often helps in their formation and in their running by helping with communication skills and problem-solving strategies. Though informal and voluntary groupings, quality circles need to be acknowledged by management who can also use them to their own ends for fostering corporate culture.

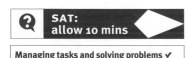

SAT:
allow 10 mins

Managing tasks and solving problems ✔

ACTIVITY 2

Look back at the research you undertook on your chosen organisation. Comment on the 'strength' of the culture in the organisation. Describe the organisation in terms of some of the cultural characteristics introduced in this session.

Commentary...

You may have described your chosen organisation as a weak culture, if there does not seem to be many visible signs of culture or a person that epitomises it, or there does not seem to be a common approach among your interviewees about what the company's business is and how it functions.

You may have described it as a strong culture if your interviewees could identify many examples of the culture, for example, logos, uniform, canteen facilities for all staff, many social outings for all staff, or a strong identification with a charismatic leader; or if they identified a common cause throughout the organisation, perhaps it is charity or a political group, and all employees share the same concern about a particular issue. There may be good team or departmental sub-cultures.

Managing culture

Before we go on to look at the organisational culture change process in detail, we take a brief look at managing culture itself, and remind ourselves of some of the pertinent issues about culture.

Following the impact of In Search of Excellence, numerous texts advising management how best to manage through values were published. Whether the writers took the position that it was relatively easy or difficult, depended very much upon how they conceptualised culture. There are basically two approaches.

MANAGING CULTURE

The more popular view held that organisational cultures are just another organisational characteristic like size and, as such, can be varied more or less at will. In this view, organisations have cultures which can be managed with relative ease.

The alternative approach held that organisations are cultures and that these given cultures are difficult to manage. This second idea is closer to the notion of culture used by social anthropologists. They use the term culture when referring to the different ways in which groups and societies live and operate. And within this meaning, organisations are regarded as mini-societies with their own characteristic way of life. Organisations then are cultures, and the culture's basic assumptions, common values and beliefs, shared meanings and actions have developed, and are developing, in response to changing shared pressures and, indeed, are solutions to the problems associated with these pressures. The organisation, as a culture, provides its members with identity, security, belonging, order and a way of making sense of the 'world'. Threats to the culture from any source, especially when it is strong, are threats to all of these things and are likely to be deeply unsettling. From this perspective on culture, managers are a part of this way of life. Culture is not something in their hands which can be changed at will.

This second view does not imply that organisational cultures cannot be managed but, rather, that the process is much more difficult than some commentators are prepared to admit. For example, Pettigrew (1990, 'Is corporate culture manageable?', in D.C. Wilson and R.H. Rosenfeld (eds) Managing Organisations: Test, Readings and Cases, McGraw-Hill) has listed seven factors which make organisational culture hard to manage:

1. The levels issue – there are three levels of culture: tangible elements of culture, values and basic assumptions. Obviously, the deeper the level the more difficult it is to change.

2. The pervasiveness issue – culture is not only deep but it is also broad. It is manifested, for example, in the mission, structures and systems, recruitment, selection, induction and training, socialisation in all of its other forms, appraisals and rewards, relationships, values and assumptions.

3. The implicitness issue – culture is partly unconscious. It is obviously quite difficult to change that which is rarely, or perhaps never, explicitly considered.

4. The imprinting issue – the weight of history, in one form or another, still leaves its imprint on the present and indeed, potentially, the future.

5. The political issue – this is the connection between culture and power groups in the organisation. It may be, for example, that certain groups have a vested interest in preserving the entrenched culture which organisational leaders are seeking to change. These groups are unlikely to submit peacefully to any change or management of the culture which threatens their position.

6. The plurality issue – different sub-cultures within the organisation may be differently affected by change.

7. The interdependence issue – the organisation's priorities, politics, structures, systems, processes and members are all interconnected with the culture.

There are only two of these issues which you have not met before – the political issue and the plurality issue – and these are interrelated. The following case study should help you to understand them better.

BUTCHER AND BUTCHER

Prior to 1990, Butcher and Butcher manufactured wooden window frames and wooden doors. The organisation was structured into three functions as illustrated in figure 3.2.

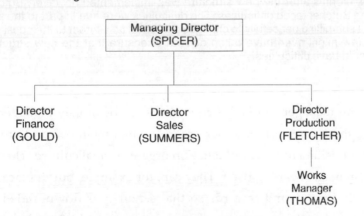

FIGURE 3.2: Butcher and Butcher's pre-1990 structure.

In 1990, the directors decided to enter a new product area by manufacturing PVC windows and patio doors. It was decided that a matrix form of organisation structure was the most appropriate structural design to help the company through this difficult transition in its manufacturing process (see figure 3.3). Two production teams were created, one for the existing wooden products and one for the new plastic product range.

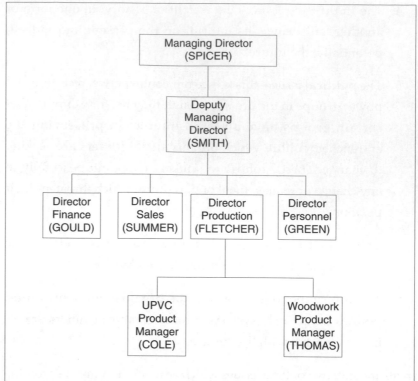

FIGURE 3.3: Butcher and Butcher's revised structure.

The decision to develop a new product area was made at director level with little consultation. Nobody had thought to ask the management and other employees how they might feel about this move. Their expertise and skills, and indeed their careers, lay in wood. Suddenly, the reorganisation of the company and its future direction could be perceived as a threat. Some employees may well have felt that they had a vested interest in preserving the traditional culture which the organisational leaders above them wanted to change.

Six months after the new structure was implemented however, Butcher and Butcher faced difficulties. The difficulties were due in part to the staff not submitting peacefully to changes perceived as a threat to their position. A few might even have taken actions to ensure that the new structure would have difficulties.

Culture management is difficult. However, obviously managers do have more control than other organisational members and are in a better position to exert influence on organisational culture. They can also manage meaning itself. They can, for example, put in place new criteria for pay and rewards so that seniority is downgraded and excellent performance in what they deem to be key activities rewarded. And this can be given intense visibility through ceremonies which can be pure theatre. Managers can plan the setting, the props, the lighting, the ritual behaviour and speech making and, of course, be there at the centre.

ACTIVITY 3

Resource 5 (in the back of the book) contains an account of the post-war history of Jaguar Cars. Read the article and review how the company sought to meet and manage changes in its environment. Comment on how Jaguar's culture has changed since 1945. Write a 500-word report on the changes at Jaguar and submit it to your tutor. Outline the key points in the box below.

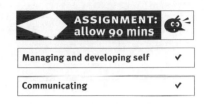

ASSIGNMENT:
allow 90 mins

| Managing and developing self | ✔ |
| Communicating | ✔ |

ORGANISATIONAL CULTURE

CHANGE

Organisational culture change

Throughout this book, change has been a recurring theme – as part of an organisation's effectiveness and performance, and as part of its adaptation and flexibility to the changing environment. We studied the process of change, its management and the resistance that change encounters in section two. We have also looked at change in relation to culture.

Changing culture itself is obviously tricky as it concerns people's values and beliefs, and norms of behaviour and may include the basic assumptions of the organisation. It is not the same as changing a procedure or introducing a new technology, because it forms part of the change itself.

We have already discussed some of the factors that initiate change – in the internal environment, and in the specific or general environment. We have looked at the types of change that are required during an organisation's life cycle, with changes in size, technology, complexity, top management, products, and competitors. We have also discussed routine and non-routine changes, how to implement them, and the role of the communication process in implementation.

Now we consider how to implement culture change. Several models of culture change have been developed by researchers that can help with the implementation of change within organisations. Before we look at these models of culture change, we first need to identify what these models have used as criteria for describing the change.

Change can usefully be described in terms of four criteria:

1. The size or scale of change is significant. Change may be small, incremental or first-order, or large, radical or second-order.

2. Change may be at varying levels: departmental, organisational, industry-wide or nationwide.

3. Change may be at varying levels within the organisation as far as the individual is concerned. It may concern their beliefs and values, or the basic assumptions of the organisation or just at behavioural level. If it concerns the latter, the change may eventually become part of the beliefs and values.

4. Change occurs over different time-scales. However, because change will occur at different rates in different parts of the organisation depending on how that part is affected, time-scale is a very complex variable.

Models for understanding culture change

We now look at five models of culture change:

1. Lundberg's model

2. Dyer's model of cultural evolution

3. Schein's life cycle model

4. Gagliardi's model

5. the composite model.

We have already met some of the ideas that underpin these models in section two, but now consider each in some depth.

LUNDBERG'S MODEL

Lundberg (1985, 'On the feasibility of cultural intervention', in P.J. Frost, L.F. Moore, M.R. Louis, C.C. Lundberg and J. Martin (eds) Organizational Culture, Sage, pp. 169–85) proposed a learning cycle of culture change following some kind of triggering event. Consider a large differentiated organisation with many subcultures. For change to occur, he suggests that two external factors are required:

1. domain forgiveness (i.e the degree of environmental uncertainty)

2. organisation-domain congruence. If there is a big gap in the congruence between the organisation and its environment or domain then the change is seen as too risky or unnecessary.

He identifies four internal conditions that allow change:

1. Sufficient change resources
   These might be the right personnel for any changes in job function, the right raw materials for making a new product, or sufficient funding for a new marketing approach. In 1995, Asda, the supermarket chain announced plans for new superstores and hypermarkets to compete with the supermarket giants – Tesco, Sainsbury and Safeway. However, it estimated it would need capital of £300 million for this redevelopment.

2. System readiness
   People are ready and willing to change. Otherwise, they realise, their jobs, or the company could be in jeopardy.

MODELS FOR UNDERSTANDING

CULTURE CHANGE

3. Communication and control mechanisms that are available to facilitate change

4. Leadership, and a team with appropriate skills to guide transition

In September 1995, Robert Allen, Chairman of AT&T, the telecommunications giant announced plans to split the company into three separate entities and to pull out of the PC business. He will need to exercise leadership to guide the company forward, especially since it will mean a loss of around 9,000 jobs. The structure and culture will need to adapt to the new strategy.

Lundberg identifies four types of precipitating pressures:

1. unusual demands for performance or production, e.g. a competitor brings out a new product or opens a new outlet

2. pressures from government, the public, etc. in the organisation's specific environment

3. pressures from organisational growth, e.g. AT&T's decision to divide into three separate companies is based on a perception that it has become too big in its present form

4. pressure from a crisis in the specific or general environment, e.g. a lack of raw materials or a shortage of staff with the necessary skills.

He identifies five triggering events:

1. Environmental calamities, e.g. recession
   The 1990s have seen world-wide recession affecting employment, global trading, inflation, etc.

2. Environmental opportunities
   These may be generated by new technology, for example, or new sources of funding. In Britain, many organisations have been rescued by money from the National Lottery. The Royal Court Theatre in London has been awarded £16 million which will be used for refurbishment of the theatre and will save it from closure.

3. Internal revolutions
   These may be caused by a change of leadership. In June 1995, the clothing and furnishing group, Laura Ashley, hired Ann Iverson as chief executive. By September, she had replaced five directors. She intends to close some stores and expand others in good locations as part of a drive to increase the company's

profits. She will eventually change the whole structure and culture of the organisation.

4. External revolution, e.g. legislation
    In September 1995, the European Commission drew up a new set of safety measures for vehicles aimed at reducing environmental pollution as well as increasing safety. If these are ratified, they could have far reaching effects for manufacturers of cars, vehicles and associated parts.

5. Managerial crisis
    This may result from incompetence or panic. We have all seen football managers come and go each season as the team succeeds or fails and the club's directors search for quick remedies.

Lundberg sees the change process as going through a number of steps starting with a cultural visioning of what the result will be, then implementation through a cultural change strategy, which involves inducement action that counter resistance and enhance readiness for change, including management actions that redefine the new culture, and stabilisation action that may mean devising new slogans, logos, training programmes, selection and recruitment procedures. He accepts that if culture change is to occur then basic assumptions need to be changed not just the visible signs. It is an iterative procedure, i.e. one repeated again and again, to induce a cultural revolution.

In his Pizza Company, Jonathan will need to change the culture from a craft-based supportive team approach with him at the helm to one that is appropriate for a mass-production factory. He will have to generate a new approach for the semi-skilled operators, and he will only be able to build this up over time with different selection and induction procedures, different working guidelines, etc.

Lundberg does not provide many answers to the many questions surrounding change, but at least he indicates how difficult it can be.

DYER'S CYCLE OF CULTURAL EVOLUTION

Dyer (1985, 'The cycle of cultural evolution in organizations', in R.H. Kilman, M.J. Saxton, R. Sherpa and associates (eds) Gaining Control of the Corporate Culture, Jossey Bass, pp. 200–29) formulated a model for large-scale change based on visible signs, rules and norms, values, and basic assumptions. It is a cycle of organisational change that tends to operate after an internal crisis and the arrival of a new leader. It is dependent on the vision supplied by the new leader and the

MODELS FOR UNDERSTANDING

CULTURE CHANGE

leadership team. Remember the new leader that was brought into Oticon to implement the major changes.

At Laura Ashley, Ann Iverson is applying 'a new broom'. She is making significant changes particularly at director level. However, she cannot dismiss all the staff, and part of 'Dyer's cycle' involves the acceptance of her new direction and culture of the company by the remaining staff. This then leads to her culture and vision for the company becoming the new way of doing things.

SCHEIN'S LIFE CYCLE MODEL

Schein (1985, 'How culture forms, develops, and changes', in R.H. Kilman, M.J. Saxton, R. Sherpa and associates (eds) Gaining Control of the Corporate Culture, Jossey Bass, pp. 17–43) identified phases of growth that an organisation passes through. Each phase is associated with a different sort of culture serving different sorts of functions (see table 3.1).

The first phase is birth and early growth when the organisation is in simple entrepreneurial mode. Culture change will probably only become an issue if the organisation has financial problems or there is a problem with the owner. If required there are four mechanisms that may enable it to change:

1. natural evolution

2. self-guided evolution through organisational therapy

3. managed evolution through hybrids

4. managed 'revolution' through outsiders.

An organisation may use one or all of these four mechanisms.

The second phase is organisational mid-life when the organisation is well established and has a complex diversified operation. Culture is also established, with strong subcultures too. Schein identifies four mechanisms whereby change can occur:

1. planned change and organisational development – unfreezing, changing and refreezing the organisation

2. technological seduction – change in work tasks, behavioural interrelationships with new technology, and also any changes in organisational goals and mission

SCHEIN'S LIFE CYCLE MODEL

Schein (1985, 'How

Growth stage	Function of culture	Mechanism of change
Birth and early growth • Founder domination, possibly family domination *Succession phase:*	• Culture is a distinctive competence and source of identity • Culture is the 'glue' that holds organisation together • Organisation strives towards more integration and clarity • Heavy emphasis on socialisation as evidence of commitment • Culture becomes battleground between conservatives and liberals • Potential successors are judged on whether they will preserve or change cultural elements	1. Natural evolution 2. Self-guided evolution through therapy 3. Managed evolution through hybrids 4. Managed 'revolution' through outsiders
Organisational midlife • New product development • Vertical integration • Geographic expansion • Acquisitions, mergers	• Cultural integration declines as new sub-cultures are spawned • Crisis of identity, loss of key goals, values and assumptions • Opportunity to manage direction of cultural change	5. Planned change and organisational development 6. Technological seduction 7. Change through scandal, explosion of myth 8. Incrementalism
Organisational maturity • Maturity of markets • Internal stability or stagnation • Lack of motivator to change *Transformation option:* *Destruction option:* • Bankruptcy and reorganisation • Takeover and reorganisation • Merger and assimilation	• Culture becomes a constraint on innovation • Culture preserves the glories of the past, hence is valued as a source of self-esteem, defence • Culture change necessary and inevitable, but not all elements of culture can or must change • Essential elements of culture must be identified, preserved • Culture change can be managed or simply be allowed to evolve • Culture changes at basic levels • Culture changes through massive replacement of key people	9. Coercive persuasion 10. Turnaround 11. Reorganisation, destruction and rebirth

TABLE 3.1: Schein's stages of growth, functions of culture and change mechanisms. SOURCE: Schein (1985).

3. change through scandal – an organisation which apparently supports values and beliefs is caught doing the opposite, e.g. polluting the environment when it is supposed to be a 'green' organisation

4. incrementalism – leaders make changes in the basic long-term assumptions by making very small operational changes.

The third phase is organisational maturity when the organisation is stable, and lacks the motivation to change. Culture may become dysfunctional if there is little dynamism or flexibility. The only ways to change are by a complete turnaround and large rapid changes or a complete reorganisation through a merger or takeover. Change may be by:

- coercive persuasion, instruction by top management

- turnaround, a combination of leadership, effective change management, and employee participation.

The fourth phase is reorganisation, destruction and rebirth.

Schein's framework is a useful way of approaching change through the organisation's life cycle. Remember how this affected the organisational structures, too.

GAGLIARDI'S MODEL

Gagliardi (1986, 'The creation and change or organisational cultures: A conceptual framework', Organization Studies, 7(2), 117–34) based his model on the notion that culture is basic assumptions and values, and visible aspects are secondary. Gagliardi sees that:

- culture changes incrementally and depends on the development of values from the leader's vision and initial power to implement change within the organisation

- subsequent organisational experience confirms the value

- the value is accepted and shared throughout the organisation and then becomes the basic assumption.

For example, when he first started the Pizza Company, Jonathan's vision was that he would make the highest quality pizzas. He was able to achieve this by setting the quality criteria for his craft bakers and directly supervising their work. As they made quality pizzas, the bakers became used to the notion that they produced the best regardless of the time and effort involved, and it became a basic assumption. With this model, you can see that Jonathan will find it hard to change the basic assumption that he is producing quality individual pizzas to just a hand-finished mass-produced pizza. And this cultural problem may be more important to the craft bakers than the actual changes in their job function or in physical manifestations of status.

For Gagliardi, culture change is one process that is driven by the leader's vision, and reinforced by his symbols and myths.

THE COMPOSITE MODEL

This model is based on the work of Lewin. We studied his three-phase model for change in section two (1952, Lewin, K., Field Theory in Social Science, Tavistock). Lewin sees his unfreezing, experimentation and refreezing phases as being associated with certain social behaviours or rites within the organisation and also a particular cognitive state. He sees the organisation in an equilibrium between driving and restraining forces. His force-field analysis seeks to reduce the driving forces that activate the restraining forces. The three phases are summarised in table 3.2.

Contextual	Social	Cognitive
Unfreezing mechanisms	Rites of questioning and destruction	Anticipation
	Rites of rationalisation and legitimation	
Experimentation	Rites of degradation and conflict	Confirmation
Refeezing mechanisms	Rites of integration and conflict reduction	Aftermath

TABLE 3.2: The composite model for understanding organisational culture change.
SOURCE: Roberts, H. and Brown, A.D., 1992, 'Cognitive and social dimensions of IT implementation', paper presented at the British Academy of Management, Annual Conference, Bradford, 14–16 September.

Lewin's original model has been modified by Schein (1964, 'The mechanism of change', in W.G. Bennis et al., (eds) Interpersonal Dynamics, Dorsey Press, pp. 199–213), Beyer and Trice (1988, 'The communication of power relations in organisations through cultural rites', in M.D. Jones, M.D. Moore and R.C. Sayder (eds) Inside Organizations: Understanding the Human Dimension, Sage, pp. 141–57) and Isabella (1990, 'Evolving interpretations as a change unfolds: How managers construe key organizational events', Academy of Management Journal, 33(1), 7–41).

This model is applicable not just to culture but to change of any type: it can apply to individuals, functional departments or the organisation as a whole. Parts of the organisation or individuals within it need not necessarily be at the same phase at the same time. For example, if technology is introduced into an organisation, it will affect departments differently, it may affect how the operating core does its actual job initially, but have a much lesser and later effect on marketing. This model provides a more detailed view of what is actually happening in the organisation when it is going through a culture change.

The unfreezing mechanisms could include presentations (either directly or by outside consultants) to employees to explain the problems, training and education programmes and involvement by top management. The next phase could include the establishment of the new systems and procedures and initiation of the employees into the new ways. In the final refreezing stage, the new ways of doing things become stable, and employees are starting to forget the old ways and regard the new ways as the 'best'.

All five of these models of organisational culture change share some common factors:

- a crisis triggers the initial change

- the leader is instrumental in making the change work

- if the organisation and individuals believe in the success of the changes, they are more likely to work

- the organisation learns about itself and its environment through change.

These models help us to understand culture change, but only partially identify when, how and what actually happens, in this very complex process. More appropriate models could be developed that take into account three culture-related factors:

1. availability of other cultures

2. the individual's level of commitment

3. the flexibility of the existing culture.

RECALL:
allow 20 mins

Identify the main features for each of the following culture change models.

Lundberg's model

Dyer's model

Schein's model

Gagliardi's model

and Composite model

Managing culture change

We discussed in section two how organisations can manage structural change. By comparison, managing culture change is more difficult because it involves not only changing an individual's behaviour but also the underlying values and basic assumptions of the organisation.

However, it can be done. We have already looked at some models of change that identify certain characteristics of culture change. There is also a framework that we can follow for change implementation, and there are ways of overcoming resistance to change. Table 3.3 summarises some general principles and guidelines to give us a starting point for our investigation.

From their review of the culture management literature Hassard and Sharifi suggest the following general principles and guidelines:

- Organisations possess values and assumptions which define accepted and appropriate patterns of behaviour.
- Successful organisations tend to be those which possess assumptions and values which encourage behaviours consonant with the organisational strategy.
- Successful culture change may be difficult to achieve if the prevailing values and behaviour are incompatible with strategy.
- If an organisation is contemplating change it first needs to check to see whether the strategy demands a shift in values or assumptions or whether change can be achieved using other means.
- Senior management must understand the implications of the new culture for their own behaviour and be involved in all the main change phases.
- Culture change programmes must pay special attention to an organisation's 'opinion leaders'.
- Change programmes must also take an organisation's culture transmission mechanisms (such as management style, work systems and employment policies) into account.
- In order to create a change in culture, channels should be programmed with new messages and old, contradictory ones eliminated.
- Every opportunity should be taken to reinforce the key messages of the new values and assumptions.

Qualifications

- The deeper the level of cultural change required (artifacts being the most superficial and assumptions being the deepest), then the more difficult and time-consuming the culture change programme is likely to be.
- If there are multiple cultures and subcultures then this will make the change programme still more difficult and time-consuming.
- Some of the easiest changes to effect are alterations in behavioural norms.
- Managing the deepest layers of an organisational culture requires a participative approach.
- A top-down approach may work when there is only a single culture or when the focus is on changing norms rather than assumptions.
- Top-down approaches yield changes that may be difficult to sustain in the long term because they produce overt compliance but not acceptance.
- Participative approaches are most likely to be successful and are the only real option if assumptions are to be altered. However, they are difficult to implement and extremely time-consuming to enact.

TABLE 3.3: Hassard and Sharifi's general principles and guidelines of cultural change.

SOURCE: Hassard, J. and Sharifi, S., 1989, 'Corporate culture and strategic change', Journal of General Management, 15(2), 4–19.

We introduced the idea of resistance to change that is encountered on an individual and an organisational level in section two and described strategies to cope with this resistance. At an organisational level, one major resistance is the culture itself. And the more major the change the greater the resistance – something that is only changing a behavioural pattern will be much more acceptable than something that is changing a basic assumption. The level of resistance is also likely to be greater in strong cultures than in weak ones.

Sathe (1985, Culture and Related Corporate Realities, Irwin) suggested the following relationship to sum up the amount of cultural resistance that we are likely to encounter. Resistance to culture change is a product of the size of change and the strength of the existing culture.

Kilmann (1984, Beyond the Quick Fix: Managing Five Tracks to Organizational Success, Jossey Bass) has suggested five steps for managing culture change:

1. surfacing actual norms (for norms read culture)

2. devising new directions

3. establishing new norms

4. identifying culture gaps

5. closing the gaps.

This is a very simple way of defining a very complex process. In the models of organisational culture change, you looked at different ideas that concerned culture at the visible level and the basic assumption level. Both levels are affected by the individual's organisational life and their leader. The ways in which an employee is hired, trained, evaluated and remunerated are an integral part of the individual's organisational life and are instrumental in developing culture.

The leader, as you have seen, is instrumental in implementation of change. So this gives us two ways of managing the change either through the human resources management approach or through the strong leadership approach.

HUMAN RESOURCE MANAGEMENT

A human resources department, if it exists, can be instrumental in the implementation of change because it controls several aspects of the individual's organisational life that form part of the culture. (See the companion workbook Managing People and Activities.) These include:

- recruitment and selection procedures, that start the process of establishing the culture in the eyes of the new employee

- induction, socialisation and training, that continue the process once the new employee has started with the company

- performance appraisal systems, that control and reward employees fairly

- reward systems, that reinforce organisational values, and assumptions, by rewarding performance of individuals and teams, also reinforce the culture.

With care, these procedures can be used to implement culture change. Let us consider Jonathan's Pizza Company again. In the early days, there would have been no human resources department. Jonathan will have drawn up many of these personnel requirements himself. When he comes to make the big production change, he can start any new employees on the right track for the new company's culture. The evaluation of their performance and the remuneration system will also be changed and modified to the new tasks and general operation of the company. Using the human resources approach will probably not work with the existing bakers, so he will have to rely on his leadership skills to persuade them to accept the changes.

LEADERSHIP

The organisation's leader is instrumental in the change process. It is his or her vision that sets the future direction of the company. And through top management decisions, tasks are reallocated, job functions are changed, the organisation is restructured and resources reallocated. Leaders can implement the culture change by using symbols and social behaviours or rites.

Symbols concern how top executives spend their time in the organisation and what they are seen to be doing by the workforce. They include the language they use when describing changes. Meetings, agendas and minutes and the settings of particular meetings are also important signals to employees.

Jonathan may have earned the respect of his craft bakers because he will stay late and get 'his hands dirty' to meet an order; so, when the major change comes they will be more prepared to follow his lead, especially if he is still seen to be coming to the shop floor and not hidden away in a grand office.

Rites are planned activities that communicate cultural messages, e.g. visible public promotion or demotion, sports competitions to reduce conflict between departments, the annual dinner with public rewards or team-building training programmes.

Jonathan may choose to announce the new changes at an annual company dinner, describing them as a positive step both for the company and for the employees. He may use the occasion to encourage staff to stay with him and this vibrant growing company. He may set up management training programmes for some of the bakers and use their experience to manage the company into the future.

MODEL FOR MANAGEMENT OF CULTURE CHANGE

We now briefly look at a model for organisational change developed by Silverzweig and Allen (1976, 'Changing the corporate culture', Sloan Management Review, 17(3), 33–49). This model allows us to bring together all the relevant factors about culture and change and its management. However, this model concentrates on the more visible signs of culture and does not address changing values and basic assumptions.

This model sees the change process as four interlinking circles:

1. The first phase identifies the change from the existing to the required state.

2. The second is a rather vague phase for employees to experiment with the new culture and to voice concerns probably through a workshop situation.

3. The third phase is actual implementation of the change.

4. The fourth is evaluating and sustaining the final culture.

Silverzweig and Allen suggest some critical areas that influence the result:

- the leader and his or her power throughout the organisation

- work-teams or departments having their own subcultures that need to be addressed

- not all departments being affected by the changes at the same time or to the same extent

- the need for information and communication processes to be effective for conveying details of the change

- the need to allow employees to ask questions and to be given feedback

- the need to address performance and reward systems, as these will reinforce the structural and cultural changes

- organisational structures, policies and procedures which will need adjusting and documenting

- training and orientation which will be required throughout the change process

- the need for sufficient resources for new job functions, the change itself, communication, training and education, new corporate image etc. (AT&T is expecting that its restructuring into three separate companies will cost US$1.5 billion)

- the need for special help for the supervisory level between the workforce and middle management – these first-level supervisors are between the culture of the management and the culture of the workforce, and will be the first to feel the effects of problems with the changes or dissatisfaction from the workforce

- the need to monitor results of the changes and to set up a system to feed back information to individuals and management.

You will have come across many of these already.

ORGANISATIONAL DEVELOPMENT

The whole process of managing organisational culture change is known as organisational development. Stoner and Freeman (1989, Management, 4th edn, Prentice Hall, p. 374) define organisational development as 'a long-range effort supported by top management to increase an organisation's problem-solving and renewal process through effective management of organisational culture'.

Organisational development may involve structure and technology, but it is primarily concerned with people. It may involve the use of outside consultants at various stages of the process; outsiders often have a clearer view of the company and what needs to be done, and the implementation of any change can sometimes be easier and more effective via a third party.

Organisational development involves collaborative management through employee participation and power sharing rather than through hierarchical authority. It also involves action research – the method through which change agents learn what improvements are needed and how change can best be achieved. Action research involves:

- identification of the problems

- data gathering to support change

- feedback of data to employees and managers

- investigation of data by employees and managers

- planning action

- implementing action.

Plans are implemented at various levels, and different approaches are suitable for different levels. These include:

- sensitivity training at individual level, where individuals are guided by a trainer in groups to develop interpersonal skills

- transaction analysis for two or three people, where groups are trained in sending clear and unambiguous messages and in developing communication skills

- process consultation for teams or groups, where a consultant works with teams and groups within the organisation, and through team-building techniques enhances effectiveness of the organisation by breaking down internal team barriers, improving the achievement of the team's tasks, and improving inter-team relationships

- confrontation meetings between groups, where inter-group relationships are improved by direct confrontation with group leaders

- survey evidence fed back to the organisation – data is collected from everyone in the organisation, and results are fed back through the organisational structure to individual members again, allowing employees to feel part of the change process and to have been allowed input which can be used to overcome some of the barriers in implementation.

PATTERSON TRANSPORT

Patterson Transport is an independent road haulage company. The company operates 40 lorries, with 46 drivers, six mechanics and five administrative staff. Most of the company's work comprises transporting road-making materials for major construction firms.

Ted Patterson, the owner, makes all the management decisions and carries out all the management functions. He employs a bookkeeper to keep the accounts and administer the wages, two clerks, and a shorthand typist. Most of Ted's time is spent negotiating contracts with construction firms or planning the operating schedules for the fleet of lorries. In the latter task, he is assisted by 35-year-old Reg Morris, a former driver who suffered an injury to his spine, as the result of falling off a ladder while painting his house. Over the years, it has become the custom for Reg to prepare the operating schedule sheets and for Ted to merely sign them for issue to the drivers.

Ted recently decided that he could no longer keep in touch with all aspects of his business and needed to appoint someone to assist him in running the company. He created the post of operations manager, to take responsibility for all vehicle schedules and maintenance. When he heard about the new job, Reg asked Ted if he could fill the post but was told by Ted that he needed someone with management experience.

David Lane was appointed to fill the post. Twenty-seven years old, David had a Higher National Diploma in Business Studies, specialising in transport studies, and previously worked as assistant manager of the contract department of one of Ted's customers. David was engaged to marry Ted's only child, Susan, and Ted hopes that he will eventually take over running the company so that he can retire. To provide an office for David, Reg was moved from the room he occupied and provided with a desk in the general office, where the other administrative staff worked. Reg was assigned the task of maintaining the company's filing system.

During the first month in post, David became aware that absenteeism among the drivers had increased. On 14 occasions, drivers had failed to work to the schedules David had issued, complaining that the schedules were impossible to follow and that they demonstrated ignorance of the transport business. In fact, the schedules were identical to schedules that the drivers had followed, without comment, in the past. David decided to take no action, in the hope that the situation would improve as the drivers became accustomed to his appointment.

Two months later the situation had not improved; absenteeism and lateness among the drivers continued, and schedules were not being kept. David convened a meeting of all the drivers and mechanics. He opened the meeting by outlining the present position on absenteeism and time-keeping, and he explained that they were meeting to explore why the present situation had arisen and what could be done to improve matters. David voiced his belief in democratic management and said that they could best achieve the goals of the company through the co-operative efforts of the drivers, mechanics and himself.

David asked for comments on the issues of time-keeping, absenteeism and the work schedules but no comments were forthcoming. He attempted to evoke comments by mentioning that they now found it impossible to follow schedules which were the same as ones previously worked. He suggested increases in traffic and revised one-way systems as possible causes, but still no comments followed. David felt frustrated by the lack of response. He asked everybody to give these matters some thought, and said that he would call a meeting in a week's time to discuss them.

After the meeting ended, the drivers and mechanics regrouped informally. The two recurrent themes in their discussions were that Lane had been foisted on them because he was marrying Ted's daughter and that the right person for the operations manager post was Reg.

ACTIVITY 4

Read the case study about Patterson Transport. In small groups, discuss how the company dealt with the appointment of David Lane.

Based on what you discussed, each write a 500-word report to answer the following questions:

1. What was the culture at Patterson Transport before and after David Lane's appointment?

2. How could the appointment of David Lane have been handled better?

3. How do you think the current situation can be best resolved? Discuss alternatives and explain your choice of option.

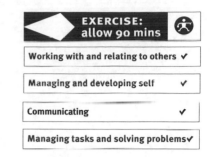

EXERCISE:
allow 90 mins

Working with and relating to others	✔
Managing and developing self	✔
Communicating	✔
Managing tasks and solving problems	✔

summary

▶ An organisation's culture contributes to its effectiveness and performance. In particular, four different aspects of culture affect an organisation's effectiveness: consistency, involvement, adaptability and mission.

▶ Culture can be managed. However, changing organisational culture is not easy because it involves not only changing an individual's behaviour but also the underlying values and basic assumptions of the organisation.

▶ There are several models of organisational culture change that look at culture on different levels and from different perspectives.

▶ Models of organisational culture change share some common features: a crisis triggers the initial change; the leader is instrumental in making the change work; if the organisation and individuals believe in the success of the changes, they are more likely to work; and the organisation learns about itself and its environment through change.

▶ Human resource management and leadership are crucial in the implementation of change.

▶ Organisational development is concerned with using organisational culture change to increase an organisation's effectiveness.

Resources

Resources

Trevor Thompson Company

The Trevor Thompson Company specialises in making fishing rods. Trevor formed the company, with a staff of five, about ten years ago to produce a new style fishing rod which he had designed. The rod was a success and, gradually, the workforce was expanded to accommodate increasing demand. The workers are mainly women, most recruited straight from school.

They work in teams of four to assemble, inspect and package a fishing rod from start to finish. The whole of the production area is partitioned so that each team works in a separate area. The walls of the partitions are decorated with posters of pop stars and with holiday postcards.

The expansion has been achieved by forming new teams comprising one experienced worker, selected from a list of volunteers, and three newly recruited employees. Workers receive a basic wage and a group bonus which increases with the number of rods produced. Newly formed teams receive an additional learning bonus for the first three months after formation.

Each team takes charge of its own quality control and discipline. If the performance of a team member falls below standard, the team decides what, if any, action is to be taken. In extreme cases, the team leader might ask the production foreperson to have an individual removed from the team. At work, team members chat mainly about their social life, and very rarely about task or company matters.

Around twelve months ago, Trevor designed another rod specifically for night fishing.

Research carried out by a consultant indicated that there was a market for the new rod. Trevor decided to put the night fishing rod into production as an addition to the company's range. Acting on the advice of the marketing consultant, Trevor decided to call in an engineering consultant for expert advice on manufacturing the new rod. The consultant recommended a flow-line production process to manufacture both the old and new rods. Trevor accepted the recommendation and secured a bank loan to finance the re-engineering of the whole production process.

To avoid a loss of production, the new manufacturing layout was introduced during the two weeks the company closed for the annual summer holiday. The workers were told that some changes would take place while they were on holiday and that there would be, in the words of Trevor, 'a nice surprise' awaiting them on their return from holiday. Most workers assumed that the production area was going to be redecorated, and removed any postcards and posters that they wished to keep.

Under the flow-line process, the manufacture of a fishing rod is broken down into five elements. Each element is given to one worker to perform. Each worker sits in line alongside a track which is in continuous motion. The basic rods are automatically fed onto the track and, in turn, each worker completes one element of the fishing rod. The finished rod is then carried to an inspection position, where it is checked for quality and then stacked. The track contains ten teams of five-person production units.

The new production process was explained to the workers when they returned from holiday. Training in the new methods of production proved difficult because the only experience that could be given was on the actual manufacturing track. The problem was aggravated by 12 newly trained workers leaving within the first two months of the new process.

Some three months after the introduction of the new manufacturing process, output of rods had stabilised but it was 16 per cent below the performance level set by the consultant. The amount of management time spent dealing with problems associated with quality of the rods produced increased by 65 per cent. After the significant level of wastage during the first two months, labour turnover returned to the previous employment pattern, but absenteeism increased by 20 per cent.

RESOURCE 2:

From: Organization Theory: Text and Cases, by G.R. Jones (Reading, MA: Addison-Wesley, 1995)

The crisis of leadership at Apple Computer

On April 1, 1976, Stephen G. Wozniak and Steve Jobs formed Apple Computer company in Menlo Park, California, with the proceeds of the sale of Jobs' Volkswagen and Wozniak's two programmable calculators. With the money they raised, and working out of Jobs' now-empty garage, they designed and built a single-board computer, which they called Apple I. By the end of the year, the demand for the computer was so high that the two founders could not handle the manufacturing needs. Lacking the funds to expand on their own, they formed an alliance with A.C. 'Mike' Markkula, who invested $250,000, became chairmen of the board, and directed Apple's first business plan. The Apple team proceeded to develop an improved computer, the Apple II. As sales took off for that machine and more and more software applications were written, the fortunes of the company rose. In December 1980, every share of the initial share offering sold within minutes. By 1982, sales of apple computers had reached $2 billion.

As the company grew, the structure of the top-management team changed quickly. Wozniak, interested in research, had no interest in managing the company. Jobs had an interest in both activities and, in 1981, replaced Markkula as chairman and took over responsibility for Apple's strategic direction. At the same time, he was the product champion who pioneered the development of a new kind of Apple computer (the Macintosh), and he used considerable organisational resources to further its development. Jobs began to dominate Apple's top-management team and its decision making, especially after Wozniak left the company after a near-fatal plane crash.

By 1982, Jobs realised that he lacked the time and ability to both manage strategy and champion new product development. He searched for someone to help him and fixed on John Sculley, Pepsi Cola's president and a known marketing genius. In 1983, Sculley became Apple's president and CEO and took over the responsibility for Apple's strategic growth and marketing plan. Jobs, as chairman, would oversee technical development. Together the two would manage Apple's growth to become a mature company capable of dominating the industry.

However, things did not work out as planned. Jobs soon found that he missed the power that control over strategic decision making gave him. He started to oversee Sculley's activities and to intervene in corporate decision making whenever he felt it necessary. Moreover, in using resources to develop the Macintosh project, he stirred discontent among other Apple project teams, and the level of politics and conflict in the organisation was rising. Finally, by spreading his talents between management and research, Jobs was causing delays in decision making, and the company was losing direction. By 1993,

however, low-cost competition was hurting Apple just as it hurt Compaq, and Sculley was forced out of Apple because the board of directors had lost confidence in his ability to lead the company through the new crisis it was experiencing.

Chrysler's new team structure

RESOURCE 3:

From: Organization Theory: Text and Cases, by G.R. Jones (Reading, MA: Addison-Wesley, 1995)

After Lee Iacocca took over Chrysler corporation, the company changed its approach to product development. Formerly, the company had an idea for a new model of car, formed a product division to take control of the idea, and made the division responsible for obtaining the inputs of the various functions. The divisions had made their contributions sequentially; so, for example, design had the idea, engineering designed the prototype, purchasing and supply ordered the inputs, manufacturing made the vehicle, and marketing and sales sold it. Iacocca saw that this approach was very ineffective. Typically, Chrysler took seven or eight years to bring a new car to market, more than twice as long as the three years needed by Toyota or Nissan. Moreover, this system resulted in products with higher costs and lower quality than Japanese products. Why?

According to Iacocca, when a company like Chrysler produces a range of complex and technically sophisticated products, getting the different functional support groups to cooperate and co-ordinate their activities to arrive at the final product design is a nightmare. One function's activities may conflict with another function's, and no function learns anything from another because of the strength of their respective sub unit orientations. The engineering department says: our aim is to develop an aerodynamic, lightweight car with good mileage, and we are not really interested in how difficult it is to assemble or how costly it is to build. The Marketing department

says: you engineers and production folks had better control your costs so that we can price this car competitively.

Iacocca was determined to change this situation. As an experiment, he used what he called a "platform team" to develop the Dodge Viper, a luxury sports car. In a platform team, which is the same as a product development team, the functions are organised around the product. A team consists of product and manufacturing engineers, planners and buyers, designers, financial analysts, and marketing and sales people, and each team has sole responsibility for getting its car to the market. The team concept encourages different specialists to interact and thus speeds communication and allows problems to be solved quickly, creatively, and efficiently. Moreover, as the specialists begin to learn from one another, the quality of the product improves, and the pace of innovation quickens. The concept was widely successful at Chrysler. "Team Viper" got the product to market in three years – record time for the organisation. Moreover, the car was a hit, and customers lined up to buy it.

With the success of the platform team concept established, Iacocca reorganised the rest of Chrysler's functionally organised product development operations into product-oriented platform teams. Chrysler now has four such teams: large car, small car, minivan and Jeep/truck. Three of these teams operate out of Chrysler's new billion-dollar technology centre in Auburn Hills, Michigan.

The Economist
29 July 1989

Reorganising the organisation

As the world changes, so too must the corporations that live in it. The first step in corporate evolution was the delegation of functions like production, finance and marketing to specialised divisions. But as product lines became more varied, and the pace of innovations faster, a single manufacturing division could not cope with all demands placed upon it. So, at firms like General motors and Du Pont, responsibility was split again. Instead of functions, divisions concentrated on products or markets, and each division had within it several functional sub-divisions for production, marketing and so on.

In the 1950s, as American companies spread across the world, innovators tried to combine the efficiency of companies organised by function with the responsiveness of those centred on individual markets. Their solution was the management matrix. In effect, each executive had two bosses: one in charge of satisfying a particular market, another in charge of a particular function. In practice, many found that the matrix resulted merely in confusion and endless meetings.

The newest trend in organisational design is almost a non-organisation: networks. The theory here is that a company is at heart little more than a network of people with specialised skills. As opportunities arise, the firm re-shapes itself into whatever form is necessary for it to prosper. Examples of successful networking include the informally assembled team that built IBM's first personal computer. Working outside the normal corporate bureaucracy, it developed one of IBM's most successful products, in record time. Now that's organisation!

From: Organisational Culture, by A. Brown (London: Pitman, 1995)

Culture and performance at Jaguar Cars

Jaguar Cars is a Coventry-based luxury car manufacturer with a chequered history of success, decline and turnaround. The post-war performance of the company may be divided into three main periods.
1945-1968
Up to 1968 its market performance was generally strong. During this period it was dominant in the UK luxury saloon and sports classes of car, 50 per cent of its output was exported, costs were kept down and pricing was competitive. In short, Lyons, the founder and chief executive achieved considerable success with the firm, which won major awards with its XJ6 and XJ12 models. Some of the hallmarks of his regime were a strong craft identification with the product, the pursuit of products engineering innovation, and a 'can-do' mentality which resulted in the meeting of many short deadlines. Lyons himself was noted for his authoritarian and interventionist style, his aversion to unnecessary expenditure, and his distaste for formal management techniques.
1972-1980
From 1972 until 1980, the strengths of Lyon's culture withered, and Jaguar Cars went into decline. Now owned by British Leyland, Jaguar was technically no longer a

company but a manufacturing location. A succession of senior mangers were imposed from corporate level, each of whom applied widely contrasting policies. Part of the problem was that BL's managers were from volume/mass production not specialist car backgrounds. On top of this came three substantial reorganisations, the dismemberment of Jaguar's finance, sales and marketing functions, and the development of divisional warfare. The result was that the 1979 series III model was beset with quality and reliability defects, production fell dramatically, and losses for its main site were running at $4 million per month. In 1980 Michael Edwardes, the British Leyland chief executive, gave notice that unless the plant broke even within a year it would be closed. 1980-

Later in 1980 a new managing director and chairmen of Jaguar, called John Egan, was appointed. There followed a remarkable turnaround in the fortunes of Jaguar, with vast increases in turnover, profitability, and productivity. Jaguar re-established its market position by restructuring its retail operation and reformulating its relations with outside bodies both in the UK and aboard. Key to the firm's success was a new senior management team and the re establishment of finance, sales and marketing, and purchasing departments. As a 'stand alone' company Jaguar was better able to reduce operating costs, raise quality standards and reliability, and improve communications. Meeting these objectives involved reducing the workforce from 10,000 to 7,000, setting up company-wide task forces to tackle 150 specially targeted problems, and making operators and suppliers directly responsible for quality.

Five features of Jaguar's survival and regeneration programme touch on issues of organisational culture: leadership, the quest for quality, communications, project management, and language:

1. Leadership John Egan provided a new mission for Jaguar, which suggested that it is now aimed 'to become the finest car company in the world'. A strategic plan was produced which dictated that $1 billion was to be invested over 5 years, expenditure on R&D was to increase dramatically, and production was set to rise from 14,000 to 100,000 cars per annum. The new set of beliefs Egan sought to create clustered around the notion that Jaguar could produce world-class cars by focusing on growth, quality market sensitivity, learning and human development, and professionalism. Some observers have noted that what Egan has done is to merge the best elements of the Lyons culture (such as product excellence and craft pride) with new beliefs (such as market sensitivity).

2. Quality The 'cult of quality' involved the devising of quantifiable standards and the establishment of new working practices. All managers were trained in statistical process control. In addition, American dealers were invited to talk directly to work stations responsible for faults, making workers immediately accountable for problems. Unlike many organisations, Jaguar's quality programme was not used as a PR device, and its substantive impact was most noticeable in terms of the new types of stories that began to be told. Instead of stories of mercy-dashes to Jaguar car owners stranded in their new cars, directors and engineers began telling stories about the number of workers and relatives who attended the new XJ40 model launch days.

3. Communications Key to the success of the quality programme was a comprehensive communications structure. This involved not just a company newsletter and monthly management bulletins, but video programmes, briefing and discussions sessions, management conferences, 75 quality circles and a set of performance and review committees which linked the shopfloor with senior executives. External consultants were also brought in to mount surveys of employee's views of the communications scheme. Given the degree of cynicism among staff at the time, this extensive communications infrastructure was vital.

4. Project management The ad hoc methods of designing cars had in the

late 1970s become a competitive liability. Throughout the 1970s they resulted in late, over-budget exercises and cars not acceptable to consumers. With Egan came a whole new approach to project management. Instead of supplying a car for marketeers to sell, engineers now ask 'What type of products do you want?' Cross-functional teams with 10-year product plan objectives have revolutionised Jaguar's approach to car design, manufacture and marketing.

5. Language Influential changes have accompanied Jaguar's programme of culture reform. In addition to the new stories mentioned above, a whole new glossary of terms such as 'programme status reports' and 'business objectives' have been incorporated into the linguistic repertoire of engineers.

Finally, it is worth noting that Jaguar's competitive renaissance has been both assisted and constrained by the 'shared assumptions' of the automobile industry as a whole. In the 1970s, the industry had a lack of faith in product planning, management training, and marketing, and Jaguar's management adopted these beliefs with disastrous results. An enormous rise in the price of oil, massive increases in imports, and changes in government policy conspired to shatter the industry's

assumptions concerning the inevitable survival of domestic producers such as Jaguar. Similarly, Jaguar's adoption of a new set of assumptions has mirrored what is going on elsewhere within the industry. Industry sector culture as much as organisational culture may thus be used to explain how Jaguar has achieved so dramatic a turnaround.

SOURCES: Rosenfeld, R., Whipp, R., and Pettigrew, A., 1987, 'Process of Internationalization: Regeneration Competitiveness', paper presented to the ESRC/EIASM Seminar on Competitiveness and Internationalisation, European Institute of Advanced Studies in Management, Brussels; Whipp, R., 1987, 'Technology Management, Strategy, Change and Competitiveness', in M. Dorgham's Proceedings of the Fourth International Vehicle Design Congress, Geneva, Inderscience; Whipp, R., Rosenfeld, R. and Pettigrew, A., 'Culture and Competitiviness: Evidence from Two Mature UK Industries', Journal of Management Studies; Williams, A., Dobson, P. and Walters, M., 1987, Changing Culture: New Organisational Approaches, Institute of Personnel Management; Goldsmith, W. and Clutterbuck, D., 1985, The Winning Streak, Harmondsworth, Penguin. Reproduced with permission.